Shakespeare   1564-1964

Brown University Bicentennial Publications

Studies in the Fields of General Scholarship

SHAKESPEARE 1564-1964

A Collection of Modern Essays by Various Hands

EDITED BY EDWARD A. BLOOM

BROWN UNIVERSITY PRESS PROVIDENCE RHODE ISLAND 1964

Editorial Committee

DESIGNED BY MALCOLM GREAR

TYPE SET IN LINOTYPE PALATINO BY CONNECTICUT PRINTERS, INC.

PRINTED BY CONNECTICUT PRINTERS, INC.

ON WARREN'S OLDE STYLE

BOUND BY RUSSELL RUTTER CO.

Contents

Introduction

Two humanistic events are joined in this volume: the founding of Brown University in 1764, and the birth of Shakespeare in 1564. The theme, however, is exclusively Shakespeare, and Brown University is content with the honor of making available a forum to scholars and critics who reflect modern directions in Shakespearean studies. When the collection was proposed, the editors agreed that no attempt should be made to assign subjects or limit approaches. In soliciting contributions, therefore, we stipulated only that each essay be composed for this occasion, that it express an original or independent point of view, and that it meet rigorous standards of scholarly and critical judgment.

Although the list of possible contributors could extend far beyond that at hand, inevitable circumstances of cost, time, and availability have helped to dictate the limits of this book. At least one omission, for instance, must be mentioned with profound sadness. Leo Kirschbaum, of Wayne State University, had been preparing for us an essay on *Troilus and Cressida*. On May 24, 1962, he wrote from Jerusalem—where he was a Fulbright Professor in Hebrew University—that he would send it within a few weeks' time. But the promise was one he could not keep, for he died suddenly. There is sadness also in noting that E. M. W. Tillyard, whose essay is included in this collection, died in England (coincidentally, on May 24, 1962) about eight months after his paper reached us. We are singularly honored to publish the essay, possibly the last before his death, although his posthumous volume on Shakespeare's comedies will soon appear. On the other side, however, we may rejoice that Hardin Craig, himself the recipient of two volumes of essays in his honor, has now contributed to this *Festschrift*.

In comparing the present commemorative volume with one published almost fifty years ago we cannot help becoming forcefully aware of the changing tone and temper of Shakespearean interest. *A Book of Homage to Shakespeare*, edited by Israel Gollancz and published in the tercentenary year 1916, is a lavish testimonial to a belletristic, often genteel, tradition. The Gollancz volume, frankly adulatory and heterogeneous, is one in which "the ready and generous co-operation of one hundred and sixty-six Homagers finds expression." Contributors, aside from the British, were drawn from the United States, virtually every country in Europe (on both sides of what is now the Iron Curtain), Japan, China, Persia. The tributes appear in all the modern languages, in the classical languages (omitting neither Hebrew nor Sanskrit), and in a variety of dialects from Bengalee and Urdu to Bechuana. If the tercentenary volume contains the remarks of such proven scholars as Colvin, Chambers, Henry and A. C. Bradley, Saintsbury, Moulton, and so forth, it also contains eulogies in prose and verse by Hardy, Galsworthy, Drinkwater, Kipling, and Wister, among others— to say nothing of those by other celebrated European and Oriental figures. Its motif that of paean, the handsome book is a stunning *tour de force*, undaunted even by World War I.

Times, we hardly need be reminded, have changed, and a modern *Book of Homage* becomes an altogether different thing. The best writing on Shakespeare, such as we think is represented here, is less ecstatic and more exacting, less impressionistic and more insightful. It is informed by painstaking knowledge of dramaturgy, history, psychology, philosophy, language, textual matters, as well as the *sine qua non*, literature. Shakespeare today is largely managed by the specialists, but the specialists are giving him back to the general public with discrimination and enhanced import. Shakespearean studies continue to thrive because Shakespeare continues to be for modern scholars and readers, as he was for a Slavic commentator in 1916, *pananthropos*. "He was *multi*—and *multi*. He never was *alone*."

The range of essays here (like the countries of their origin) is necessarily limited, but it reveals predominant critical concerns. Much of the emphasis, though on the tragedies, proceeds from Shakespeare's devotion to human values, his awareness of inner tensions and social relationships. But if he is treated as psychologist and philosopher, he is also treated as artist and man of his times. Although the comedies receive less attention quantitatively, the essays based upon them contribute toward a whole view of Shakespeare's accomplishments. And so also do the essays on his poetry, his education, and the rising curve of his influence. Despite the eclecticism of these contributions and even some amicable disagreements about certain fundamental issues—for instance, the presence or absence of an orthodox Christian ethos as a measure for judging Shakespeare—they can be read not only as individual pieces but as parts of a unified whole.

The constant image in Shakespeare's world is man, but man himself is variable and ambiguous; it is thus that he is portrayed and thus that we are called upon to understand him. To apprehend the art of Shakespeare, then, is a way of coming to terms with ourselves. To see his illusions—no matter how wonderful—only as illusions is to miss the truth of human experience. The paradox of Shakespeare's creations, as Robert Ornstein asserts, is that "of the disparity between the outward appearance and the inward reality of man's moral nature."

In this vein, William T. Hastings tells us that the puzzle of Hamlet's procrastinated vengeance is indicative of such a disparity, but it is one that we are made to accept as an artistic measure of the protagonist and not as an exercise in logic. "Hamlet the character is what makes the play—the illusion of him, if you wish—as a young man with a desperate task to perform which somehow reveals havoc in his life and in all the lives around." The power of Shakespeare's illusions is such, to return to Mr. Ornstein, that they cause us to revaluate our notions of what is and is not real. As both illusionist and realist, Shakespeare uses the make-believe world of the theater to bare man's inner truth obscured by superficialities of experience.

Like Mr. Ornstein and Mr. Hastings, Robert B. Heilman is concerned with Shakespeare's revelation of "true" human nature, the inner strain or ambiguity which our commonplace preoccupations too often prevent our recognizing. This split in personality Mr. Heilman examines specifically under the theme of "manliness," that is, a polarized concept that man may fulfill himself in two different ways, through patience or intemperance, through forbearance or ruthless retaliation. This Shakespearean view of human contrariety is likewise incorporated by Mr. Hastings with regard to Hamlet, who is at once "the perfect avenger" and the reluctant avenger cursing "the malice of Heaven" in assigning him his task. For neither Mr. Heilman nor Mr. Hastings are these poles of "manliness" contradictions to be explained. Rather, they are inescapable truths of personality.

Other critics, however, feel that the deepest utterances of Shakespeare must be probed even beyond the plane of psychological, secular experience. The search for meaning, they imply, is incomplete unless it transcends the mortal. That is, Shakespeare is held up to the assertions of theological Christian dogma. Urging precisely such an interpretation of *Hamlet*, Fredson Bowers treats the "play's moment of final suspense" as the Christianization of a classical device. In defying fatal omen, Hamlet avows his faith in orthodox principle which culminates in "catastrophic victory." Religious assumptions for Shakespeare's dramatic art are further adduced by Kenneth Myrick, who concentrates upon a theme of Christian pessimism in *King Lear*. For both Shakespeare and his audiences, in the judgment of Mr. Myrick, man's tragic experiences could be meaningful only according to the terms of Christian faith. The despair which permeates *King Lear* is based upon pessimistic—though not hopeless—attitudes characteristic of Elizabethan Christianity.

Arguments like Mr. Bowers' and Mr. Myrick's, dependent on the premise that Shakespeare's vision is that of a Christian poet writing in a Christian environment, are winning much respectful attention. Opposition to the theological view, however, is equally vigorous and persuasive. Nicholas Brooke, thus, far from regarding *King Lear* as a "Christian play," finds evidence that in it divinity has been rejected. It is, indeed, a great play for him in the complete and superb energy of its negation. *King Lear*, Mr. Brooke maintains, compels us to adjust to a world of disorder, even though it does not deny the existence of "*values* good and evil." Similarly, Adrien Bonjour challenges theological interpretations of *Antony and Cleopatra*, a play no more to be treated as Christian allegory than is *Snow White*. Urging closer attention to its dramatic and psychological properties, he rebukes the rapturous "theologians who would turn it into a hymn to the resurrection of the body."

Although R. A. Foakes agrees in substance with Mr. Bonjour's rejection of a Christian theme in *Antony and Cleopatra*, his argument is even less concerned with dogma as such than with questions of total experience not only in *Antony and Cleopatra*, but in *Timon of Athens* and *Coriolanus* as well. Having conceded that the heroes of *Hamlet*, *Othello*, and *King Lear* support a Christian order, Mr. Foakes holds that the later tragedies—with *Macbeth* in a transitional role—represent for Shakespeare a change in tragic intention. That is—in *Timon*, *Coriolanus*, *Antony and Cleopatra*—the earlier absolutes of good and evil are now "inextricably mixed," and the issues turn to human wholeness with stress on the psychological (as in Mr. Bonjour's thesis). Shakespeare's later tragedies suggest to Mr. Foakes the fashion set by Jacobean drama, which he denies makes morality central.

Turning to the two essays on the comedies, we discover a shift of attention from the world of man to the demiworld of fairies and daemons. Mr. Tillyard is intrigued by the story of *König Drosselbart* or *King Thrushbeard*, finding enough resemblances between the fairy tale and *The Taming of the Shrew* to plead for an analogous relationship. While agreeing with other critics that the fabliau tradition is an important ingredient of the play, he also suggests that as a whole it reveals an even greater affinity with the fairy tale. But the dramatist "in his loyalty to both . . . was cheated of the unity at which surely he must have aimed." There is no such doubt in the mind of Robert H. West about the success of *The Tempest*, which he treats as "a look into as fearful a face as life shows to a discerning man." In this play, as in the tragedies, Shakespeare brings human and nonhuman mystery into conjunction, demonstrating ways in which the supernatural—"the outer mystery"—is brought to bear upon our mortality. So even in comedy, the illusion is but an aspect of reality.

Mythic, symbolic, textual, and analytic problems enter into the discussions of the nondramatic poetry. Thus Christopher Butler and Alastair Fowler advance an interesting thesis about number symbolism in *Venus and Adonis* as a clue to a fresh understanding of that poem. Relating their mathematical discoveries to the temporal or seasonal meanings of the myth, as understood in the Renaissance, Messrs. Butler and Fowler see philosophical and cosmological meanings within human events. Additionally, they find evidence for identifying young Southampton with Adonis. An altogether different aspect of Shakespeare's poetry, the textual puzzle of Sonnets 127–54, engages Brents Stirling. Joining those critics who believe the original order of the sonnets had been disarranged in the 1609 text, he is more optimistic than most that a restoration can be achieved. In addition to offering his own restored version, Mr. Stirling also considers reasons for the disruption of Shakespeare's sequence. And finally, with regard to the poetry, Kenneth Muir has addressed himself to the task of renewing interest in the neglected "Lover's Complaint" and of confirming his belief in Shakespeare's authorship. Arguing from both critical and textual evidence, Mr. Muir acknowledges that the "Complaint" is a lesser achievement than either *Venus and Adonis* or *Lucrece*. Nevertheless, he asserts that it has moments of brilliance and a distinctive flavor, and is a positive contribution to our total impression of Shakespeare's poetry.

The three concluding essays in this volume may for convenience be classified as biographical and bibliographical. In the first, education—and the education in particular of an Elizabethan schoolboy—commands Hardin Craig's erudite and witty attention. Linking the matter of the trivium to the notion of "concrescence" postulated by Alfred North Whitehead, he develops the effect of Shakespeare's grammar-school studies upon his artistry, with specific application to *King John*. Then T. J. B. Spencer traces the history of Shakespeare's rivalry in England with the great classical dramatists, showing how he slowly won his own acceptance among English audiences as a writer of classic stature. But the terms of acceptance, even by the beginning of the twentieth century, were often grudging and comparative.

The rivalry now consigned to history, it remains only for Irving Ribner to summarize the critical eminence which is indisputably Shakespeare's. Analyzing the mainstream of Shakespearean criticism of the last sixty years, Mr. Ribner observes the significant influence of five men writing at the beginning of the present century: Edward Dowden, A. C. Bradley, Richard Moulton, Walter Raleigh, and Robert Bridges. In them and their successors is solidified a great tradition (derived in turn from Dryden, Johnson, and Coleridge) which is both moral and philosophical, and which emphasizes "always the value of Shakespeare's plays as the embodiment of important truth about human experience." Almost every essay in this volume is in its own way a reflection of this critical engrossment. In another respect, also, the contents which follow support Mr. Ribner's summation. The various approaches may be heterogeneous, but even seemingly contradictory attitudes may be reconciled when they are committed to a common purpose, a better perception of Shakespeare's meaning and art.

One of the most gratifying features of a venture of this kind is the spirit of cooperation and community of interest which make it possible. The Shakespearean zeal of those immediately concerned is not adequately acknowledged in a formal statement. Even impersonally, however, the editor would not omit expressing his admiration for the enthusiasm and responsiveness of his distinguished contributors. Nor would he fail to state his deep debt of gratitude to his colleagues in the English Department of Brown University who patiently and knowledgeably served as his associates and counselors: Professors George K. Anderson, Leicester Bradner, Elmer M. Blistein, Andrew J. Sabol, and John W. Shroeder. Special thanks are owing to Mr. Howard Shawcross for scrupulous examination of quotations and for astute questions. And finally appreciation must be recorded for the generous encouragement of the Bicentennial Publications Committee and the Corporation of Brown University. In celebrating its own anniversary, Brown makes this book its gift to those who celebrate Shakespeare's.

EDWARD A. BLOOM

Shakespeare   1564-1964

Character and Reality in Shakespeare

By Robert Ornstein

One of the important turning points of Shakespeare criticism occurred some forty years ago in the writings of Levin Schücking and E. E. Stoll. Their insistence on the role of artifice and convention in Shakespeare's plays marked not only the end of a long period of character study but also the beginning of the modern investigation of those aspects of Shakespeare's art which had been largely ignored by nineteenth-century criticism. Plays that had been for Romantic critics sublime and timeless revelations of the human heart became for modern critics masterpieces of poetic form and dramatic composition, shaped by the conditions and traditions of the Elizabethan stage and imbued with the values of Elizabethan culture. If the history of criticism were properly Hegelian, the clash of thesis and antithesis—of Mrs. Jameson and Professor Stoll—would have produced a new synthesis of opinion about Shakespeare's portrayal of character and a new understanding of the relation of the dramatic image to the actuality of experience. But if there has been a dialectical synthesis, it has been obscured by the development of new critical approaches which have made the very issues Stoll raised seem old-fashioned and irrelevant to the interpretation of the plays. The knowledge of Shakespeare's art which earlier critics sought through impressionistic character studies, modern critics would gain more objectively by analysis of the patterns of language and imagery which express Shakespeare's poetic vision, or by scholarly investigation of the moral and theological schemes of the plays, which endow the characters with emblematic and allegorical significances.

Although the advance of criticism may well have outdated Stoll's inquiry into the nature of Shakespeare's art, I think we often beg the questions which Stoll sought to answer by treating the plays as if they were poems or tracts that were only incidentally intended for dramatic performance. Assuming, as Stoll did not, that the findings of criticism need not accord with the impression which we receive of a play in the theater, we reduce the infinite variety of Cleopatra to a cautionary lust in the pages of scholarship, and discover from close verbal analysis that Horatio and the Sentries are waiting for Godot, not for the Ghost. Lacking the perspective of the theater we tend to see too much or too little, to find meaning in every rhetorical detail, or to insist that the tone, rhetoric, and imagery of the speeches of Prince Hal have no bearing on his moral character. At the same time that we examine some plays with minute particularity, we advise readers not to look too closely at the problem comedies lest they puzzle over questions of motive and plot which would not have bothered an Elizabethan audience. The notion that we are too modern, too serious, and too unromantic to accept the conventions of Shakespearean drama would be more convincing if we found as many problems in the late romances as in the problem comedies—if we were as troubled by Prospero's intrigues as by Duke Vincentio's. But it seems unlikely that we are naive enough to accept the romantic fables of *The Tempest* and *The Winter's Tale* yet not naive enough to accept the folklore elements in *All's Well That Ends Well* and *Measure for Measure.*

Granted that there are eccentricities of interpretation on the stage as well as in works of criticism, it does seem to me that the theater restores our sense of the plays as dramatic actions, and it does remind us of the rich humanity of characters who appear in the pages of criticism as conventional dramatic types and simple embodiments of passion or principle. I think that if we are to speak authoritatively of what is conventional in Shakespeare, we must deal with the impression of his plays in performance, because time and again we discover in a theater the credibility and naturalness of passages which appear artificial and conventional in the printed text.[1] Moreover, those who would explain Shakespeare's art by reference to the unique conventions of the Elizabethan stage must also explain why his plays are so well received by thousands of modern spectators who know nothing of Elizabethan drama.

Stoll believed, of course, that even when not conventional, Shakespeare's art aimed only at a theatrically effective semblance of reality. He saw Shakespeare, not as a great portrayer of life, but as a superb craftsman of the theater who fashioned striking if improbable dramatic situations, and who contrived the vivid impressions of personality in his great characters through a mastery of verbal gesture and manner.[2] Because this view of the plays makes of Shakespeare a superior Beaumont and Fletcher, it has not been widely seconded by later critics. Yet many who would grant Shakespeare's profound understanding of human nature would agree with Stoll that his plays did not pretend, as does modern drama, to imitate reality. They argue that Shakespeare could not have attempted a verisimilar depiction of life in plays that were presented on a relatively bare sunlit stage and acted, so we are told, in a formal, somewhat declamatory style. The Elizabethan audiences, we are to imagine, did not really suspend disbelief in the playhouse; they saw the play as play, as dramatic fiction and entertainment, and were satisfied if the speeches were eloquent, the action exciting, and the theme edifying.

It is ironic that while we admire Shakespeare's freedom from the restrictive conventions of the modern realistic stage, our insistence on the conventionality of his art seems to imply that in drama only the realistic is real, only a literal imitation of human speech and behavior can persuade an audience to suspend disbelief. Moreover, we seem to contrast Shakespeare's poetic "conventionalism" against a norm of prosaic naturalism that cannot be found in the masterpieces of the modern stage, which are suffused with poetic symbolism and more concerned with the extraordinary life of fantasy and illusion than the ordinary norm of daily experience. It is one thing to kick at the stones of art to test whether they are real; it is another thing to claim that only stones of the same size and color as those we trip over daily seem real to us on stage. Unless we recognize that drama has the power to extend as well as mirror experience and to deepen our perception of reality, we shall stand incredulously over the bodies of Shakespeare's tragic heroes, even as Judge Brack stands over Hedda Gabler, exclaiming that people don't do this sort of thing.

Brack is a fascinating example of critical incapacity: he does not lack intelligence or understanding of human nature, but since he has no capacity for illusion he is unable to fathom the depth of the illusion that destroys Hedda Gabler. Indeed, he is too much of a realist to know the extent to which illusion and fantasy are a part of the reality of other men's lives. When we speak of what is real in the theater we cannot assume an audience made up of Bracks, nor can we assume an audience that has never read a psalm or a sonnet, never heard a fairy tale or a ghost story, never listened to eloquence in the pulpit or the courtroom, and never participated in the ceremonial rituals of church and family life. Above all, we cannot assume that an audience in the theater shares our critical awareness of the means by which a playwright achieves his artistic effects.

To be sure, no effort at realism can blind an audience to the fact that an illusion is being created on stage. When we sit in a theater we are aware of the physical presence of a dimly lighted building; we are aware of being part of an audience which has gathered to watch actors perform. But we can be aware of the artifice of the stage at the same time that we are convinced of the reality of the dramatic world which it creates, because our response to the art of the drama is finally distinct from our response to the artifice of the stage. When we go to the theater for casual entertainment we are prepared to make allowances for the incredibility of character and plot; we accept the artificiality of the dramatic portrayal for the sake of a sentimental release or because the play is genuinely amusing without being too demanding of our attention. When we watch a performance of a great play, however, the only allowances we need make are for those actors who are not adequate to their roles. To be sure, we do not literally identify the actors with the characters they represent. As Dr. Johnson suggested, if we believed that the woman who plays Desdemona on the stage is strangled in the last act, we could not bear to watch a performance of *Othello*. But, on the other hand, if we did not believe that Desdemona is murdered, a performance of *Othello* would not move us. The truth, I think, is that when Shakespeare is performed, his characters are real to us even though we know that the actors who take their parts belong to the make-believe of the stage.

The power of a dramatic illusion to alter our sense of what is real and what is make-believe is brought home to us by a performance of *Six Characters in Search of an Author*, because Pirandello seems determined to strip away the flimsy pretenses of dramatic realism. Before our eyes the veil is lifted from theatrical illusion; we are taken behind the scenes to witness the company meeting on the naked stage to rehearse their next production. When the Characters appear we share the Actors' incredulity at the hypothesis of artistic creation; we agree that you have to be crazy to think that a character born of a playwright's imagination can be real. Yet as the action proceeds our confidence that illusion and reality are discrete and easily distinguished from one another is undermined, because soon the Characters with their histrionic poses and gestures, their bravura speeches and melodramatic stories, become intensely real to us, while the Actors, so realistically drawn, so perfectly natural in their speech, behavior, and affectations, remain synthetic figures, except when they try in their fumbling way to imitate the Characters.

No doubt Pirandello's mock revenge on the theater has its serious side; no doubt it expresses a real irritation at the vanity and stupidity of actors and the crassness of the commercial stage. Certainly it exposes the folly of a realistic convention which demands that the significant appear ordinary and the ordinary significant. Yet *Six Characters* is an act of love, a practical joke apparently aimed at the actors but turned by their skill against the audience, which finally understands that the exposure of illusion is an illusion in itself. It is all done with mirrors, or more correctly, with dummies who move, speak, and live only within a histrionic make-believe but then are animated with the terrible truth of human passion. We know in Shakespeare as in Pirandello when we are being duped by a play within a play or by allusions to the stage which contrast the reality of a dramatic action against the artifice of the theater,[8] but we do not protest because we also know that the dramatic illusion is not a capricious deception or sleight of hand. To create a masterful artistic illusion one must be nothing less than a realist; one must know exactly how the world appears to men and why they see it as they do. One must know how their minds distinguish between the pretended and the actual, or how their eyes measure the relative size of objects in perspective. Like an optical illusion, a dramatic illusion is an exercise in perception that serves to expose the shallowness of common-sense realism.

Though we do not ordinarily see life with the poetic vision of a Shakespeare, we assent to the truth of his vision because it accords with our intuitions, because it is familiar to us though perhaps never seen before with such clarity or understood with such compassionate sympathy. At its most fanciful the dream of his art is familiar to us if only in that it evokes the memory of childhood make-believe. To enjoy *A Midsummer Night's Dream* we need not believe in fairies; we need only have heard enough fairy tales, for the enemy of romance is not common sense but a too sensible upbringing. Moreover, when art grows fantastical our poetic faith is only momentary and even then superstitious. We demand a sign and it is given to us. On the stage as in life, seeing is believing; we cannot deny the reality of Shakespeare's Ghosts and of Pirandello's Characters when they appear on stage, particularly when they appear to a skeptical Horatio and an exasperated Director, who exemplify the common-sense incredulity of the audience.

In Fletcherian romance the laws of emotional gravity are suspended as passions soar fantastically on the wings of improbable events. In Shakespearean comedy the laws of character seem far more natural because it is through character that Shakespeare domesticates the wild enchantment of romance. In every Shakespearean dream there is a dreamer like Bottom; in every Shakespearean Wonderland there is an Alice like Viola or Rosalind romantic enough to join in its pretendings but unwilling to surrender completely to its make-believe. Even when the Shakespearean isles and woods are enchanted, the dramatic issues are familiar and familial; we witness courtship and marriage, marital difficulties and expectant motherhood. We are not amazed that Shakespeare's husbands and lovers grow jealous or that his untried virgins speak as knowingly as college girls of sexual matters. For his comedies are not escapes from reality; they are at most escapes from the serious business of the world (the greed, ambition, and malice of Duke Frederick's court) into a holiday of innocent pranks and pretendings, and of harmless affections and affectations. We could say that the holiday world is irresponsible except that it attends to the necessary business of renewing life and is ruled by a benign providence, thinly disguised as coincidence, which rescues the characters from their ineffable talents for confusion. We could say that it is an artificial world except that we see beneath its literary posturings the wry and tender truth that romance is a masculine game of songs and sonnets, melancholy poses and self-indulgences, while marriage is a woman's destiny, a practical affair for which an Orlando or Orsino must be properly educated. We learn from Shakespearean comedy that it is as difficult to separate literature from life as it is to separate custom from nature, because love is at once the most instinctive and conventional of human emotions. Though perhaps not invented by Provençal troubadours, it has a natural affinity for poetry, from which it derives its madness, raptures, symptoms, and codes of behavior. The trouble with Phebe and Silvius is that they have read too many sonnets. The trouble with modern audiences who are bored by *As You Like It* is that they have read too few; their romantic dream is a Hollywood starlet, not Sidney's Stella.

Shakespearean comedy does not lie because it does not pretend to tell the truth; or rather it does not lie because it does not pretend to tell the whole of human truth. Whereas the horizons of tragedy seem to us the utmost bounds of human experience, the delight of comedy we know as a single aspect of experience bounded by the harsher facts of human nature, which can intrude only in the comic transformations of a Malvolio or an Oliver. If there are no clocks in the Forest of Arden, there is an ever present sense of the movement of time that turns the poetry of courtship into the prose of marriage and replaces the eternal pastoral spring with wintry wind and rain. And when the holiday of *Twelfth Night* comes to its joyous end, we half suspect that in a more workaday world Malvolio will someday have his revenge. We need no Prospero or Camillo to tell us that romantic hope belongs mainly to the young, whose confidence in life is as yet unsullied and who have yet to learn that beauty fades and that love is often time's fool. Even as the anguish of tragedy is defined by its moments of "comic" joy and tenderness—the laughter of the Osric scene, the song with which Desdemona prepares for bed—so too the joy of comedy is the more affecting because of its melancholy overtones. The poignancy of love's triumph in the comedies, as in Sonnet 116, derives not from a sense that it is only a dream, but from a knowledge of the many impediments that bar love's fulfillment: the hostility of circumstances, the human bendings, alterations, self-deceits, and vanities which make the purely generous affections of a Viola or a Juliet seem the more precious and miraculous.

We can say that the happy ending of Shakespearean comedy is determined by romantic convention so long as we remember that the tragic ending of *Romeo and Juliet*—the blasting of the bud of love—is equally conventional and traditional in romantic literature. Indeed the themes and conventions of romance are so varied and contradictory that no dramatist could depend on "conventional expectation" to lend probability to a romantic plot. The expectation of an audience must be cued by poetic and dramatic means, by the control of tone, by anticipatory ironies, by the foreshadowing effect of thematic imagery, and by the management of plot which makes a specific ending seem inevitable even though the characters, as in *Romeo and Juliet*, are as suitable for comedy as for tragedy. The festive mood of *As You Like It* leads us to expect that chance, which often plays a vicious role in tragedy, will redeem itself in Arden through fortuitous meetings between fathers and daughters or brothers and lions. In the star-cross'd world of *Romeo and Juliet*, however, accident and coincidence seem naturally to weave a pattern of tragic fatality; and it is not accident alone that makes a furious Tybalt seek out Romeo on his wedding day or that causes Mercutio to intervene in the quarrel, for in Verona fate is the conjunction of unfortunate circumstance and passionate temperament.

If a student questions Oliver's sudden change of heart at the close of *As You Like It*, we can only advise him to change his course of study. But if a student questions why Juliet agrees to the subterfuge of the potion when her obvious and instinctive course of action is to run away and join Romeo in exile, the answer is not so easy. For though an audience must accept the *données* of romance (and the flight of a heroine to join her lover *is* a *donnée* of romance), a playwright must in turn contrive his plot so as to lend probability to romantic events. We might tell the student that this question occurs because he is naively thinking of Juliet as a real person, but the chances are that just the opposite is true: the question occurs because the play has not become real enough to him as a work of dramatic art. He knows the incidents of the plot, but he does not know the plot as a dramatic progression that unfolds on stage with irresistible emotional force and logic. He has not felt the ever quickening tempo of the action, the suddenness of Capulet's insistence on the marriage to Paris, the desperation of Juliet, who, abandoned by her family and the Nurse, fiercely demands a solution from her only remaining ally, the timorous Friar. We need not say that convention allows the "improbabilities" of plot in *Romeo and Juliet* when in fact the plot seems conventional and improbable only when our response to the play is unpoetic and unimaginative.

In a sense the credibility of the potion scene is created externally to the character of Juliet by the dramatic and poetic evocation of a highly romantic world in which such radical cures for the illness of love are necessary and "natural." We do not say of Juliet, as Quiller-Couch remarked of Isabella, that she is "the kind of woman who will commit herself to any deed without question if it be suggested by a priest." Nor do we conclude from a careful psychological analysis that Juliet is the kind of oral personality who *would* drink a potion. Yet if it were not for the convincing portrayal of emotion in Juliet's soliloquy on the vial, the drinking of the potion would seem to us nothing more than a romantic fiction. Although some critics contend that Shakespeare cared more for dramatic effect than psychological truth, I think it is more accurate to say that his characterizations—Juliet, for example—are psychologically valid though not fundamentally conceived as psychological studies. A playwright uninterested in the psychology of motive, as Chapman is in most of his plays,[4] provides his characters with the most obvious passions of love, hate, envy, or ambition which will turn the machinery of his plots. But although Shakespeare found obvious, logical, even elemental motives for the behavior of Brutus, Iago, and Macbeth in his sources, he did not casually or indifferently transfer these motives to his plays for purposes of plot. Brutus, Iago, and Macbeth do not puzzle us because their motives are too crude and obvious; they puzzle us because their motives seem undefined or illogical. I do not mean that Shakespeare deliberately obscured Iago's motives in order to create a mystery for his audience to unravel; on the contrary, his artistic aim was always clarity. But as his moral imagination complicated and deepened Cinthio's tale of Italianate intrigue, it necessarily complicated and deepened the motives and moral natures of Cinthio's characters.

We can appreciate the subtlety and profundity of Shakespeare's characterizations without falling into the trap of psychologizing criticism, which treats the characters as if they were mysteries to be unraveled by ingenious conjectures. We may speak all we wish of different levels of critical response and interpretation, but if we assume that Shakespeare's imagination was truly dramatic, then it follows that his conceptions of character are fully communicated in the theater to his audience—or at least to the most sensitive fraction of his audience. Although Shakespeare is one of the rare playwrights who can manage a subtle depiction of character in a rapidly moving and eventful dramatic action, his genius does not remit the natural law of the theater against obscurity. For no dramatist can expect his audience to ponder what a character *really* meant by a speech in Act I while it also attends to the dialogue in Act II. Though a dramatist need not tell all about his characters' motives, he must make clear at the crucial points of his plot that a speech is hypocritical, that a reason is a rationalization, and that a seemingly casual remark is weighted with extraordinary feeling. The irrational, obsessive, and ambiguous nature of human emotion can be effectively presented on stage only when an audience sees the characters far more clearly than they see themselves. For psychologizing critics a character's words and deeds are clues to a hidden unexpressed or inexpressible depth of motive and emotional response. But to an audience watching a Shakespearean play a character's words and deeds are the total expression—the total reality—of his personality; they offer an immediate and fundamental knowledge of the character's moral and psychological nature.

Only superficially, however, is Shakespeare's portrayal of character in conflict with modern psychological theories of the submerged depths of the human personality. For Shakespeare's art does not presume the transparency of character; it creates that transparency at the same time, paradoxically, that it leaves a deep impression of the disparity between the outward appearance and the inward reality of man's moral nature. Instead of falsifying life by placing the truth of personality on the surface of word and deed, Shakespeare offers in the opening dialogue of *Othello* a dual revelation of Iago: we see the surface gruffness, the apparent candor, and the hearty outspoken cynicism which make him seem "honest," at the same time that we see what is hidden from Roderigo: the ruthless contempt, the intense craving of unsatisfied ego, and the inured duplicity. Thus the portrait of Iago is psychologically true, but our apprehension of Iago's nature is an "artificial" way of seeing, an immediate intuitive insight made possible by an art that discloses the essential nature of a character in a dozen superbly contrived lines of poetic dialogue.

One doubts that Shakespeare had a theory of the human personality that could be abstracted from his plays. What we do find in his plays is an artistic method of presenting character which is significantly different from the psychological portrayals we are accustomed to in modern literature. It is hardly an accident that the novel is the dominant literary form in an age of depth psychology or that the psychological interests of nineteenth-century novelists foreshadowed the investigations of modern professional psychologists; for the form of the novel lends itself naturally to the tracing of inner reactions to experience, unspoken reveries and associations of idea, and barely conscious processes of mind and memory. One would imagine, however, that the psychological exposition of character which we find in the novel is inherently at odds with the nature of dramatic art because it allows so little genuine immediacy of action, that is, it so clearly predicts in advance what a Madame Bovary will say and do in moments of crisis.

Yet because modern dramatists share the interests of modern novelists, the psychological exposition of character is in itself the central action of many contemporary plays. A modern tragedy, for example, is often closer in form to the last chapter of a psychological novel than to a Shakespearean tragedy in that the fate of its hero is the consummation of a psychological process that began in the earlier years of his life. Thus while the plot moves forward in modern tragedy, the revelation of character is often regressive. We learn about the hero as we learn about his past, and we know him completely, not when he completely reveals himself in action, but when he recalls the traumatic experience or the corrupting familial and social influences which maimed him psychologically. The slowly unfolding actions of modern drama permit leisurely expositions of character and situation. The protagonists, though already set in their tragic attitudes when introduced, seem at first view far more opaque than Shakespeare's heroes; the dramatic situations are also opaque at first and often ambiguously "normal": we eavesdrop on a casual dinner party at the Werles' or witness the uneventful arrival of a sister-in-law at the Kowalski flat. Then slowly, scene by scene, the opaque surface of character and situation is rubbed away. The initial amorphous impressions of character crystallize, giving us at last a poignant view of the anguished fantasies or destructive impulses of a Miss Julie, a Hedda Gabler, a Blanche DuBois, or a Willy Loman.

Even when Shakespeare approximates in *Macbeth* the pattern of modern tragedy, his tragic action is conceived in a radically different way. When we first see Macbeth he is not, like the modern tragic hero, already marked by the sickness which will later destroy him; nor can we predict from Macbeth's early behavior the nature of his coming spiritual degradation, though we know from his soliloquies before the murder of Duncan and from the way he commits the murder that he will not be able to live with the deed. Only in the soliloquy "To be thus is nothing" (III.i) do we discover that Macbeth will try to "adjust" to the terrible memory of his crime by committing it again; and then this irrational need to kill again and yet again seems to us Macbeth's ineluctable fate. Where the tragic action of a modern play unfolds with the relentlessness of a syllogism, the tragic action of *Macbeth* seems, despite its inevitability, to mimic the spontaneous, unpredictable form of human experience because it is not so much a logically articulated narrative as a series of intuitive perceptions. We see Macbeth just after the murder of Duncan and not again until the very moment when his despair seeks release in bloody purpose, but these two views of Macbeth are so perfectly congruent—the soliloquy in Act III releasing the flood of bitterness, hatred, and fear pent up in his speeches to Macduff and Lennox in Act II—that there seems no hiatus in the forward leap of the dramatic action. Though only two co-ordinates, these scenes trace the full downward curve of spirit that leads Macbeth to a private hell.

Only in the mature tragedies is the consciousness of the hero the moving center of Shakespeare's dramatic actions. In the earlier plays, where the dramatic action is focused on external event, we find a more oblique revelation of emotional processes. A fateful commitment will be reflected in an unexpected turn of a dramatic situation, not directly revealed to us in a soliloquy. The moment of crucial decision for Juliet, for example, comes in the hectic rush of the fifth scene of the third act, where we see her parting from Romeo, bullied by Capulet about the marriage to Paris, deserted by her mother, and at last advised by the Nurse to abandon Romeo. We half expect that Juliet's brief attempt at independence will end in an Ophelia-like submission; but at the extreme of bewilderment and despair when her spirit seems hopelessly crushed, she is quietly determined as she addresses the Nurse: "Speakest thou from thy heart? . . . Amen!" Although there are earlier signs of Juliet's growing maturity, Shakespeare does not attempt to explain or predict what is unexplainable and unpredictable—the moment when the unreasoning, unpremeditating will becomes free in refusing to bow any longer before the demands of circumstance.

As Shakespeare's art develops it boldly oversteps the sequential narrative logic that demands so many brief transitional scenes in *Richard III*. Instead of depicting Brutus' and Cassius' flight from Rome, Shakespeare "saves" the drama of their response to disaster for the scene at Sardis, where they seem almost to exchange personalities. The philosophical Brutus is as unreasoning in his contempt for Cassius' failings as Cassius was in his scorn of Caesar's disabilities. The thin-skinned Cassius, who murdered Caesar rather than bow before him, now bows before Brutus' fury, unable to find fault with Brutus, whose erring judgment ruined all, even as Brutus had been unable to find fault with Caesar, who had already become Dictator of Rome. What has happened to Brutus and Cassius between Rome and Sardis we do not know and we need not conjecture, because the revelation of character in the scene at Sardis is all-sufficient. The news of Portia's death and of the execution of the Roman Senators accounts for Brutus' anger and his need to cling to the ideality of the assassination. The old harshness, scorn, and cynicism of Cassius, which reappears soon enough in later scenes, is here muted by his response to Portia's death and by his abject need for Brutus' love. At first we are struck by the daring way in which Shakespeare unexpectedly softens his portrayal of Cassius, but on reflection we realize why there is no inconsistency or, indeed, sense of alteration in the portrayal. Cassius' weakness and growing dependence on Brutus were suggested earlier in the play; by his own admission he would have followed Caesar if given the chance, and now though all is lost through Brutus' mistakes, Cassius is content to have a hero he can worship.

To the extent that Shakespearean drama differs in form as well as substance from modern drama it poses different critical problems. We are rarely puzzled by the behavior of characters in modern plays because they are carefully explained to us as psychological entities; what we are not sure of is how we are supposed to judge their behavior, with what degree of sympathy or condemnation, pity or contempt. In Shakespearean drama the reverse is true: our emotional response to Cassius is immediate and unequivocal. But since the logic (or illogic) of Cassius' behavior is intuitively felt, not psychologically explained, Cassius becomes a problem when we reflect on our responses to the play and try to explain to ourselves why the portrayal of Cassius seems consistent even in its apparent inconsistencies. To reflect in this way on the integrity of Shakespeare's characters is not to confuse literature and life. We confuse literature and life only when our concern with character leads to gratuitous amplifications of Shakespeare's dramatic portraits. That is to say, we cannot deny the right of A. C. Bradley to ponder Macbeth's conscience-ridden choice of evil or the right of John Palmer to study Richard III's sudden failure of nerve at the height of his success. We can, however, object when their psychological hypotheses would in effect tell us what happened to Brutus and Cassius between Rome and Sardis. To infer as Bradley does what Macbeth's state of mind must have been before he met the Witches,[5] or to infer as Palmer does how Richard must have reacted to the fulfillment of his ambitions when he gained the crown,[6] is not to make explicit what is implicit in the plays. It is rather to piece out the supposed imperfections of Shakespeare's plots by inventing scenes and soliloquies which theoretically should have been in the plays because without them the plots are perplexingly "incomplete." We have to insist that Shakespeare's dramatic actions are fully realized and coherent, though not logically articulated in the way of prose narrative. Our task is not to imagine what is left unsaid in Shakespeare,[7] but to grasp the imaginative contiguity of his dramatic scenes, which, like the successive frames of a motion picture film, create on stage the impression of a continuum of action though in fact they depict only successive stages of that action.

Because the printed page lacks the perspective of the dramatic scene on stage, our view of character in a dramatic text may be distorted even as a globe is distorted when flattened into a map. On the page Shakespeare's minor characters may seem like disembodied voices in that they are given only the one or two traits of personality essential for their dramatic function. On the stage, however, seen from the proper esthetic distance, they are as convincing as background figures in a landscape. The humors character seems artificial because it is artificially flattened and conceived as a human synecdoche. But the Duchess of Gloucester, who speaks just a few words in *Richard II*, is a lifelike figure because we know her as we know the people on the periphery of our acquaintance—through a single unguarded remark that exposes a depth of loneliness and pride. The art of creating minor dramatic figures is like the art of perspective in painting. Proportion matters more than detail, and a barely sketched peripheral character is as convincing as a fully realized protagonist so long as both are seen from a single consistent point of view.[8]

Unlike the humors character, who is frozen in the attitude of his ruling obsession, most of Shakespeare's characters seem, like Cassius, to change as they are portrayed in new circumstances and relationships, or as more of their personalities is revealed by their participation in the dramatic action. Although Webster's characters spring, like Shakespeare's, into immediate and vivid life, the initial impression of their personalities rarely develops because they are always seen in the same emotional light. The larger range of moods and situations in Shakespeare's plays, however, allows a more dynamic unfolding of dramatic personalities. While the character of Claudius does not really change —he ends as he began, a murderer who twice commits a nearly perfect crime— it seems to develop because it is progressively revealed to us during the dramatic action. His responses to Hamlet's stratagems, to Polonius' death, to Ophelia's madness, and to Laertes' challenge enrich the initial impression of his character, so much so that we cannot say we know Claudius fully until the last moment of the play when he watches his beloved Gertrude drink the poisoned cup rather than prevent her by disclosing his murderous plot.

In plays as in life actual changes in character are rare, and rarest of all character changes is the spiritual transformation of the tragic hero. Yet this does not mean that Shakespeare's tragic heroes are uniquely characterized, or, as Arthur Sewell suggests, uniquely endowed with a spiritual inwardness.[9] Though briefly portrayed, Ophelia's madness is as deeply imagined and as profound a study of inner torment as is Hamlet's melancholy. But Ophelia's anguish, though touched by songs and flowers, is painful to watch because it is a blind and merely pitiable suffering like that of a stricken animal. Hamlet's anguish, in contrast, seems to us incomparably beautiful because we apprehend it not as suffering but as poetic vision, as a heightened sensitivity to life and a deepened awareness of self and world. The truth is that we witness a kind of spiritual change in the character of Juliet even though we see her "from without," and we find a remarkable study of psychological process in the portrait of Iago, who does not change as a character. Having neither moral need nor sensitivity from the start, Iago progresses from petty swindling to murderous intrigues without seeming to fall or to be further degraded. He does not, like Macbeth, find a perverse fulfillment in shedding blood; his instinct for murder is first aroused by Othello's murderous rages, and, coward that he is, he bungles the ambush of Cassio and kills Roderigo and Emilia out of blind desperation; he is caught in his own machinations. As we follow the course of the action in *Othello*, Iago does not appear to be a psychological enigma, for we see how he is led from petty malice to moral enormity by his genius at improvisation as well as by the almost sexual pleasure of his sadistic satisfactions. The problem of motive in Iago arises when, abstracting his character from the dramatic action, we try to explain his last vicious, completely irrational schemes (which can succeed only if everyone else involved is murdered) by reference to his initially mean and "reasonable" desire to spite Othello. To see the continuing evolution of Iago's motives and his chameleonlike response to the darkening color of Othello's thought is to realize that he is not simply an incarnation of diabolical evil.

There are, of course, genuinely emblematic Shakespearean characters, particularly in a play like *King Lear* where the moral action is extensive and panoramic, not intensively and psychologically focused as in *Othello*. Yet the absoluteness of moral characterization in *Lear* is not Shakespeare's usual practice. The moral spectrums of his other plays are more limited in scope and more delicately shaded; and his characters usually vary not only in the moral attitudes they exemplify but also in the ways that they are morally engaged in his dramatic actions. Northumberland, for example, seems more of an emblematic figure than does York in *Richard II* because he has no doubts as well as no scruples. An energizing catalyst of political change, he is untouched and unchanged by the process of rebellion he helps to initiate; from beginning to end he is consistently a political opportunist. York is more difficult to place on a moral spectrum because, though he would be neuter, he is caught in the moral toils of the plot. Shaken by the assault of circumstances on his deepest certainties, and bewildered by conflicting emotions and opposing loyalties, he is a more complex figure than Northumberland in that his needs are moral and emotional as well as political. Above all he needs to be a devoted patriot—to Bolingbroke if not to Richard.

As is clear in York, what we call psychological depth or complexity in many of Shakespeare's characters might more accurately be called a mirroring in character of the moral themes which are more largely embodied in the dramatic actions of the plays. For Shakespeare's vision of character is, in essence, moral, and the perfect clarity of that vision is blurred only when we attempt to explain by means of a psychological hypothesis the dilemma of a character like Hamlet, who faces a baffling problem of moral action. It is significant, however, that we do not find in Shakespeare, not even in *Hamlet,* the dilemma which modern French dramatists love to depict. There are no Shakespearean analogues to Anouilh's Creon and Sartre's Orestes, decent, compassionate, eminently civilized men who calmly decide that they must act brutally for the public good. The reason perhaps is that Shakespeare is more existential than modern existentialists; he will admit no split between moral theory and moral emotion. He cannot imagine a character who thinks as Angelo does but who feels as Cordelia does. To commit Angelo's acts in a Shakespearean play one must be what Angelo is, because the moral outlook of a Shakespearean character is an expression of his emotional being; only those who see the world feelingly in Shakespeare see it truly. Thus Shakespeare's psychological insights are not simply used to complicate his moral characterizations or to sophisticate in York and Angelo the Morality *psychomachia.* The authority of Shakespeare's ethic does not derive, like that of a Morality, from embodied doctrine; it derives from unerring insight into the nature of man's moral experience. He does not argue a particular moral hope; he does not exhort assent to a particular moral belief. He offers an incontrovertible knowledge of moral and spiritual realities.

That Shakespeare delighted sensuously, as painters and sculptors do, in the things of this world is evident to the most casual reader of his poetry. Less evident is the extent to which the form of his art, like the form of sculpture, answers to the grain, texture, and "natural form" of the artistic material it shapes; that is, the imagined experience it bodies forth. The astonishing range and variety of imagined life in his greatest plays find expression in an equivalent range and variety of poetic and dramatic styles which extend from the quiet naturalism of a conversation in *Othello* to the exalted expressionism of the heath scenes in *Lear*, where the depicted experience is at once chaotic and visionary. A rigid or naive standard of realism will not suffice for an art so varied in its decorums. We need a critical approach to Shakespeare that will allow us to share his poetic discovery of truths that lie beyond the scope of common sense and common perception.

Manliness in the Tragedies: Dramatic Variations

By Robert B. Heilman

I

Shakespeare's tragedies[1] are bursting with ideas of what man is and what he should be and do. In defining "man" and the "manly," speakers reflect their own make-up, their moods, and their intentions, of course; but at the same time their views provide a remarkably full and varied account of man as he is understood to be, and can be, and ought to be. Naturally he must shun the qualities and the conduct that belong to woman. Friar Lawrence rebukes Romeo: "Thy tears are womanish; . . . Unseemly woman in a seeming man" (III.iii.110, 112);[2] Laertes, Lear, Enobarbus upbraid their own tears or fight them off.[3] Hamlet resists a misgiving of "such a kind . . . as would perhaps trouble a woman" (V.ii.225–26), and Coriolanus fears "of a woman's tenderness to be" (V.iii.129). This sort of thing could become a cliché; Shakespeare fights off the hackneyed by introducing reversals. So Antony, thinking Cleopatra dead by her own hand, must "condemn myself to lack / The courage of a woman" (IV. xiv.59–60), and Portia can claim a "man's mind" (II.iv.8). But what catches the eye especially is the freedom in the symbolic use of tears: the very thing that man fears, may prove a virtue. We approach this in Macduff's words after the slaughter of his family, "O, I could play the woman with mine eyes" (IV.iii. 230). Since he has already spoken of feeling the disaster "as a man" (221), the tears of grief actually become manly. Timon, seeing his faithful steward Flavius shed tears for him, cries out:

> *What, dost thou weep? Come nearer. Then I love thee,*
> *Because thou art a woman and disclaim'st*
> *Flinty mankind, whose eyes do never give*
> *But thorough lust and laughter. Pity's sleeping:*
> *Strange times, that weep with laughing, not with weeping!*
> (IV.iii.489–93)

Beneath the lines is a paradox: man, fallen into hardness—an excess of qualities natural to him—may recover by being more like woman.

Yet Shakespeare sees how deep the fear of effeminacy is. By means of it one
man may work on another, as does Cassius in trying to stir Casca to rebellion:
"And we are govern'd with our mothers' spirits; / Our yoke and sufferance
show us womanish" (I.iii.83–84). Man is always struggling to be of his own
sex, to have its quality. Friar Lawrence rates Romeo: "Art thou a man?" and
"Fie, fie, thou sham'st thy shape, . . . Digressing from the valour of a man"
(III.iii.109, 122, 127). The King taxes Hamlet with "unmanly grief" (I.ii.94).
Whatever Iago's ends, the moral force of the manliness to which he regularly
appeals remains axiomatic. To Roderigo: "Come, be a man!" (I.iii.340). To
Othello: "Are you a man?" (III.iii.374). And then a long derisive admonish-
ment of an Othello now completely under his thumb: "Would you would bear
your fortune like a man!"—"Good sir, be a man"—"A passion most unsuiting
such a man"—"all in spleen, / And nothing of a man" (IV.i.62, 66, 78, 89–90).
When Macbeth quails before the ghost of Banquo, Lady Macbeth's sharpest
spur to self-control is "Are you a man?" and "What, quite unmann'd in folly?"
(III.iv.58, 73). The manly virtue that is in contrast with these unmanly excesses
of feeling[4] is summarily imaged in Hamlet's "Give me that man / That is not
passion's slave" (III.ii.76–77). He has led up to this by praising "blood and
judgement . . . well commingled" (74). The opposite forbidden territories of
the true man are hysteria and policy.

Unmanly hysteria may seem "womanish" or even bestial. Romeo's gesture
of suicide, Friar Lawrence declares, shows "The unreasonable fury of a beast,"
and he adds, "Unseemly woman in a seeming man, / And ill-beseeming beast
in seeming both" (III.iii.111–13). Man's need to avoid being a beast is paradoxically turned against Macbeth by Lady Macbeth. When he insists with
standard male defensiveness, "I dare do all that may become a man; / Who
dares do more is none," she retorts that he then was a "beast" to "break
[broach] this enterprise"; yet by carrying through what he started he would
"Be so much more the man" (I.vii.46–51). Her sardonic equation is: the more
the beast (if that's the way you want to play the game), the more the man. In
defining his father, Hamlet approaches the opposite formulation: the more the
god, the more the man. On his father "every god did seem to set his seal / To
give the world assurance of a man" (III.iv.56–62); and Cleopatra needs images
of a vast deity, coextensive with the cosmos, to picture "such a man" as she
dreams of (V.ii.79–94). But Hamlet can praise "a man" only a little less ad-
miringly than he does his father: "What a piece of work is a man! How noble

in reason! How infinite in faculty, in form and moving! How express and admirable in action! How like an angel in apprehension! How like a god!" (II.ii. 315–18). On the other hand Desdemona, in a fairly important moment in her learning process, coaches herself: "Nay, we must think men are not gods" (III.iv.148); and Agrippa, discussing Antony's mixed nature, concludes, "you gods will give us / Some faults to make us men" (V.i.32–33).

Shakespeare never falls into a thin or one-dimensional theory of man. Man must avoid the womanly, but the womanly may be a virtue. Man must avoid the bestial, yet it is always a threat. Man is not a god, but the divine is an indispensable measure of his quality. The sense of the nature of man is expressed in both descriptive and evaluative terms; his identity embraces *is*, *can*, and *ought*; in other terms, the *is* is a sum of actuality, liability, and potentiality. Some observers are biased toward the *errare humanum* view; to others, man is identical with his potential. Thus Hamlet, saying of his father, "He was a man" (I.ii.187). Thus Kent, calling himself "A man"—one who "professes" to "serve," "love," seek wisdom, fear the Day of Judgment, and be loyal to the state (I.iv.11–18). Thus Antony, having "Nature" say of Brutus, "This was a man!"—a man without "envy of great Caesar," with a sense of the "common good," of "gentle" (noble) life (V.v.68–75).

II

In whatever sense man is conceived, every man is obliged to be a man. At this point we can see the obligation taking, normally, a twofold form aptly summarized in Hamlet's phrase "blood and judgement . . . well commingled" (III.ii.74), or, as Ortega y Gasset has put it, "reason" and "spontaneity." "Judgement" implies both maturity (hence "boy" is a handy term of abuse)[5] and, above all things, the possession and use of reason. Friar Lawrence calls Romeo's transports not only unmanly but "unreasonable" (III.iii.111); Hamlet declares that "a man" who does not use "god-like reason" is "a beast" (IV.iv. 35, 38); Kent, as "a man," wishes "to converse with him that is wise"[6] (I.iv.16–17). But Shakespeare also sees how reasonableness in man can become a different thing. When Cominius advises Coriolanus, "And manhood is call'd foolery when it stands / Against a falling fabric" (III.i.246–47), the reason that belongs to manhood is metamorphosed into the common sense required for strategic retreat. This in turn approaches opportunism in Edmund's assurance to the Captain that "men / Are as the time is" (V.iii.30–31). From this it is just a step to Timon's sense of material self-interest in men: "were your godheads to borrow of men, men would forsake the gods" (III.vi.83–85; cf. IV.iii.391).

On the side of "blood" or "spontaneity" there is a comparable range in the sense of what is manly, but here the variations are explored much more fully because "blood" is the very substance of drama. And here Shakespeare moves into basic contradictions in ideas of what "a man" is, and hence into fascinating uses of theme for dramatic and tonal effect. A key episode is Kent's recklessly explosive countering of insults to Lear: "Having more man than wit about me, drew" (II.iv.42). "Wit" names judgment shrunken into policy; "man" is honest feeling that must be released. It is an integrity that disdains concealment. It is what Emilia appeals to in Iago after Othello has credited him with revealing Desdemona's infidelity: "Disprove this villain, if thou be'st a man"[7] (V.ii.172). It is what Coriolanus claims for himself in defending his intransigence before the plebeians: "Would you have me / False to my nature? Rather say I play / The man I am" (III.ii.14–16).

"Blood" means forthrightness, hence recklessness rather than reckoning the cost: it is the general realm of courage. Macduff must grieve for his murdered family, but also he is adjured to "Dispute it like a man"; and when he resolves to fight "this fiend of Scotland," he is praised: "This tune goes manly" (IV.iii. 220, 235). Youths fighting against Macbeth assert, as Lennox puts it, "their first of manhood" (V.ii.11); and young Siward, with his "hurts before," dies "like a man" (V.viii.43). Macbeth, learning that Macduff was not "of woman born," acknowledges that "it hath cow'd my better part of man" (V.viii.18)— that is, his courage. War is a major arena of manhood from the early *Titus* to the late *Coriolanus*. Titus can feel pride in "one and twenty valiant sons, / . . . slain manfully in arms" (I.i.195–96). Volumnia describes her joy in her young son Coriolanus' success in war, and Cominius tells more fully of Coriolanus' almost premature development of manhood-by-war at sixteen:

> When he might act the woman in the scene,
> He prov'd best man i' th' field, and for his meed
> Was brow-bound with the oak. His pupil age
> Man ent'red thus, he waxed like a sea . . .   (II.ii.100–103)

Let us take it a step further: between the brave man and the man of honor there is a close nexus. To Volumnia it is the same thing to say that Coriolanus fought well, that he "proved himself a man," and that he "won honour" (I.iii. 4 ff.). Conversely, Antony's flight at Actium violated "manhood, honour"[8] (III.x.23). But we come to a different sense of that somewhat unstable word "honor"[9] when Goneril in one breath sneers at Albany for being deficient in manhood and for being unable to distinguish "Thine honour from thy suffering" (IV.ii.53). In Goneril's use honor means resentfulness of slights—not, as with Kent, slights to one's lord, but slights to oneself; Goneril is speaking for a version of manliness that in modern parlance is called "quick on the trigger," that is, ever ready for retaliatory attack. This manly-honorable ideal comes up in illuminatingly different tones in *Romeo and Juliet*: playfully when Mercutio quips that Romeo is "dead; stabb'd with a white wench's black eye; . . . and is he a man to encounter Tybalt?" (II.iv.13–17); more seriously when Sampson challenges the Montague servants, "Draw, if you be men" (I.i.69); and still more seriously when Mercutio applies the term "dishonourable" to Romeo's effort to avoid a duel with insolent Tybalt (III.i.76). The duel sensibility is carried a step further by Alcibiades in *Timon* when he defends a friend who in "hot blood" and with "honour," when he felt a "noble fury" at a threat to his "reputation," killed another man (III.v.11–19). By now manly integrity of feeling, which may appear as bravery or desire for honor, has come very close to what we call aggressiveness. It may utilize the accepted form of the dueling code, or may appear in an unmeditated passional act, or, as we shall see, may cross the line into plotted murder.

To have traced these variations is to show how far Shakespeare is from univocal simplicity in his treatment of the manly. But even in a single episode he can suggest different perspectives; for instance, he does not treat "Draw, if you be men" as an ultimate, unexaminable invitation to manliness. In a punning speech Mercutio says that Tybalt "may call" Romeo "man" because Romeo will be his "follower" to the (dueling) "field" (III.i.61–62); when Romeo, called "villain" and "boy" by Tybalt, tries to fend off the challenge by argument, Mercutio exclaims, ". . . dishonourable, vile submission!" (76) and precipitates the fight. Mercutio's style is the conventional "manly" one, and it can count on cheers from the pit. But Shakespeare also makes clear that everyone else's failure to understand Romeo is what brings on the disaster. Hence we see in Mercutio's "dishonourable" not a final judgment that cannot be questioned, but simply one point of view. That point of view is under dramatic pressure from Romeo's two conciliatory speeches to Tybalt, for these embody another

way of responding to insolent challenge: the slighted party can actually con-
strue a deliberate insult as an error, and reject a retaliatory blow in favor of a
plea for understanding. Tybalt's offensive "boy" makes us sense Romeo's relative maturity, that is, his own different approach to manliness. The maturity,
we know, passes; in the perspective of the ideas of manliness competing in this
scene, the saddest words are Romeo's "O sweet Juliet, / Thy beauty hath made
me effeminate" (118–19), for now he reverts to the dueling convention and
seals all their dooms. But this reversion does not obscure the fact that, even in
this early tragedy, Shakespeare's imagination is entertaining forgiveness as an
alternative manly virtue.

Shakespeare offers more explicit critiques of the man-honor-fight dogma.
Capulet himself rejects the touchy honor in whose name Tybalt wants to attack
Romeo at the masked ball: he calls Tybalt "goodman boy" and "saucy boy"
and directly challenges the manly credit Tybalt hopes to snatch: "You will set
cock-a-hoop! You'll be the man!" (I.v.79–85). The subtle movement of manliness toward a heedless self-gratification appears even in Kent; though in him
impolitic explosiveness is charming enough, still there is some justice in beaten
Oswald's complaint that Kent had "put upon him such a deal of man / That't
worthied him" (II.ii.127–28)—a rather neat hit at the self-glorifying and excessive in Kent's style. If Oswald's role leads us to resist his insight, we quickly
yield to that of Volumnia when she criticizes Coriolanus for a comparable out-
rush of integrity in which self-indulgence is more unmistakable. To his somewhat sulky defense for being contentiously "the man I am" in a political context demanding restraint, she retorts, "You might have been enough the man
you are, / With striving less to be so" (III.ii.15–20): she puts her finger on a
strained, self-conscious manliness that mistakes an aversion to even a tactical
self-discipline for moral quality.

We have seen how, as an expression of "blood," the manly can leap from
fortitude over into the explosive, the combative, or something beyond; how
the ideal can slide into the histrionization or indulgence of self. In the catalogue of manly traits, Shakespeare says in effect, there is only a hair's breadth
between the courageous and the outrageous. "Draw, if you be men" puts us
right in that slender space. When Titus Andronicus tells of "one and twenty
valiant sons, / . . . slain manfully" (I.i.195–96), this hyperbole of ultimate manliness introduces an atrociousness of experience that threatens to discredit the
ideal invoked. When Antony, having twice assured his crowd of plebeians that
they are "men," suggests that therefore Caesar's will must "inflame you, . . .
make you mad" (III.ii.147–49), the manliness implied is that of furious, self-

seeking vindictiveness. But it is in later tragedies that Shakespeare is more fully concerned with the imposing of a noble form upon flagrant attitude and deed: he observes the resolute slipping over into the callous and brutal, and courage becoming readiness for outrage. He notes that for some men the outrageous is the natural expression of courage.

In *King Lear* two complementary scenes turn on this transvaluation of the manly: in one, an admirable character is charged with failure as a man; in the other, the image of manliness is used to suborn murder. In the earlier scene, Albany reveals that he at last sees the situation straight; this is a sign of moral recovery in the kingdom. But Goneril is full of contempt for him, and she accuses him of a defective manliness. Two facts are equally striking: Albany is secure enough in his new sense of truth to be invulnerable to charges that by long tradition might be expected to be shattering; and the ideal of the manly has been taken over and used as a weapon by a pitiless and calculating power-grabber. Goneril might have accused Albany of, say, family and political disloyalty, but in seventy lines she has only one tune—Albany's failure as a man: ". . . our mild husband" she calls him to Edmund and Oswald; she sneers at "the cowish terror of his spirit," and carries it a step further, "I must change arms at home, and give the distaff / Into my husband's hands" (IV.ii.1–18). These charges of effeminacy are her response to Albany's welcoming the French invasion, pitying Gloucester, and showing antipathy to Edmund and Goneril. Albany "dares not undertake," Goneril specifies: he is not opportunistic and aggressive. He does "not feel wrongs / Which tie him to an answer" (13–14)— that is, he does not have the duelist's hypersensitivity to slights and his readiness for violence. Then she extends the idea of the manly in a way that is remarkable for its infrequency in Shakespeare and for its relative frequency in other writers. Edmund has what Albany lacks—"O, the difference of man and man!"—and hence he is sexually attractive: "To thee a woman's services are due; / My Fool usurps my body" (26–28). The very drive for power in the world has a sexual charm that invites women to succumb.

This climactic definition of manhood, spoken to Oswald after Edmund's exit, is not repeated to Albany. Otherwise Goneril attacks him to his face just as she has done behind his back: "Milk-liver'd man! . . . Who hast not in thy brows an eye discerning / Thine honour from thy suffering, . . ." (50–53). The scene contains a meaningful antithesis of moral judgments: Albany accuses her of being a fiend, and she accuses him of being less than a man. Goneril closes the scene with a contemptuous summation: "Marry, your manhood—Mew!"[10] (68)

Counterfigure Edmund dares to "undertake": he gets the Captain to murder

Cordelia and Lear (though Lear gets to the murderer before becoming his second victim). Edmund appeals to the Captain's desire to get on in the world, striving to undercut possible objections by invoking the nature of "men," who, he says, "Are as the time is," that is, opportunists (V.iii.31–32). He adds, "to be tender-minded / Does not become a sword": the subtle conversion of sword-bearing manliness into readiness for any killing. Then come the revelatory words of the Captain's commitment: "I cannot draw a cart, nor eat dried oats; / If it be man's work, I'll do 't" (V.iii.38–39). The Captain's "rough humor,"[11] as Kittredge calls it, could not exist did not many human beings see the outrageous as the logical form of manly courage. If the Captain spoke as he does but did not kill, his remark would be an ironic commentary on the nature of "man's work"; but spoken by a murderer the words, whatever their facade of jovial cynicism, clearly say something felt to be literally tenable.

Now let us imagine Shakespeare asking himself a question: what if both parties to this dialogue were more intense, more uneasy people? It is a question we could suppose him to be answering in his very next play: in *Macbeth* he takes the same scene of subornation of political murder by a shaky power-holder fondly seeking security, and expands it from 14 to 69 lines. And he expands proportionately the dramatic importance of the concept of the manly. Macbeth has much more sense of having to make a case to the Murderers whom he is setting on Banquo, and the motive he appeals to is love of revenge: he works on them by implying that they could not let themselves be found indifferent to revenge. Thus he elicits the sought-for reply, "We are men, my liege" (III.i.91). This is the key line; it shows what manliness means to the Murderers, and Macbeth leaps in to press his advantage. He says, in effect, Yes, but what kind of men? Just men by classification? Or something more? If, he argues climactically, you are "Not i' th' worst rank of manhood, say't" (103), and I'll show you how to get even with Banquo and get in with me. So they establish the quality of their manhood; both, having been victims, are now ready to be plungers; as the first puts it, "I am reckless what / I do to spite the world" (110–11). As soon as the manly is understood by all to embrace retaliatory violence, Macbeth can lay out a blueprint for murder.

In 1605–6 Shakespeare was clearly interested in the way in which the concept of manliness could be used as a weapon or as a persuader to action. He sensed in certain men a susceptibility to the argument from undefined manhood, whether through an impulse to violence that thus achieved a quasi-ethical sanction, or through some fear of a deficiency that made it needful to accept all invitations to exacting tests of mettle. His concern led him twice to portray

a commander pushing an underling into "manly" murder, and twice
tray a noble wife bringing pressure against her husband on the score/
ness. In Albany, Shakespeare presents moral security against taunt.
Macbeth he shows the moral situation—doubleness of motive—that creates
vulnerability to the idea of the manly as that which cuts through every inhibit-
ing scruple. Nowhere is that idea put more unreservedly than in Lady Macbeth's "unsex me here" speech: to be unwomaned would be to gain "direst
cruelty" and freedom from remorse, from whatever might "Shake my fell purpose" (I.v.42–47). Later Macbeth himself puts it in other terms: "Bring forth
men-children only; / For thy undaunted mettle should compose / Nothing but
males" (I.vii.72–74). He says this after Lady Macbeth has whipped him back
into line and sketched the tactics against Duncan. Before this, when he hesi-
tated, she attacked him subtly, with insinuations about his "love" and his willingness to "live a coward in thine own esteem" (39, 43). It is a two-edged attack, designed to elicit, and play on, fear of manly insufficiency; it drives
Macbeth to a response remarkably like that which he himself will draw from
the Murderers later: "I dare do all that may become a man" (46).

Lady Macbeth catches the defensive I-can-take-a-dare note, the need to
prove the man that outweighs the will to discriminate morally, and she pounds
the weak spot relentlessly. When you first dreamed of this, she urges, "You
were a man"; act as you dared dream, and you will "Be so much more the
man." But now the actual opportunity appears, and this itself "Does unmake
[unman] you" (49–54). She closes her rhetoric by picking up her "unsex me
here" note in the wild image of dashing out the brains of the sucking babe. It
works: if she can be so little the woman, he must be so much more the man.
Feebly he shifts ground: "If we should fail?" She brushes the fear aside: "we'll
not fail" if you "screw your courage to the sticking-place" (54–61). Courage
again: the manly virtue to sanction the outrageous deed. Lady Macbeth has
learned how to hold Macbeth in line, and she immediately tries the same strat-
egy at the next crisis—Macbeth's panic when he sees Banquo's ghost: "Are you
a man?"—"What, quite unmann'd in folly?" (III.iv.58, 73). Again Macbeth insists he dares, but with a revealing increase in volubility: I "dare look on that /
Which might appall the devil."—"What man dare, I dare."—"I am a man
again" (59–60, 99, 108). Shakespeare uses the resemblance of the scenes to un-
derline the changed times: what confronts Macbeth now is not a scruple but a
vision, not what is to be done but what has been done. His clutching to his manliness is an ironic automatism, for his ideal of the manly is irrelevant to the
claims that the moral order is making against him.

III

What Shakespeare gets hold of is the immense psychic force exerted by man-liness as an ideal—a force so compelling that quite different kinds of conduct claim the color of the ideal. When bloody violence is demanded in the name of the manly, few men can resist the challenge. Albany is virtually unique in de-fying the blandishments of "Be a man." Normally, when "Be a man" rings in the air, man as destroyer must act; other imperatives waver, and the challenger or situation may not be inspected. "Be a man" works thus even though the exhortation comes from an outright scoundrel or someone morally ambiguous. More often than not, the appeal to manliness is used to suborn or justify mur-der; in this sense Shakespeare places a common ideal in very ironic perspective. But at the same time he develops dramatically a counterview of manly action, one that permits us to sense a dramatic struggle, direct or implicit, between different values that find a sanction in the nature of man. For instance, Tybalt's "Boy" and Mercutio's "dishonourable, vile submission" seem to miss the mark beside Romeo's gentle, reasonable explanatory reply to the insolently provoca-tive Tybalt: his desperate cry, "forbear this outrage!" (III.i.90), has a balance and maturity lacking in the conventional responses of the others. Whereas at the Capulet ball Tybalt cried, "I'll not endure him" (I.v.78), Romeo says in effect, "Let us endure him." His "forbear this outrage" might well be spoken by Brutus when, in the plotting against Caesar, he argues against the bloodi-ness that characters in the tragedies often identify with manliness. Brutus' style may not be a popular one today, but in trying to prevent a slaughter he is clearly the man of principle that Antony will later eulogize in "Nature's" sum-mary phrase, "This was a man!" Kent's definition of himself as "a man" in-cludes one phrase of great significance here: "to fight when I cannot choose" (I.iv.17–18). Though Kent hardly acts on his principle, the important fact is that in theory fighting is treated as a last resort, not as a manly virtue per se. Kent asserts and Romeo tries to practice what Macbeth fears the Murderers may have instead of a desire to kill Banquo; so Macbeth has to sneer at "Your patience" and ask with heavy sarcasm, "Are you so gospell'd / To pray for this good man . . . ?" This brings them into his school: "We are men, my liege" (III.i.87–91).

Shakespeare recognizes, then, two different poles of manliness, two differ-ent ways of self-fulfillment for man as man: the way of patience, and the way of striking back; of explanation, and of counterblow; of repenting, and of resenting; of give and forgive, of bear and forbear, and on the other hand of take and "undertake" (Goneril's term). There are two countermovements of personality: the holding back of the self, or the ruthless assertion of the self over others. When Kent, who in different moods has different ways of being manly, says that as "a man" he professes "to serve him truly that will put me in trust," his words reveal one way in which humility and subordination are compatible with manliness.[12] This is not quietism, passivity, or withdrawal; one must always act with courage ("fight when I cannot choose"). But this surrender of primacy for the self is quite different from the self-aggrandizement that leads toward outrage, from the pathological likeness of courage that creates tests for oneself and threats for others, from the sense of honor that demands blood and must revenge all slights, from that aggressive imposition of the will which has as its end the death of whoever means a constraint upon the self.

This latter manliness Shakespeare examines repeatedly in his last three years of tragedy-writing—in *Lear* and *Macbeth,* as we have seen, and then again in both private and public life in the last plays. In *Timon* the banishment of Alcibiades stems from his unremitting defense of a hero-turned-murderer. In proposing his own war wounds and those of his friend as arguments for showing mercy to his friend who has killed, Alcibiades implicitly invokes the ideal of the manly that we shall see most unqualifiedly developed in Coriolanus. The friend, to judge from the opinions of the Senators who condemned him, must have been cut from the Tybalt cloth: the Second Senator calls him a "sworn rioter," who in "beastly fury / . . . has been known to commit outrages" (III.v. 68–72). "Outrages": again the term that seems most appropriate to signify an extreme and perverse employment of courage. It is exactly "valour" that Alcibiades praises his friend for; indeed, he pictures him as an admiring friend might picture Tybalt, that is, as a quick-tempered man of honor. He is "a man, setting his fault aside, / Of comely virtues"; he acted "in hot blood" and without "cowardice"—

> An honour in him which buys out his fault—
> But with a noble fury and fair spirit,
> Seeing his reputation touch'd to death,
> He did oppose his foe . . .   (11–20)

Though the word "man" is little used, Shakespeare is clearly permitting Alcibiades to make the strongest possible case for honor-blood-and-death manliness, indeed in its name to attempt a justification for the impulse to murder.

In *Coriolanus* the theme of manliness is developed, though with a somewhat altered formulation, in an eminent public figure. Though Coriolanus is not a plotter or suborner of murder, his stiff-necked insolence is a variation of the self-promoting manliness propounded by Goneril and Lady Macbeth. It is more than a coincidence that the arrogance which distinguishes Coriolanus should appear in a man of all but excessive achievements in blood-and-honor manliness. Volumnia has wanted only "honour" for her son; when Coriolanus[13] was but "tender-bodied" she sent him to a "cruel war," where he "proved himself a man"[14] (I.iii.6–19). She has a happy image of Coriolanus going out with "bloody brow" to "mow" down Aufidius. Blood, she insists, "more becomes a man / Than gilt his trophy," and she claims an ultimate loveliness for Hector's forehead "when it spit forth blood / At Grecian sword" (37–46). Coriolanus is a literally bloody conqueror ever talking about blood in his double contempt for Volscians and Romans defective in manhood. Cominius eulogizes Coriolanus for his battle feats at age sixteen, when "He prov'd best man i' th' field" (II.ii.101). Then, "His pupil age / Man-ent'red thus," he was the star of seventeen battles. "He was a thing of blood, whose every motion / Was tim'd with dying cries" (102–3, 113–14). He ran "reeking o'er the lives of men, as if / 'Twere a perpetual spoil" (123–24). To this gory praise Menenius adds an amen in the form "Worthy man!" (126). Of this man it could be predicted that he would wear badly "The napless vesture of humility" (II.i.250), would give demagogues plenty of raw material for raising a revolt against him ("You speak o' th' people / As if you were a god to punish, not / A man of their infirmity"—III.i.80–82), and would justify his impolitic behavior thus: "Rather say I play / The man I am" (III.ii.15–16).

In this last tragedy Shakespeare makes a new and very penetrating approach to the theme of aggressive manliness. The rampant ego expresses itself equally in the destroying of enemies and the contemning of "the people." It is not as simple as that, of course, for the destroying of enemies is an act of patriotism, and the contemning of the people is centered in a reluctance to truckle that has its moral appeal. What we are compelled to do, in the end, is to recognize a sort of frenzied destructiveness in this man with the warrior's traditional virtues, and a self-worshiping inflexibility in the man of what we now call "integrity." We could make a modern genetic approach to this amalgam of virtues and their distortions and theorize that his mother made him what he is, thrusting him prematurely into duels with death and allowing him, for psychological and emotional sustenance, only a code of ego-enhancing loveless valor; so that, in the end, he can never consent, but must only resent, can never yield, even ceremonially, but must always conquer. But genesis is less important than the consistency of apparently independent manifestations of the personality: the manly destruction of enemies is paralleled, or re-expressed, in the active contempt for the citizenry. It is not going too far to say that Coriolanus, with a style that is an extension of Kent's explosiveness, comes close to a symbolic murder of the citizens. The problem is that even a great hero cannot murder everybody. But omnicide (to risk a coinage) is the logical extreme of a manliness that implies the autonomy of the will in the self and the mastery of the world by the self.

IV

The later tragedies would be interesting enough for their portrayal of the manliness that needs a triumph of the self, through whatever mingling of pride easily inflated into insolence, and strength ever driving toward violence. But it is a provocative fact that in these later plays Shakespeare is also exploring, either in itself or as a dramatic alternative, the manliness that yields, endures, or even pities. To her treasurer Seleucus Cleopatra says bitterly, "Wert thou a man, / Thou wouldst have mercy on me" (V.ii.174–75); Cleopatra has her own ends, of course, but she is never naive enough to invoke a concept that would only bring smiles. Against Alcibiades' arguments for the bravery and honor of his hotheaded homicidal friend, the Athenian Senators vehemently thrust a countervalue so far from the aggressive that it is close to turning the other cheek. The First Senator not only accuses Alcibiades of "too strict a paradox," of making "an ugly deed look fair," and of "set[ting] quarreling / Upon the head of valour," but formally denies Alcibiades' "hot blood" notion of valor: this, he says, "Is valour misbegot," the spirit of "sects and factions"[15] (III.v. 24–30). Then he makes the major ethical leap and propounds an alternative valor of self-control and tolerance:

> He's truly valiant that can wisely suffer
> The worst that man can breathe, and make his wrongs
> His outsides, to wear them like his raiment, carelessly,
> And ne'er prefer his injuries to his heart,
> To bring it into danger.   (31–35)

Though a note of self-preservation creeps into the definition, it is clear that at the heart of it is the assertion of a spiritual quality; the Senator sums up, "You cannot make gross sins look clear; / To revenge is no valour, but to bear" (38–39). Valor is manliness; here, the manly is the surmounting of resentfulness and punitiveness, and it approaches Christian forgiveness. Alcibiades derides "enduring" (cf. Tybalt), "valour in the bearing," "wisdom . . . in suffering" (44, 46, 51); in this view, he sneers, women are "more valiant" (47). Shakespeare writes extremely vigorous lines for both Alcibiades and the Senators who oppose him, and the scene is one of great tension; but behind the conflict of personalities is a tense drama of ideas that crop up repeatedly in the tragedies. Here the course of the action (the rejection of Alcibiades' appeal, the banishment of Alcibiades) makes one of Shakespeare's most emphatic rejections of the eye-for-an-eye theory of the manly.

In *Coriolanus* Shakespeare returns to make still another reply to the hypersensitive, revengeful male ego. From very early in the play, indeed, he uses Virgilia, Coriolanus' wife, to offer at least a mild criticism of the blood-worshiping Volumnia, who had driven her young son into military manliness in a "cruel war." "But had he died in the business, madam, how then?" Virgilia asks (I.iii.20–21). And she exclaims, "His bloody brow! O Jupiter, no blood!" (41). Later, when Coriolanus is said to be coming home wounded, Virgilia's "O, no, no, no" balances Volumnia's "O, he is wounded; I thank the gods for't" (II.i.132–34). Virgilia's is a small voice, but it is enough to prevent the drama from being run away with, so to speak, by Volumnia's blood-and-glory sense of manhood. But when the Volumnia code is to be most powerfully challenged, Shakespeare manages it as effectively as possible by having the challenge made, not by the gentle Virgilia, but by Volumnia herself. We first see a modification in her position when, in answer to Coriolanus' "I play / The man I am," she retorts, "You might have been enough the man you are, / With striving less to be so" (III.ii.15–20). Partly she is urging him to practice tact and tactics, to "play politics"; but also she is observing something excessive and self-indulgent in his total unwillingness to curb self-will, however much it wears the dress of uncompromising integrity ("The man I am"). She urges him to bow his head, "correcting thy stout heart" (78), but his replies center on his "honour" (121, 144).

When his last effort to be politic fails, and he leaves to join Aufidius and get "revenge" on Rome, Volumnia furiously curses the demagogues who were opposed to him, and she exhibits a disgust with Rome almost equal to his own. This is dramatically important, for it shows that when she pleads with Coriolanus to save Rome, she is not merely the voice of mechanical patriotism but has also to control her emotions. The son to whom she appeals is in love with his "rages and revenges," is determined to resist pleas that he "forgive" and to reject "woman's tenderness," to deny "instinct, but stand / As if a man were author of himself / And knew no other kin" (V.iii.35–37, 44, 85, 129). Coriolanus here embodies all the conventional manliness of self-love: readiness to deny all restraints and to assume, in the style of Macbeth, the tincture of divinity. Volumnia makes a very striking approach: she attacks him on his own ground, the ground of honor and overvaulting manliness: "Thou hast affected the fine strains of honour, / To imitate the graces of the gods" (149–50). And from that she goes on to formulate a plea that is as remarkable in her, with her old faith in blood-manliness, as it is in the public life portrayed in the tragedies: "Think'st thou it honourable for a noble man / Still to remember wrongs?" (154–55). In the tragedies, these words of hers make the most unqualified presentation of manliness as the ability to yield and forgive, and they lead to the dramatic climax in which Coriolanus relinquishes his own hardness of spirit and gives up the attack on Rome. Shakespeare could imagine this as possible even in the personality nurtured on blood-letting and stiffened into a more than usually rigid willfulness. Yet he guards the achievement of spirit against the sentimentality that always lurks in the train of forbearance: Coriolanus has got himself too deeply involved with fell opposites for magnanimity to be compatible with safety. And Aufidius now becomes the voice of ruthless repayment of wrongs: in effect he rejects Volumnia's identification of the manly and forgiving by interpreting Coriolanus' saving of Rome as "set[ting] thy mercy and thy honour / At difference in thee" (200–201) and Coriolanus as "a man by his own alms empoison'd, / And with his charity slain" (V.vi. 11–12).

V

Shakespeare's range in characterization is due in part to the conceptual inclusiveness with which he looks at the nature of man as a class. He might use "man" and "manhood" as if each had a set meaning, but for him they are never clichés seeking stock responses, however narrowly a character may use such a word. His wisdom in viewing man emerges as esthetic resourcefulness; we have not aphorisms, but ideas in action. Shakespeare presents man as not-god, not-animal, not-woman; his portrait embraces man-as-he-is and man-as-he-ought-to-be; his sense of man-as-he-is-thought-to-be opens up a vast panorama of relativities, with different personalities in different moods and contexts proclaiming that man is ungrateful, fearful, courageous, resolute, controlled, envious, opportunistic, angelic. Man in a generic sense, as well as the mass of individual men, embodies a multiple, discordant, and yet somehow appropriate reality. "He is a man" can mean so many different things that any systematic paraphrase of it may appear impossible. But in fact "he is a man" is not used at random, or in an infinite series of disjunct situations; indeed, the generic views of man, various as they are, tend ultimately to gather about two polar conceptions—of manliness as the restraint of the rampant and aggressive self, and of manliness as the expression of the assertive and conquering self. On the one hand man can exhibit his generic nature by yielding, forgiving, enduring injury; here is the manliness of the soft answer, of the generous act, of the acceptance of whatever imperative modifies the surging, combative ego. In these responses is the kind of moral security that can produce the saint, and the very potentiality implies something of an obligation. When the action turns on an individual's sense of where manhood lies, Shakespeare's management of the drama invites admiration and respect for the generous and disciplined man. But he has a very lively sense of the power over men of that other manliness which also demands valor but in which the act of courage moves toward or becomes outrage, the self expresses itself in some triumph by might, and the impulse to injure or destroy, whether it act in public causes or private quests, reveals the pressing male ego. For many men the call of that destructive impulse is virtually a moral imperative.

Shakespeare looks from many angles at this version of the manly in which the id flares up and the outward drive of energy makes every barrier seem a humiliation. One must surge through barriers—enemies, public or private; injuries and slights; sanctions and scruples. Slights and scruples are equally burdensome to the manly free spirit; they are to be thrown off as rivals are to be thrown down. Here is the link between Tybalt the challenger; Goneril and Lady Macbeth, who cry for men that will dare all to snatch the world; Edmund and Macbeth, who plot murder; Alcibiades' friend, who would brook no infringement of honor; and even Coriolanus, the bloody patriot to whom an all-but-decided political engagement must be a total triumph, untainted by even a ceremonial submission.

Shakespeare's understanding of this primitivist version of the manly ideal appears also in his copious animal imagery, a good deal of which comments on the bestial element in man that constantly endeavors to take over. But the animal imagery normally embodies a moral judgment: rarely do people want to be beasts, or admire the beast in others. All men, on the other hand, are torn by the desire to be "men," and to many this means seizing or conquering or destroying. That the impulse to triumph over men and scruples has found some share in the sanction of manliness—of that biological-moral norm which few are willing to fall short of—reveals the urgency of the impulse. Literature periodically shows its force, in evil men of course, but more importantly in average sensual men. It is a very ordinary fellow, a representative good friend, who will not face death with Everyman but who assures him cheerfully: "But and thou wilt murder, or any man kill, / In that I will help thee with a good will!" (281–82) Since Bunyan's characters are highly representative figures, we are safe in assuming that his Shame spoke for a popular attitude when "he said that a tender conscience was an unmanly thing; and that for a man to watch over his words and ways, so as to tie himself up from that hectoring liberty that the brave spirits of the times accustom themselves unto, would make him the ridicule of the times."[16] "Unmanly" and "hectoring liberty" place Shame exactly in the Shakespearean gallery of "men" of a certain type. When Michael Henchard, in Hardy's *Mayor of Casterbridge*, traps Donald Farfrae into a wrestling match with the intention of killing him, he tells Donald that now they are "man and man," that is, creatures of physical strength only.[17] In Conrad's *Victory* Heyst is of a totally different stamp: he has sought a fugitive and cloistered virtue—a rejection of the "brave spirits of the times" and the "man and man" views. Indeed, he acknowledges that he may lack "courage," at least "the sort that always itches for a weapon." He adds, "No, I've never killed a man or loved a woman"—and, musingly, "To slay, to love—the greatest enterprises of life upon man!"[18] Even in Heyst there is a faint philosophical nostalgia for a kind of valor that he has rejected and could never practice.

Heyst's "to slay, to love" reflects the ancient love-death nexus that appears often in literature. We can illustrate the drift of manliness (of the predatory-retaliatory type) toward sexual prowess by an arrangement of approximate synonyms: manliness—masculinity—maleness—virility (cf. the folk phrase "in the manly state"). It is interesting that this spectrum of meanings, which could bridge the gap from Bunyan's Shame to Byron's Don Juan, is hardly developed in Shakespeare's tragedies. It is true that the love-death nexus is active more than once: in *Romeo and Juliet*, *Othello*, and *Antony and Cleopatra*. But sex rarely enters the definitions of manliness; the self-assertive male, who is always a potential death dealer, is hardly ever the sexual hero. Edmund is briefly this kind of hero when Goneril openly and vigorously asserts her sexual response to him; Antony might be such a hero, but in the treatment of the Antony-Cleopatra relationship, with the constant pressing toward romantic transcendence, there is little tinge of the potent male. The manly-as-virile flourishes in Restoration drama and in the Fielding side of eighteenth-century fiction, and then goes underground until its resurrection in the somber evangelical form of D. H. Lawrence's "essential maleness" or "savage maleness." But here the predator of old has thinned out into the antifeminist, and his longing to lose the self in "blood consciousness" is a far cry from longing to assert the self in bloodletting.

Still Lawrence is talking about "maleness," and the very word reveals an underground reservoir of common feeling somewhere beneath the manliness of love and the manliness of war. If Shakespeare does not tap the reservoir at one point, he does at the other, and hence we can see a marked line of connection between an aspect of his thought and an aspect of contemporary thought. The manliness that is rooted in physical strength and that easily branches out into killing—the manliness which Shakespeare understood very well—has a strong hold on the twentieth-century imagination. It shows in the ceaseless representation of male merit by the images "red-blooded" and "guts," which are not used to laud the pacific and forbearing; in the unformulated ethics that dominate the subterranean phenomena of "gangs" and the massive above-ground phenomena of the popular cinema, which almost invariably identifies moral excellence with sterner fist and more agile pounce; and finally in an art which purports to be less simple—the literature, fiction largely, of strain and danger, in difficult exploration, hunting, and fighting. In the rather voluminous literature that speaks for this sensibility the most conspicuous writer is Hemingway, with his sanguinary adventuring, bullfighting, campaigning. One need not disparage Hemingway to suggest that even after four hundred years our view of this manliness tends to be more naive than Shakespeare's: we more readily regard it as an uncontingent virtue, less readily place it in a context of choices and consequences.

An essay on Shakespeare is not the place to speculate on the needs that may underlie an apparently unusual craving for manliness as an assertion of the self over things and other beings. But if unexpected doubts, tensions, and challenges stir up a longing for proof of manly valor, and if blood-shedding, the most ancient reassurance, is not easily available in its plainer forms, we have at least the conquest of nature and animals to fall back upon. In life, as in our response to Hemingway themes, we make much of hunting, that sterilized version of the old blood-and-death manliness. And on this side of his personality, modern man finds a remarkably complete Shakespearean prototype—in Macbeth when he is terrified of Banquo's ghost. What is in the forefront of Macbeth's mind is the necessity of asserting his manly valor, of insisting that his confusion and terror do not make him less a man. "What man dare, I dare" is his self-rehabilitating vaunt (III.iv.99). And he argues it thus to Banquo's ghost: ". . . my firm nerves / Shall never tremble" if you "Approach . . . like the rugged Russian bear"—the bear pit (cf. the Spanish bull ring); or if you approach like "The arm'd rhinoceros, or th' Hyrcan tiger"—hunting in Africa; or if you "dare me to the desert with thy sword"—ask me to "step outside" (100–104). The scene is archetypal: it reveals the depth of the fears, the pressure of guilt, that lie behind the need to establish manliness by bloody sports. Bears, tigers, duels to the death: all better than ghosts and impalpable dangers, all substantial, faceable, reassuring man that he is man. For two acts more, indeed, *Macbeth* goes on in a related vein that has become equally familiar to us: it is the most modern of the tragedies. For if the world is meaningless, a tale told by an idiot, signifying nothing—is absurd—nothing remains for man but the pride of fighting on alone: ". . . tell pale-hearted fear it lies" (IV.i.85); "Fear not" (V.iii.6); "I'll fight till from my bones my flesh be hack'd" (V.iii.32); "At least we'll die with harness on our back" (V.v.52); "I must fight the course" (V.vii.2); "I will not yield" (V.viii.27).

It is the contemporary feeling for this manliness of the militant self, no doubt, that makes Shakespeare's understanding of it, almost four centuries ago, seem extraordinary. But it is more extraordinary that he had equal understanding of it and at the same time of that other manliness of the pacific, forbearing self.

Is *Hamlet* a Hoax?

By William T. Hastings

I invite my hypothetical reader to share with me in an impossible adventure—the attempt to say something true and not wholly trite, something slightly enlightening if not comprehensive, about the most familiar, the most written and talked about—many would say the greatest—of Shakespeare's plays. Fifty years ago in the stacks in Gore Hall in Cambridge there was a whole shelf devoted to books about *Hamlet;* how many shelves in Widener the past half century of commentary occupies I do not dare to guess. In a college lecture course the teacher may well devote a third of his time on the play to a survey of *Hamlet* criticism. Here I must disregard, except for unconscious assimilation or slaps in passing, what others have thought and said about the play and its protagonist. I must assume it is known by heart. I must hew to a line, however much that would be interesting or significant for reader or spectator is left aside.

My "line" is vaguely and facetiously indicated by my title, but the point of view needs some expansion. It is certain that the appeal of the play is due to the appeal of the character, what he is, what he says, what he does. In the attempt to define that appeal criticism has described him variously as the conventional hero, as charming and frail, cowardly, too philosophical, too Christian; as melancholy, as a type study of *the* melancholy man, as hysteric, neurotic, victim of an Oedipus complex, even as mad. Professor Stoll almost argues that he is no character at all.[1] Mark Van Doren, in contrast, becomes mystical: "We do not know why he was created or what he means. We simply and amply perceive that he exists."

Inevitably a critic must at least glance at the unsolved mystery of Shake-speare's art. Was it conscious or instinctive? Was it grounded in philosophy and didactic, or superficial and photographic? Ben Jonson said Shakespeare had both "nature" (natural gift) and "art." Shakespeare tells us nothing him-self. Did he write histories, as Tillyard thinks, to glorify Tudor England, with *Respublica* his protagonist? Did he have a theory of tragedy, involving types of tragic action and of tragic hero, and a concept of the tragic flaw, of fate, of decorum? He uses the word "decorum" once in the technical sense, though he violates the principle consistently; but this provides little basis for generaliza-tion. His "mind and hand went together," but what went on in the quick forge and working house of his thought before he wrote we can only guess. Did he start with an idea, a character, a situation, or a scenario? Or with various com-binations of these? To what extent did he write to order? To what extent is the cynical so-called "box-office" theory of his motivation justified? There is no clear answer, and therefore in the examination of each play criticism must be wary, and so far as possible without preconceptions. It must avoid the pedantry of categories and classifications, trying to see the thing simply as it is.

The pre-Shakespearean *Hamlet* has not survived, but from contemporary allusions and from the legendary history on which it was based we can recon-struct it to some extent. It was extremely popular and was in the repertory of Shakespeare's company in the mid-nineties. It was violent, declamatory, and bloody in the best tradition of the Senecan revenge play. The perfect hero had no doubts; he was delayed in his revenge by external obstacles; and when re-venge was achieved, in the original legend at least, it was a holocaust. It began with the ghost appearing on the battlements "on a frosty morning," as does our play; and this and other correspondencies justify us in assuming that, as so often, Shakespeare took over the scenario of his source. And, as always, he gave the story depth and meaning.

Is it too fanciful to suppose that one day when he was watching a perform-ance of the *Ur-Hamlet*, or perhaps, as legend suggests, playing the ghost, it suddenly struck him that a greater and more moving drama, a genuine tragedy, would be created if the shallow, bloody-minded Prince were transformed into an intelligent, nice young man of late sixteenth-century rather than early thir-teenth-century characteristics? The delay, without which there could be no drama, and which in the original story is made incidental to the self-protec-tive fencing of two brutal antagonists, uncle and nephew, would have to be handled more subtly, and the fencing would be elevated to an intellectual thrust and parry. This, I believe, was the start. To the highly intricate result many other things contributed, as the dramatist's creative thought went on.

In all Shakespeare's greater plays, even though he begins with a plot, it is his triumph to make the developing action seem grounded in character; the traits of the characters, for good or evil, seem to converge upon the crisis and compel the denouement. There is a complex of astute characterization here, but in large part I must disregard it. I must take for granted an understanding of the good and evil, strength and weakness, in Claudius, Gertrude, Polonius, and Ophelia (not to mention Rosencrantz and Guildenstern, the sentinels, the grave diggers, and the rest), and what their traits mean to the play. Attention must be fixed, so far as possible, upon the protagonist, for though there has been some critical disagreement about all these other characters, the great fury of interpretation has eddied around that slight figure dressed in black whose entrance in Act I, scene ii, is so moving and so significant.

Shakespeare seldom leaves us in any doubt as to a character: his emotions, his morals, his mentality; whether we are to feel admiration, sympathy, delight, tolerant amusement, hatred, or contempt. When the character acts, therefore, we understand the logic of his action and are ready to applaud or condemn; ready, in short, to say, or think, "That is just like him, my hero" (or, variously, "that freak," "the fool," "the scoundrel"). How does he prepare for, make clear, the behavior of his characters? He did not write prefatory essays like Bernard Shaw or, with two or three partial exceptions, extradramatic author's prologues addressed to an audience. The information is all within the play. It is sometimes, by a convention still alive, begun in a preparatory conversation between minor characters. It is sometimes developed by contrasting characters as in *Julius Caesar*; sometimes by the use of a formal chorus, as in *Henry V*, or a so-called chorus character, like Queen Margaret in *Richard III*; sometimes by the remarks of a confidential friend or associate, like Enobarbus in *Antony and Cleopatra*. Often, in a technique now frowned upon, it is conveyed in the spoken thoughts, or soliloquy, of the character himself. And finally, of course, what is said about him by himself or others and the suggested parallels or contrasts with other persons in the drama are supplemented or corroborated by the acts of the man himself. At least, criticism thinks, they *will be* in a well-ordered piece. Hence all the critical turmoil over *Hamlet*.

The essential problem of interpretation is outlined in Act I. In the presence chamber scene (ii), Hamlet, before he has heard of the ghost, is melancholy, courteous to his mother, rude to Claudius, and when left alone records the deep loathing of life caused by his father's death and his mother's remarriage to an uncle whom he intensely dislikes. In the ghost scenes which conclude the act

there is much that is significant: the calm loyalty of Horatio, the physical courage of Hamlet, and more particularly the latter's shifting moods. We must find
the congruity within a "real," that is, a self-consistent, character of these
things:

First (speaking to his father's spirit):

> *Haste me to know't that I, with wings as swift*
> *As meditation or the thoughts of love,*
> *May sweep to my revenge.*

Second: His distracted speech after the ghost's withdrawal, which seems to
Horatio "but wild and whirling words."

Third: The binding to secrecy if he puts on "an antic disposition" (that is,
pretends madness—for no stated reason).

And fourth: The very conspicuously placed exit lines,

> *The time is out of joint;—O cursed spite,*
> *That ever I was born to set it right!*

Already in these scenes there is clearly suggested to us the character Ophelia
is to describe as

> *The courtier's, soldier's, scholar's, eye, tongue, sword;*
> *The expectancy and rose of the fair state,*
> *The glass of fashion and the mould of form.*

And at the same time we observe an emotional disturbance which seems partly
out of control. Let us forbear to put a label on it, since to use the words "depressed," "melancholic," "hysteric," or "frantic," to say nothing of ringing in
"complexes," will be to commit ourselves too soon. It is impossible to overlook
the fact, however, that Shakespeare has made his hero speak first the language
of the perfect avenger—"Sweep to my revenge"—and then a little later conspicuously curse the malice of Heaven in assigning him this task. Is the dramatist counting on our not noticing the contradiction?

Act I is concerned with two nights and the intervening day. Then begins
the usual Shakespearean double time, the continuity clock and the lapse-of-
time clock. There must be implied lapse of time so that events will seem to
stretch out normally; but there must be continuous action, not only because it
is a stage convention but also so that our avenger's delay will not be too conspicuous. Thus between the day of Act I and that of Act II there has to be
time for the ambassadors to go to Norway and return and for the king, dis-

turbed by Hamlet's mood, to call to court his school friends, the antiphonal Rosencrantz and Guildenstern. Yet after the "antic disposition" proposal of Hamlet in the concluding lines of Act I, the entrance of the affrighted Ophelia in Act II, scene i, to report meeting Hamlet with his doublet unbraced, his stockings down, and a mad look in his eye, seems to be the next morning; and it is on that day that the ambassadors return. There is a similar interval for Hamlet's departure for England and unexpected return, made inconspicuous for us by the Laertes-Claudius business and the madness and suicide of Ophelia. But such technicalities to one side, let us note, as briefly as we can, what Hamlet says and does, or doesn't do, which is relevant to our understanding of the dramatic intent.

In both the public (full stage) and more private scenes throughout the play we see the Hamlet of former times, courteous, friendly, even gay, the perfect gentleman, the "observed of all observers," as in his first greeting of Horatio and the sentinels, the welcome to his old school friends and to the players, and as late in the play as his mimicking of Osric, the "water-fly," his expression of regret to Laertes, before the fencing match, for his unintended killing of Polonius. But when something or someone reminds him of his moral situation, he becomes gloomy, strained, unpleasantly mischievous; he is insulting to Polonius, darkly threatening to the king, savage and cruel to Ophelia and to his mother. Some of this strange conduct is being "idle," as he calls it, playing the madman—for concealment or for emotional release. But his more violent moments are desperately sincere.

What guidance does the dramatist provide us for the interpretation of these changing moods? What for the delay of vengeance to the last moments of Act V? Let us turn first to the soliloquies. At the end of Act II, which, remember, is the night of only the second day of the action, the Player's tears over Hecuba startle Hamlet out of the relaxed mood of his reunion with old friends into violent self-condemnation for his inaction. (We are not given time to decide which clock to look at to estimate the length of his delay—twenty-four hours or a month or two. We accept his word for it.) He calls himself a dreamer not possessed by his obligation, a coward submissive under insults; and passes from screaming at himself to crying out at Claudius

> *Bloody, bawdy villain!*
> *Remorseless, treacherous, lecherous, kindless villain!*
> *O, vengeance!*

Then he breaks off, drops in tone, turning his scorn upon himself because he

> *Must, like a whore, unpack my heart with words,*
> *And fall a-cursing like a very drab . . .*

And then, with a return to something like normal self-control, he proposes—as if now first thought of, though already he has arranged it with a player—the play within the play, containing "some dozen or sixteen lines" added as a test of the ghost's reliability. He concludes: "I'll have grounds / More relative than this" (that is, than the words of the ghost on the battlements, which up to now apparently have been wholly accepted)—and goes off tranquil.

In Act IV, scene iv, Hamlet, on his way to embark for England, sees the army of Fortinbras, and dismisses his unprotesting attendants, who according to one theory are holding him virtually prisoner, forcing him away. How simply the dramatist waves his wand and dismisses this external obstacle! Hamlet dismisses his attendants so that he can respond to this second stimulus to self-condemnation. The soliloquy, though more composed, has the same general character as the "rogue and peasant slave" outburst at the end of Act II. His spirit of revenge is "dull"; he is merely living, which is bestial. Then come the critical words:

> *Now, whether it be*
> *Bestial oblivion, or some craven scruple*
> *Of thinking too precisely on th' event,—*
> *A thought which, quarter'd, hath but one part wisdom*
> *And ever three parts coward,—I do not know*
> *Why yet I live to say, "This thing's to do,"*
> *Sith I have cause and will and strength and means*
> *To do't.*

He concludes the speech, after a fervid apostrophe to the soldiers of Fortinbras who are willing to die "for a fantasy and trick of fame," with the personal exhortation,

> *O, from this time forth,*
> *My thoughts be bloody, or be nothing worth!*

And, turning his back on bloodshed, he marches down to the harbor to take ship for England!

Do these two soliloquies do what a good soliloquy should? Do they reveal the speaker's character, his purposed action, and his motives? They lack the crude explicitness of Richard III's first address to the audience, "I am determined to prove a villain"; and the slyness of Iago's recurrent gloatings: "I'll have our Michael Cassio on the hip"; or his prediction that Othello "will as tenderly be led by th' nose / As asses are." They are ambiguous, almost self-contradictory; at least, words and action do not perfectly correspond. In the first one, after lashing himself for inaction, Hamlet proposes a substitute for direct action. Why? Is it justifiable? Some critics learnedly argue that it was the right course for a true hero. The psychologists see it as an evasive mechanism. Some argue that the soliloquies are the words of a resolute man exhorting himself. Some fall back on the "beautiful but weak" or the "melancholic paralysis" formula to explain the discrepancy between words and deed, the appearance of "irresolution." Some would escape trouble by arguing that the soliloquies are a mere convention and mean nothing, meant nothing to the writer himself.

All these desperate attempts to save our hero, to protect him in our minds from his action or non-action, we must set aside. If we look at the two soliloquies squarely, we must see their ambiguity, see that without supplementary data they support at best only a tentative opinion. Hamlet twice calls himself a coward, and he is not. He accuses himself of insensitiveness, of an animal's forgetfulness of its parents, of mere raving; and we know that this is all unjust. The most arresting remark is in the passage quoted a moment ago: "I do not know / Why yet I live to say, 'This thing's to do.' "

And to the confusion—it should confound them—of more than one school of critics, he then declares that he has the physical strength, the resolute will, and the opportunity which are necessary. All we can conclude is that he admits his obligation, condemns himself for inaction, swears to act—all in most sincere and moving words—and does something else.

To the solution of the mystery what do character contrasts contribute? Fortinbras, as calm as Horatio, goes about righting a wrong with entire competence, and quite uninterestingly. The function of Laertes, as we know, is partly to develop another contrast. Like his father and his sister he is a simple soul, a little vain, a little impatient, and rather easily led; brave and loyal, however. Like Fortinbras he is a man of action rather than of thought. He is of sharply different temper from the calm Horatio and the subtle Hamlet. His promptness, however wrongheaded, in seeking to avenge the death of Polonius, throws into relief Hamlet's delay, and reduces to nonsense the argument, foolish anyway but thus squarely confuted, that Hamlet could not act sooner than he did because of the king's Swiss guard. That we prefer the delaying Hamlet to the impetuous and shallow Laertes is too obvious to mention; but the latter's activity helps the dramatist with the basic problem of the delay.

For Horatio, the self-effacing, we come to have an affection second only to that for Hamlet himself. He is the model friend, quiet, cheerful, loyal, and dependable. He has the wit which resides in reticence and understatement. His traits are clearly suggested in the ghost scenes of Act I and are elaborated by Hamlet in their important conversation which precedes the play within the play. In that talk Hamlet praises his friend for qualities in which he feels himself deficient: for his serenity in both good and ill fortune.

> *A man that Fortune's buffets and rewards*
> *Hath ta'en with equal thanks. . . .*
> . . . .
> *. . . Give me that man*
> *That is not passion's slave, and I will wear him*
> *In my heart's core, ay, in my heart of heart,*
> *As I do thee.*

Again, after the king's flight from the play which enacts his crime, Hamlet's rather wild jocosity is contrasted with Horatio's calm, brief replies. And the same sharp definition of character is revealed in the long conversation between them at the beginning of the last scene of Act V, when Hamlet is telling of the interrupted trip to England. The contrast is most conspicuous when Hamlet at the end of the story of the plot against his life sums up the evil deeds of Claudius and asks superfluously

> *. . . is't not perfect conscience*
> *To quit him with this arm?*

Horatio, who is no fool and certainly is fully aware of the delay, evades a direct answer, merely cautioning

> *It must be shortly known to him from England*
> *What is the issue of the business there.*

But to me the most interesting fact about Horatio is that instead of being, like Enobarbus, the voluble friend who tells all, he is throughout carefully drawn as the reticent friend whose modesty and taciturnity prevent him from serving as the interpreter.

We have, then, a hero who doesn't understand himself, and a *confidant* who understands but will not speak. It is as if, in this play as in no other one, Shakespeare before starting his demonstration of magic had bound himself hand and foot.

Over two fragments of the action which immediately follows the play within the play we must pause briefly. On his way to upbraid his mother, Hamlet comes upon the king at prayer, and after a "Now might I do it pat," he sheathes his sword to await a "more horrid hent" when the king is engaged in something damnable rather than in prayer. He withdraws with a characteristic threat, "This physic but prolongs thy sickly days." Every critic must fit this opportunity to act and its relinquishment into his theory of the play; an extraordinary ingenuity has been devoted to doing it. For the moment we note the fact, remark its ambiguity, and pass on.

The second fragment is the dialogue between Hamlet and the ghost when the latter enters Gertrude's chamber at the height of Hamlet's almost paroxysmal tirade.

> Hamlet.   *Do you not come your tardy son to chide,*
> *That, laps'd in time and passion, lets go by*
> *Th' important acting of your dread command?*
> *O, say!*
> Ghost.   *Do not forget! This visitation*
> *Is but to whet thy almost blunted purpose.*

Hamlet again accuses himself, and the ghost agrees. The purpose of the intervention is in part, of course, strictly dramatic. It brings the ghost back again and at an important moment. But the words spoken must have some relevance to our problem.

No doubt if we should let ourselves turn the pages, many other relevant details would catch our eye, until we almost agreed with Mark Van Doren that nothing short of the whole play will serve as adequate commentary. But I will deny myself that privilege. Two other bits, however, I cannot resist introducing. The first is in the famous "To be or not to be" soliloquy, which till now I have passed over, because it seems to be a general reflection on life and death, rather than directly related to our problem. Hamlet is remarking that we choose to remain alive partly because of our uncertainty about the life after death. This leads him to a general remark that because of our feeling of uncertainty about the consequences of our acts

> *enterprises of great pitch and moment*
> *With this regard their currents turn awry,*
> *And lose the name of action.*

There is a half-rejected personal application of this idea in "thinking too precisely on th' event," already quoted.

Another facet of the problem of action or non-action is touched on, as it were accidentally, in the conversation between the king and Laertes which leads up to the poisoned-rapier fencing match. In gradually working the young man up to his knavish proposal, Claudius asks Laertes if his father was dear to him, and justifies his inquiry by a discourse on how love fades as do other things. He goes on,

> *That we would do,*
> *We should do when we would: for this "would" changes,*
> *And hath abatements and delays as many*
> *As there are tongues, are hands, are accidents;*
> *And then this "should" is like a spendthrift sigh,*
> *That hurts by easing.*

This witty description of the emotional release and the moral deterioration from admitting an obligation and not fulfilling it, though not at all associated by this speaker with the problem of Hamlet's character, inevitably brings that problem to mind. Is it introduced with conscious intent by the dramatist, as a direct contribution to our understanding? as an indirect reinforcement of the words to the ghost, "laps'd in time and passion"? Or is it a psychological accident, springing from something not fully defined in the author's consciousness? There seems no way to tell.

It is high time to "draw toward an end," as Hamlet said to the corpse of Polonius. And it must be done summarily, without returning over our circuitous path to pick up all the hints dropped along the way.

Hamlet must be established as hero. He is so established, in terms acceptable to the contemporary audience and to us, inspiring respect and admiration, delight, understanding, pity. The author's wit and subtlety and his power of poignant phrasing were never more fully employed. But Hamlet's behavior must not be in conflict with the portrait otherwise delineated. Then comes the central dilemma of the delay. The duty of immediate revenge must remain unexecuted till Act V and the postponement must not reflect adversely upon character; indeed, in the Shakespearean as against the original story, it must be based—in part at least—upon character. What then does the magician do?

The play is full of tricks, intended to prevent the spectator from thinking of things that he shouldn't. In this respect, in a limited sense, the play is a hoax; as are, indeed, other works of literature, for literary art involves giving the sense of three-dimensional life to what exists only selectively within the pages of a novel or on the boards of a theater. (The stupid ask: Did Orsino the sentimentalist make a good husband to Viola? Would Macbeth have committed suicide if Macduff had not slain him?) But the hoax, the legitimate and necessary trickery, is greater here than usual. The double time scheme justifies by its slow clock Hamlet's self-accusations; time has elapsed, though, you recall, on review we find only one day of dramatic time between the ghost and the "peasant slave" soliloquy. By its fast clock it reduces to a minimum his opportunities for action, and this is highly important. It is well enough for him to accuse himself; but we should not *see* him constantly postponing. We do, we must, see him recognizing one opportunity and justifying delay—in terms which satisfy himself—in the scene of the king at prayer. But what besides?

After the message from the grave, Hamlet and the king are seldom shown together. In the play scene they are just grouped on stage. There his initial excitement leads Hamlet to uncharacteristic vulgarities, and by a natural carry-over of mood conceals the fact that when he gets the proof he was seeking, instead of springing into action he dances a jig and declaims doggerel. They meet again after the death of Polonius is revealed. Now Hamlet is again rude and vulgar, hardly even speaks daggers, certainly uses none, though he might perfectly well have done so, and when told he is to go to England, merely utters an enigmatic "Good." In the scene of the quarrel with Laertes at the grave of Ophelia the king is composed, and Hamlet plays mad assiduously. In the final scene of the fencing match, Hamlet is the courteous gentleman to Laertes and also, please observe, to the king. There is not the slightest sign of an intent to kill Claudius, even with rapier in hand. And the dramatist here, as in the earlier conjunctions, is deploying all his skill not to have us think about it and say, sitting on the edge of our seats, "Now might he do it pat," while he is talking about chameleon's fare or asking if the foils are of the same length. No, the hero must be protected from the adverse judgment of an audience which thinks such a thought. And when under sudden stimulus, just as when he thrust through the arras at Polonius, he leaps up on the dais and at last kills the king, we rejoice at duty done and crime rewarded, asking no questions. This is certainly Shakespeare the illusionist, the sleight-of-hand artist, at his best.

A few critics, like Professor Stoll, have been quite aware of this artistic duplicity. But their seeming inference that the character is no character is wrong. If that were so, the play would never have moved our hearts as it has done. It would simply be a supershocker. Hamlet the character is what makes the play

—the illusion of him, if you wish—as a young man with a desperate task to perform which somehow wreaks havoc in his life and in all the lives around. If he were no character, or a mere football hero who has taken a course in philosophy, or a self-pitying neurotic, the play would have no meaning except as action. The meaning of the play is the tragic meaning to Hamlet of his task.

And with a daring which because it succeeds may be considered supreme craftsmanship, Shakespeare has made us feel this, accept this, while declining to state that tragic meaning, in the words of Hamlet, of Horatio, of the queen, or of the action itself.

Did he formulate it clearly in his own mind? Only his ghost come from the grave can tell us that.

The Moment of Final Suspense in Hamlet:

"We Defy Augury"

By Fredson Bowers

Just before the catastrophe in Greek tragedy, the protagonist may be given a last chance to escape the fatal consequences of the tragic act that is now on the threshold of retribution. But the logic of character and events is inexorable: the *hubris* that engendered the original error still blinds the protagonist, and he rejects (or does not recognize) the offered alternative that might, even so late, save his life or prevent the crime that is intended. One element of this device is certainly suspense for its own dramatic effect. But, simultaneously, the audience is doubly assured of the justice of the catastrophe when it sees, ironically presented, the same lack of self-knowledge repeated as in the original error: evidence that the protagonist, at the brink of disaster, has not learned through experience the significance of his initial misstep.

An example may be found in Sophocles' *Oedipus Tyrannus*. The Messenger's narrative, in destroying the accepted picture of Oedipus' paternity, reveals the truth to Jocasta, who tries to dissuade Oedipus from demanding the fatal revelation that she knows will follow on the summons to the herdsman. Oedipus' blind pride leads him to misunderstand her motives. Thinking that Jocasta is ashamed of what appears to be his base origin, he avows that his deeds mark him as Fortune's child—therefore of worth—and despite her repeated pleas he orders in the herdsman who brings the light that will make him blind in fact. This device is sometimes known as "the moment of final suspense."

Another form of this "moment" may appear as an omen that the protagonist in his *hubris* fails to understand or chooses to ignore, although his awareness of its significance, or (better) his willingness to admit its significance, would have saved him. This is the augury that Hamlet defies. Cassandra's prophetic fit in Seneca's *Agamemnon*, containing her veiled warning to Agamemnon that she herself does not understand, is an example, in the classical drama.

The events leading directly into the catastrophe of *Hamlet* move with exceptional speed. Hamlet has returned from the abortive English voyage to come most unexpectedly upon Ophelia's funeral. Immediately thereafter he recounts his adventures to Horatio, accepts Laertes' challenge, and the fatal match is on.

In this action Shakespeare has built up a moment of final suspense that is of some complexity. The acceptance of the fencing match is the key action leading to the catastrophe, for the agreement to meet Laertes means that Hamlet has walked into Claudius' trap and is doomed. Characteristically, Shakespeare treats the episode itself in a comic light that serves by his habitual principle of contrast and parallelism to intensify the underlying serious purport of the action which the audience knows but which is not seen by any of the characters directly involved.

In the disparity between the agent and the action, between Osric and the King's plot, lies just such contrast as is found in the Clown bringing the asps to Cleopatra, the Fool counseling Lear, and even the Porter in *Macbeth*. We do not know whether the choice of such an innocent lapwing[1] was intended by Shakespeare to be a manifestation of Claudius' Machiavellism to conceal the deadly purpose, or whether Shakespeare merely seized on the occasion to show Hamlet in an innocent fencing match of words, which he wins while losing, as contrast to the oncoming match which he loses though truly winning—and not just at the odds. It is a characteristic feature of the density of Shakespeare's dramatic writing that even this simplest of actions, the delivery and acceptance of a wager, is not huddled through in bald terms but becomes a part of the human complex.

Is Hamlet's unsuspicious acceptance a fault, like the blindness of Agamemnon or the egoistic obstinacy of Oedipus? In a sense it is, but not in any deep sense—certainly not one that involves the audience's acceptance of the catastrophic justice of Hamlet's death-in-victory.

Hamlet's defense that the deaths of Rosencrantz and Guildenstern do not lie on his conscience leads naturally to his recapitulation of the justice of his retaliation on Claudius. Respectfully, Horatio intimates that Hamlet can expect Claudius' next crime to be directed against himself in repayment for the deaths of Rosencrantz and Guildenstern, a fact that must soon be known. This speech, of course, implicitly warns Hamlet that he must act without delay.[2] Both men seem to assume that Claudius will be quiescent until he is stirred to further action by the revelation that Hamlet discovered the plot against his life and may have evidence to present in the matter. In this belief they are mistaken, as the audience knows, for Claudius has not waited to mount his counteraction, which therefore strikes a Hamlet who is unprepared.

Is the mistake a culpable one? It is worthy of note that Horatio shares in it, and as a result the audience has no clear lead from a touchstone character. Hence the assumption must be that in itself the error is not a tragically characterizing or justifying one wherein the audience is invited to sit in judgment on the decision. Claudius is not helpless, nor do Hamlet and Horatio assume that he is. What seems to be contained in Hamlet's confident pronouncement "the interim is mine" is a belief that the balking of Claudius' plot has robbed the King of the initiative until a new one can be contrived. The new plot will evidently rest on using the Rosencrantz and Guildenstern execution to Hamlet's disadvantage. Until this new plot will be started by the receipt of the evidence, Hamlet takes it that he himself is in command.

In fact, this diagnosis might well have been correct if a complementary mistake had not followed. Hamlet's generous nature cannot conceive that Laertes will turn villain. Hence there is extreme irony in his regret that he had lost his temper with Laertes at Ophelia's grave, "For by the image of my cause I see / The portraiture of his." Laertes has legitimate grievances, which Hamlet can understand; they are two young men who have been wronged; Hamlet's wrong has sat for the portrait of Laertes'. He feels pity for Laertes and proposes to "court his favours." That Laertes may be feeling toward him as he feels toward Claudius—and is proposing to act upon the feeling—does not, apparently, cross Hamlet's mind, so strong is his assumption that they have a common bond. It may be that Hamlet believes he is secure in his alibi of madness, the theme of his attempted reconciliation with Laertes before the fencing match. It may be that his recognition of his own innocence of intent, corresponding to the innocence of unhinged madness, which cannot act from premeditation, makes him too self-confident and unsuspicious. It is clear that he does not envisage Laertes as a revenger of blood, and thus he cannot suspect that Claudius will immediately have formulated a counteraction utilizing Laertes as a tool.

If this error in estimating Laertes is to correspond to the classical use of the moment of final suspense, a fault in character or in attitude as evidenced by a want of a proper self-knowledge must be shown. Moreover, this generosity of mind (which at least evokes no warning comment from Horatio) is repeated in the indifferent choice of the rapiers at the duel, another error at the final moment, and so is of a piece. A lack of due suspicion of the world; an innocence, or generosity, that can be a luxury in time of peace but is criminally careless in time of danger—if this is to sum up the view of Hamlet that Shakespeare wanted the audience to hold at such a crucial moment (in the manner of Sophocles portraying with intensity the willfully blind Oedipus driving himself to destruction), then we should have had good evidence earlier in the play of such motivation. Also, earlier in the play, we should have been introduced to a characterization that emphasized what Milton was to call unwariness, or levity, a serious charge in context. Moreover, we must suppose that the moment of final suspense as logically used by the Greeks should confirm the original tragic error.

Here, at least, we are on safe ground in rejecting any such view: if Hamlet's tragic error were his generosity of mind—his incapacity to deal with a barbaric duty—we should find the play's climax centering on this tragic flaw. But the climax of the play centers not on his incapacity but on his capacity for killing. The murder of Polonius, mistaken for the King, when Hamlet gives way to a moment of unbearable temptation,[3] has nothing to do with this part of Hamlet's characterization, his generosity of mind. We must conclude, therefore, that the events immediately antecedent to the delivery of Osric's message are not structural, in the sense that they have not been designed in the classical manner to illuminate or to exemplify the initial tragic error. That they illustrate an element in Hamlet's characterization is undeniable; but that this strand, through the illustration, is structurally involved in the tragic web itself —this we may deny.[4]

Let us, then, pass on to the last of the possible escapes before the start of the fatal action of the fencing match. This episode involves the presentiment of evil that Hamlet feels after his acceptance of the wager. "But thou wouldst not think how ill all's here about my heart. But it is no matter." Horatio protests; Hamlet in reply associates the misgiving not with manly caution but with female fears, that is, with an irrational impulse. Horatio continues to take the omen—for that is what it is—more seriously than this, and he shows his agitation at its import by giving Hamlet the second direct piece of advice he allows himself in the play (the first having been his attempt to restrain the prince from following the Ghost). Hamlet rejects the counsel with an appeal to the reason of men who, like Horatio and himself, rely not on superstition but on the acceptance of God's overriding Providence, His active care for the world. With this rejection of Horatio's prudent advice, the tragic die is cast.

Omen and augury, which are interchangeable, were favorite devices in classical drama to lend dignity and inevitability to the tragic action of the conflict of the wills of men and gods. Sometimes the augury chastens human will that has broken divine law, as Creon has done with his cruel decree in Sophocles' *Antigone*. Ironically, in this play, the import of the augury is first rejected, and then accepted too late to prevent the tragic disaster.[5] On the contrary, in Seneca's *Agamemnon* the simple understanding of the augury would have saved the protagonist.

The contrast in Shakespeare's use of the device as against that in classical drama is clear. The Elizabethan audience can only approve Hamlet's rejection of pagan superstition in favor of a Christian reliance on Providence. One can scarcely discover here the final irony of lack of insight as in Greek tragedy.

At this point it should be evident that Shakespeare has piled up in the episode the characteristic devices of classical tragedy (whether found in the Greeks or in Seneca) but that he has fundamentally altered their import and structural purpose. The most causal use of this moment of final suspense by the ancients[6] emphasized the protagonist's tragic blindness in repeating the substance of his original tragic error while Nemesis was poised to strike. One moment of humility, or enlightenment, might have saved the victim, as Creon could have been saved from irreparable crime by instant obedience to the chosen of the gods. But this self-knowledge and understanding do not come; tragic *hubris* persists, and the protagonist ironically brings about his own downfall.

The difference lies in the fact that Shakespeare has Christianized the ancient pagan device. Indeed, Hamlet's opposition of Providence to pagan augury is intended to emphasize the change. Little doubt can exist that Shakespeare intended a close equation between Hamlet's serene ". . . the interim is mine, And a man's life's no more than to say 'one,' " and the biblical overtones of "we defy augury; there's a special providence in the fall of a sparrow . . . the readiness is all."

The point of the catastrophe is Hamlet's death-in-victory with its reconciliation and Divine acceptance of the penalty he must pay for his tragic error.[7] It follows that the faults that blinded the classical protagonist to his last chance to escape must be taken as virtues in Hamlet that demonstrate the clearing of his understanding as manifested by his refusal to evade the required payment for his past error. Only thus can he be brought to the characteristic Shakespearean final ennoblement of experience that persuades an audience to accept, even with satisfaction, the tragic end of a sympathetic protagonist.[8] In any

Christian view of life, nobility equals humility, the understanding and acceptance of God's will instead of the dictates of one's own. If Hamlet comes to understand the nature of his error in the slaying of Polonius, and if this clarification of his self-knowledge leads to a resubmission of his will to God's, then the line of the play from the climax to the catastrophe must bear on this theme. It is my contention that this is, indeed, the movement of the play.[9] If so, it is idle to query why Hamlet should be so confident that the interim will be his, although obviously he has no plan for action. This confidence derives from his recognition on the English voyage that his ministerial function in dealing justice has been restored, and that he is once more in the hand of God, Who has promised vengeance for all earthly crimes.[10]

It would be equally idle to accuse Hamlet of weakness in failing to suspect Laertes of villainously revengeful motives, or of tragically unwary inaction in supposing Claudius to be checkmated for the moment. Last, it would indeed be folly to accuse Hamlet either of *hubris* or of weakness in linking his own fate to the fall of a sparrow.

The Christianization of the classical moment of final suspense reinforces not the protagonist's tragic error and continued blindness that draw on his doom, but (on the contrary) his dearly bought enlightenment that justifies his regeneration. Instead of ironically contributing to his downfall, the Christian fortitude that Hamlet exhibits in the moment of final suspense leads him to choose Providence over pagan augury. The offer of an alternative precisely reverses the classical device, for an escape at this moment would have ruined, not saved, him. Shakespeare changes the opportunity to escape, making it instead a subtle temptation to evade responsibility. When Hamlet resists Horatio's two suggestions that he attempt to alter the events to come, which belong to God,[11] not to him, he justifies his catastrophic victory. Flights of angels can, indeed, then sing him to his rest.

Christian Pessimism in King Lear

By Kenneth Myrick

Ever since Tate gave *King Lear* a happy ending nearly three centuries ago, students of Shakespeare have puzzled over the meaning of the tragedy. Dr. Johnson, who was no sentimentalist, was so shocked by Cordelia's death that he never reread the play until he came to edit it. Lamb persuades most of us that a happy ending would be violently out of keeping with the preceding action, but he hardly considers the other basic problems that later critics find in the seeming chaos of events, and in the extreme sufferings of the nobler characters as contrasted with the long prosperity of the wicked. The narrow moralism of commentators like Ulrici is of no avail. Unless we accept the idea that the philosophical assumptions in the play are Christian or, as Hiram Haydn suggests, that they are Stoical, the problem seems to be unsolved except in the minds of those who have found in the play a philosophy of nihilism—like Swinburne, who heard "the keynote of the poem" in Gloucester's outcry against the gods, "They kill us for their sport"; or like Hazelton Spencer, who saw in Cordelia's death a cosmic "malevolence which . . . is invincible and unassailable." Even the wise humanist and gifted critic Prosser Hall Frye found the catastrophe a "blind and bloody shambles," because "there is no reassertion of the moral order."—"Shakespeare has blundered somehow." Bradley found Lamb's defense of the unhappy conclusion unsatisfying. The end of any tragedy, Bradley says, ought to seem inevitable, and the ending of *King Lear* "does not seem at all inevitable."[1]

Before we agree that so great an artist has blundered, we may reasonably ask whether we have perhaps missed some important points that were clearer to Shakespeare's first audiences than to later scholars.

One of the most remarkable recent developments in Shakespeare studies is the large and growing number of students who are interpreting his plays in Christian terms. Professor Hardin Craig has observed that in *King Lear* the hero's sanity is coextensive with his religious faith. Professor O. J. Campbell describes the tragedy as "an exalted morality play set against a backdrop of eternity," and dwells on "the redemption of Lear." Professor R. B. Heilman shows the justice of the gods, and the pervasive Christian feeling in the play, as seen in the utterances of all the sympathetic characters. It is harder to agree with those who like Geoffrey L. Bickersteth attribute to Shakespeare "a consciously didactic purpose," and see Cordelia as a type of Christ because she, like Christ in the myth of the harrowing of hell, "enters a kingdom already divided against itself, which is the Christian definition of hell," and because "she, like her prototype, was hanged."[2]

Allegorical symbolism seems to me impossible to prove in Shakespeare, and quite out of keeping with his dramatic method. A deliberately didactic purpose is almost as hard to show. A Christian interpretation of *Lear* has for many years seemed to me the only kind that can make sense.

Here let me guard against a possible misapprehension. The doctrine that Shakespeare wrote as a worldling or pagan seems to me an egregious error. Yet I have for it a good deal of sympathy. The creator of Falstaff and Cleopatra seldom—perhaps never—took religion for his ostensible subject. He wrote primarily of the secular world, and for an audience that gathered in a secular mood. He was no prophet-seer like Dante or Milton, but a humanist who held the mirror up to nature. He dwelt, as has been said, at the very center of human nature and wrote about what he found there. But what a man sees depends a good deal on what he is conditioned to see. And when Shakespeare looked searchingly into man's tragic experience, I believe that the meaning he found was a genuinely Christian meaning. It was also the meaning which his audience would most readily grasp. Neither he nor they, when confronted with the ultimate mysteries, could divest themselves of the Christian ideas in which from childhood they had clothed their most serious thoughts.

Each of Shakespeare's plays is of course unique, and each requires the closest study before we can generalize. As I read them, a large number are touched if not permeated with Christian thought and feeling, which Shakespeare, with his artistic tact, does not force upon us, but quietly suggests to our imaginations. In the histories, there is that able patriot but ambitious egoist, Boling-broke, who frees England of Richard's misrule, but brings on disastrous civil wars, yearns to cleanse his soul and unite his people in a holy crusade, and dies praying forgiveness for himself and a blessing on his country and his son. We think of Henry V kneeling in prayer at Agincourt, imploring God's pardon for his father's wrong in compassing the crown. In few plays is the Christian content more significant than in *The Merchant of Venice*, where I believe the Elizabethans saw that the spirit of the law is opposed to the letter, and that mercy seasons justice. In *Measure for Measure*, however we interpret it, we cannot avoid certain religious implications. A similar frame of reference is seen in the redemption of King Leontes after his sixteen years' penance. It is still clearer in Prospero's forgiveness of his enemies, "though with their high wrongs [he is] struck to the quick," and in the blessing which the good old Gonzalo calls down on a pair of royal lovers:

> *Look down, you gods,*
> *And on this couple drop a blessed crown!*
> *For it is you that have chalk'd forth the way*
> *Which brought us hither.*[3]

In an article published over twenty years ago,[4] I discussed how Shakespeare uses the idea of damnation in *Hamlet, Othello*, and *Macbeth* to intensify the tragic pity and terror by raising the question whether Claudius, Gertrude, Macbeth, Lady Macbeth, Othello, and others may be doomed to an eternity of pain and despair. *King Lear*, though its setting is entirely pagan, has perhaps even deeper religious implications than the three other major tragedies.

The dark pessimism seems not to differ markedly from the old Christian pessimism about the present life of man, which, though it had begun to decline, was still very much alive in Shakespeare's time. The improbabilities in the plot, which to many moderns have suggested an irrational world governed by chaotic forces, would have suggested to Elizabethans the rule of providence as described by Christian thinkers for more than a thousand years. This would have been particularly obvious in the sudden downfall of every wicked character. The unparalleled sufferings of Lear and Gloucester are made the very means to a deep change of heart and mind that seems indistinguishable from Christian repentance. And the death of Cordelia is the result not of a tragic flaw, but of a willing sacrifice which implies that above the order of nature there is the order of grace, which Professor Woodhouse has shown to be so significant in *The Faerie Queene.*

I

Christian Pessimism

Those who say with the able British scholar Professor Clifford Leech that "the tragic view is incompatible with the Christian Faith" seem not to have considered closely the popular religious handbooks of the Elizabethan era. Obviously, the writers often betray a spirit that nobody in his senses would attribute to either Shakespeare or his audience. Consider, for example, *The First Booke of Christian Exercise,* first published in 1582, the year of Shakespeare's marriage. The author dwells for twenty pages on the pains of death, for thirty on the horrors of hell, and devotes his longest chapter to showing "why Christ so hateth and abhorreth this world." Among other things that he condemns here are "desire of worldly honor," "worldlie wisdome," and "corporall beautie." This is hardly the religion of Shakespeare. Think of his hero-king kneeling in humble prayer at Agincourt and then a few minutes later telling his warriors,

> *If it be a sin to covet honour,*
> *I am the most offending soul alive.*

Consider the depth and range of Shakespeare's worldly wisdom and the corporal beauty not only of his heroines, but of the young man celebrated in the sonnets, or Hamlet's kingly father, on whom

> *every god did seem to set his seal*
> *To give the world assurance of a man.*

In this same chapter of the *Christian Exercise,* the author warns against "all pleasures and carnall recreations: as banketting, laughing, plaieing and the like," clinching his argument by observing that "Christ . . . wept often. . . . But he is never read to have laught in all his life."[5]

What could this pious writer have made of Puck, Falstaff, Autolycus, Romeo, Othello, or nine tenths of Shakespeare's thousand other characters? Had he ever visited the Globe Theatre, he could not have approved a single play.

Today we associate this narrow kind of zeal with the Puritans. But this man was no Puritan. He was the archenemy of all Puritans and all Protestants: Robert Parsons, the leader of the English Jesuits. Yet his general spirit was shared by large numbers of Christians of every faith, if we can judge from the strange history of the book. It quickly became so popular that a certain Edmund Bunny purged it of all specifically Catholic doctrine and republished it as a guide for Protestants, and as an indication of the common ground on which both Protestants and Catholics could stand. In one version or another it was constantly republished, running through some forty editions in sixty years.

Clearly it is not enough to say, with the late S. L. Bethell, "that the interpretation of life that Shakespeare presents is a profoundly Christian interpretation, one, that is, which harmonizes exactly with the Christian scheme."[6] Define orthodoxy as you choose—in Catholic or Anglican or Puritan terms—and you will find hundreds, or thousands, of the orthodox reading Parsons' book with reverent approval. But orthodoxy is no guarantee of a large and humane spirit. If we call Shakespeare a Christian, let us add the saving reservation that he was a Christian humanist.

Parsons, however, cannot be merely labeled as a zealot and then ignored. An able and passionately earnest man, he was deeply aware of social injustice and of man's tragic lot.

> Hee that wil . . . walk out into the streets . . . shall see justice solde, veritie wrested, shame lost, and equitie despised. He shall see the innocent condemned, the guiltie delivered, the wicked advanced, the vertuous oppressed. Hee shall see manie theeves florish, manie usurers bear great swaie, manie murtherers and extortioners reverenced and honored, manie fooles put in authoritie, and divers, which have nothing in them but the forme of men, by reason of monie to be placed in great dignities, for the government of others.[7]

Here, in a book of devotion, is the pessimism of Lear: "See how yond justice rails upon yond simple thief. Hark in thine ear. Change places and, handy-dandy, which is the justice, which is the thief? . . . A dog's obeyed in office."[8]

Lear's speech sounds almost like a paraphrase of the passage in the *Booke of Christian Exercise*. Both describe the same hypocrisy and corruption in high places, the same injustice and cruelty of man to man, the same terrible power of entrenched evil. Both express "the deepest social pessimism," which Hardin Craig has pointed out in the passage from *King Lear*.

Beside the words of Robert Parsons let us put another passage:

> Christians and persecutions close together, like Christ and his crosse. As Christ was made to beare his owne crosse: so they are made to hold their

cheekes to the nippers, their faces to be buffeted, their backs to be scourged, their eies to be pulled out; their peace is persecution, their rest labour, their riches pouertie, their glory reproches, their libertie imprisonment; although they be the sons of God, the brethren of Christ, the only heires of heaven; yet because they must suffer their hell here, they must be content to be sub-iect to their enemies, to bee abiects to their kinsmen, to be hated of most, to be contemned of all, to be persecuted ouer the earth, a very hauen and re-ceptacle of troubles. . . . *Many are the troubles of the righteous.* For they must be made examples of patience, they must suffer their hell heere.[9]

Henry Smith, who spoke these eloquent words, was the most famous preacher in London during Shakespeare's earliest years there. People thronged to hear him at St. Clement Dane's, so that latecomers could scarcely find seats. A liberal Puritan, he, like Parsons and Bunny, spoke for a large segment of the Elizabethan public. Like them, too, he spoke with deep pessimism about the human scene. If there is a difference in tone, it is that the passage from the *Booke of Christian Exercise* contains more indignation at man's evil, and the passage from Smith's sermon more compassion for the undeserved sufferings of the righteous. In reading the latter passage one is reminded of Cordelia. Smith, like Shakespeare and unlike some of his commentators, saw clearly one of the most terrible facts of human experience: that the virtuous may suffer untold agony through no fault or "tragic flaw" of their own. For Smith under-stands a deep Christian paradox. Why, in a world ruled by divine power, are the righteous visited with poverty, contempt, imprisonment, and torture? It is because only then can the rest of us learn to what heights man can rise. With-out the example of unjust suffering nobly endured, life on earth would be far poorer than it is. Again we think of Cordelia.

Whether Shakespeare ever opened Parsons' book of devotion or heard a sermon by Henry Smith is of no particular relevance. What is important is that Smith and Parsons are representative. It would be absurd, of course, to say that every religious writer of the age was gifted with the tragic sense. Many love to dwell on the worldly prosperity that will reward virtue and diligence. But the frequency of the tragic note in Elizabethan Christianity is undeniable. The pre-vailing mood of the "judicious Hooker" is a sane and tempered optimism, and yet it is he who tells us, "Almost the only complaint in all men's mouths, and that not without great cause, is, 'There is no justice.' " Hooker is referring here to men's dealings with one another. But even God's justice in his dealings with men, he continues, is very often called in question "by those repining accusations wherewith the hard and heavy casualties of the righteous, contrari-wise the impunity and prosperity of godless persons hath been from time to time complained of. With such kind of pleas books both prophane and sacred are full."[10]

In asking why the righteous endure "hard and heavy casualties" while the godless enjoy "impunity and prosperity," Hooker, like Henry Smith, is raising the ultimate problem of both tragedy and religion, the problem of evil. Shake-speare forces it upon us in his most terrible picture of the world. The religious writers of that age return to it again and again, expending their most earnest thought in the endeavor to find honest and convincing answers in terms of Christian faith. It is no accident that half a century later Milton took up the same theme in his two greatest works. Laity and clergy, common men and women as well as great thinkers, had long been pondering the question of God's justice when Shakespeare wrote *King Lear*.

This Christian pessimism is radically different from despair. Hope is a cardi-nal virtue, despair a mortal sin. But for most men the doom of suffering is a necessity if they are to know the profundities of life. The fact, therefore, that in *King Lear* Shakespeare raises the problem of evil with unexampled force does not distinguish his outlook from that of the most pious man in England. Among the leaders of religious thought were men of ardent faith and high ability who had a most realistic insight into man's tragic potentialities. When Shakespeare forces the problem on us, therefore, the question we should ask is not why he paints so dark a picture, but how he expected it to be under-stood.

II

Special and General Providence

The power that most informed men saw at work in nature and human affairs was not an inevitable causal necessity, but the providence of God. For more than a thousand years, men had held this doctrine as it had been formulated by Boethius early in the sixth century. In the words of Aquinas, "The will of God is the cause of all things" except sin. He manifests His will chiefly in two ways. The first is in the rational order of the universe, where He has ordained that effects shall "proceed from fixed causes." The second is in incalculable turns of events, which to the unreflecting man may have the appearance of chance, but which are—to use the still current legal phrase—in reality "acts of God," revealing His direct guidance of events. To the first aspect of the divine rule theologians commonly gave the name "general providence," and to the second, "special providence." A special providence which brought disaster to a flagrant sinner was called a "judgement."[11]

The term "miracle" was sometimes loosely applied to special providence, particularly in popular writings like John Reynolds' *God's Revenge Against Murther*. But strictly speaking, a miracle was thought to occur only if the divine will set aside a natural law, as in raising the dead, or causing the sun to stand still for the convenience of Joshua. Special providence was thought to be manifested through natural or human means, but in ways mysterious and unpredictable. A favorite example was the great tempest which annihilated the Spanish Armada after its defeat by the little English ships. Most Elizabethan Protestants were certain that miracles had ceased with the Apostles, but they were wonderfully quick to see special acts of God where the modern sees luck. Which interpretation is the more naive may be debated.

Special providence is opposed to the idea of blind chance or fortune, and general providence to blind fate. They are indeed precisely the Christian alternatives to these pagan ideas which they had replaced in the early Christian centuries.

The terms "fortune" and "fate" appear often in Elizabethan writings, but how literally they are to be taken is open to question. The concept of fortune, as Patch has shown, was popular in the Middle Ages among the laity, both high and low, and in the Renaissance it was central in Machiavelli's philosophy of history. In Shakespeare's England, which was "more than half medieval" in outlook, many persons must have taken it for granted, particularly those among the less educated who had not been touched by the religious ferment. The neo-Stoic philosopher Justus Lipsius insists on using the word "fate." But he means by it a beneficent though stern necessity, and explicitly subordinates it to the divine will. Very different is the "blind and callous Fate" which Brandes finds in *King Lear*. Lipsius' concept of fate seems to be identical with general providence, or an aspect of it.[12]

No consistent Elizabethan Christian could admit to a belief in either "irresistible destiny" or "the loose uncertainty of fortune and chance. Between which two extremities of error," declared Richard Hooker, "the only true mean is that doctrine of divine providence." "In the necessity of this infinite power," wrote so secular and so bold a thinker as Sir Walter Raleigh, "all the reason of man ends and dissolves itself."[13]

Theologians often differed in their emphasis on general and on special providence. For the "God-intoxicated" Calvin, "every year, month, and day is governed by a new and particular providence of God." "Not a drop of rain falls
but at the express command of God." "Men cannot even speak a word but
what he chooses." Hooker, with his majestic concept of law, avoids this extreme. There is a "law eternal which God himself hath made to himself," as his
pattern in governing creation. There is a law for angels, a law for man, a law
for nature. "See we not plainly that obedience of creatures unto the law of nature is the stay of the whole world?"[14]

The contrast with Calvin is striking, but it is largely one of emphasis. Calvin
seems to deny any laws in nature, but he finds in the very order of nature one
of his strongest proofs that God exists. Hooker is reluctant to overemphasize
God's special interventions, but he envisions no such absolute reign of law as
Zeno had proclaimed three centuries before Christ or as Huxley was to pro-
claim in the Victorian Age. "God will not have great things brought to pass,
either altogether without means, or by those means altogether which are to
our seeming probable and likely."[15] This is a far cry from Aristotle's or the
modern critic's "law of probability or necessity."

It is very close, however, to what we actually find in Shakespeare's plots. In
general the modern rationalist finds them satisfying, but if he chooses he can
find improbabilities in most of them. How did it happen that the wild storm
which annihilated the Turkish fleet let every one of the Venetian ships go by
unscathed? How likely is it that when Hamlet leaped on board the pirate ship,
not a single Dane would follow him before the pirates pulled away? How probable is it that the messenger to whom Friar Lawrence entrusted his letter for
Romeo would be quarantined because of an epidemic of which we have never
heard before? "To our seeming" such events are hardly "probable and likely."
The modern reader almost invariably sets them down to chance. But what interpretation does Shakespeare suggest?

"Unhappy fortune!" exclaims Friar Lawrence when he hears of Friar John's
failure to reach Romeo, and he speaks of "this lamentable chance" when he
finds Romeo and Paris steeped in blood. But his second thoughts are different.

> *A greater power than we can contradict*
> *Hath thwarted our intents.*

And when all comes clear at the end, the Prince of Verona attributes the course
of events to providence.

See what a scourge is laid upon your hates
That heaven finds means to kill your joys with love.

In like manner, Hamlet discovers in his whole experience at sea, which delivered him from his foes, "a divinity that shapes our ends." Even in little things "was heaven ordinant."[16]

Obviously the "inevitability," which today is so important to makers of dramatic theory, simply cannot be found in these and many similar passages. But such events are precisely the kind which to the intelligent Elizabethan, whether Catholic, Puritan, or Anglican, suggested the hand of God. Because we today have forgotten the centuries-old doctrine of special providence, we commonly pay slight heed to passages such as I have just quoted. A modern mind so independent as Prosser Hall Frye's will see in them mere "accident and fortuity" and condemn Shakespeare for failing to suggest any "reassertion of the moral order." In the Elizabethan frame of reference, these passages are quiet but solemn reminders of a divine order.

III

"Judgements" in King Lear

To the Elizabethans the providential order was perhaps most obvious in the sudden downfall of each villain. The modern reader is appalled by the prolonged agonies of the more virtuous characters, as contrasted with the long prosperity and very brief sufferings of the wicked. Except Cornwall, who lingers for a few hours, none of the criminals suffers more than a few moments. To our forebears, however, any suffering in this life seemed relatively brief as compared with what might await them in eternity. Many pious writers love to dwell somewhat naively on the mental torments of reprobates, and Shakespeare frequently portrays such agony of remorse. Othello, Posthumus, and Leontes show a real change of heart, Claudius and Macbeth none. In his sternest tragedy, however, Shakespeare has drawn the horrifying and perhaps more realistic picture of flagrant evildoers untouched by compunction. Yet here he is no more realistic than Bishop Hall, who—anticipating the findings of modern criminologists—observes that "the wicked have peace in themselves," and adds with cryptic irony that the devil will not make "war with his own subjects." "There cannot be," he says, "a greater proof of God's disfavour than for a man to prosper in wickedness." And two generations earlier, Robert Parsons stated the same conviction: to "live in continuale prosperitie is a dreadful signe of everlasting reprobation."[17]

The unbroken prosperity, however, was commonly illusory. Elizabethan Christians saw clearly the principle stated by Plato: evil is self-destructive. It is the same idea that Whitehead stated during the era of Mussolini and Hitler: "Machiavelli wrote the blueprint for a fifteen years' success." The false security of flagrant evildoers, as the Elizabethans heard from many a pulpit, ends in sudden ruin. "Gods iudgements are most suddaine, and when men are in greatest delights," observes one famous preacher. "It is a dangerous slumber wherein they are cast by the heaviness of sin, wherein they lie fatting in all delights, but at last they come to the everlasting slaughter," we learn in one of the best-known religious manuals. Not for nothing does the English liturgy contain the petition to be delivered from sudden death—a prayer which the wise Hooker defends, in his sane and temperate manner, against a Puritan who thought it was papistical.[18]

No one described the false security and dramatic downfall of evildoers with sharper precision than did Henry Smith. The passage occurs in a sermon on Nebuchadnezzar—a king whose arrogance, wanderings in the wilderness, madness, and repentance remind us forcibly of Lear.

> First, God takes him in his fault, that he might see his fault. . . . Then he takes him suddenly, because he contemneth his warning. . . . Thirdly God takes him where hee is pleasantest and lustiest, and safest.[19]

Now Shakespeare, in depicting the downfalls of all the five wicked characters in *King Lear*, has followed with exactitude the formula of Henry Smith. On each of them vengeance falls (1) while he is "in his fault," (2) "suddenly," and (3) when he supposes his situation to be "pleasantest and lustiest, and safest":

On Cornwall while he is blinding Gloucester, confident that no one can call him to account, and while he is hoping eagerly to be king of all Britain.

On Oswald while he is trying to murder Gloucester, confident that there is no danger to himself, and counting on a splendid reward from Regan.

On Regan soon after her order for Gloucester's murder, while she eagerly expects to marry Edmund.

On Edmund almost instantly after his order for the murder of Cordelia and Lear, while he is sure of marrying one princess or the other, and of becoming ruler of half Britain, or king of the whole.

On Goneril just after she has poisoned Regan, has joined Edmund in ordering the murder of her father and of Cordelia, and is expecting to murder her husband, marry Edmund, and rule with him as queen of all Britain.

"Vengeance doth stay until sinne bee ripe, and watch the time when they are most occupied, then iudgement steps foorth, like the Angell to stop Baalam in his way, because the punishment is more grievous and terrible when they look not for it." One by one, the five villainous characters in *Lear* are destroyed in the exact circumstances in which the Elizabethan had been trained to see and dread the judgment of an angry God. But Shakespeare, as Kittredge has emphasized, is like all Elizabethan dramatists in taking pains "to make every significant point as clear as daylight." To give emphasis therefore to what would be self-evident, the poet has expressed through Albany and Edgar the thought that would naturally occur to any spectator.[20]

> *This shows you are above,*
> *You justicers, that these our nether crimes*
> *So speedily can venge!*

> *The gods are just, and of our pleasant vices*
> *Make instruments to scourge us.*

> *This judgement of the heavens, that makes us tremble,*
> *Touches us not with pity.*[21]

These well known speeches have often been understood as expressing merely the individual attitudes of Albany and Edgar. Professor Charlton, indeed, has studied all the religious utterances in *King Lear* as essentially personal to each speaker, and has shown in a most interesting way the particular emphasis that is characteristic of each. But the words of Edgar and Albany express far more than merely private opinions. They are choral utterances. For they come at great climactic moments of wonder and awe, when the members of the audience are most fully united in a common feeling, and when their minds are most open to imaginative suggestion. The thought in these choral utterances would already be half-formed in their own minds.

Indeed, a part of Edgar's speech is less natural to him than to the spectators. The lines

> *The dark and vicious place where thee he got*
> *Cost him his eyes*

seem self-righteous and cruel as coming from a man to his dying brother, even though the brother be a traitor to their father. Yet Edgar is in reality both humble and gentle. Only as a general comment, voicing the spontaneous feeling of the audience, are his words truly appropriate and dramatic. For on occasions like Edmund's fall, it was second nature for both the common man and the philosopher to see the hand of God. "If we after consider the circuit, wherein the steps of his providence have gone, the due consideration thereof cannot choose but draw from us . . . [St. Paul's] words of astonishment: . . . 'O the depth of the riches of the wisdom of God.' "[22]

This comment from so great a thinker as Richard Hooker assures us that in Shakespeare's audience both wise and simple would see the downfall of the wicked not merely as sudden or arbitrary. Each fall results from human agents whose deeds so intertwine with one another as to form a pattern which none of them could ever guess in advance. What to so many modern readers suggests a merely irrational world would suggest to the Elizabethans the power of a superintending wisdom and justice.

How impressive to the Elizabethans this providential pattern was can be seen in John Reynolds' enormously popular collection of pious and bloody short stories, *God's Revenge Against Murther*, first published in 1621. Any commonplace incident—the murderer's drunkenness, a quarrel with his wife, or the stumbling of his horse—can set in motion the forces that will destroy him; and always the same lesson is repeated like a refrain: "God's Providence and Justice is miraculous." Particularly significant for the study of *King Lear* is this fact: Any sudden idea in the mind of a good person is almost sure to be seen as the direct inspiration of Heaven. When the police had searched a garden for a murdered body without avail, "at last the Lord put it into the Provost's mind to search the well." "They bring up the dead body. . . . But behold the mercy and justice of God!" Christeneta, who instigated the murder, is identified because a small boy notices in the mouth of the corpse a piece of cloth. This turns out to be a handkerchief which Christeneta herself had used to stifle the victim's cries, and which had her name embroidered on it in red silk letters. "God's Providence and Justice is miraculous."[23]

There is a vast difference between the naive Reynolds and the wise Hooker, but their concept of the providential guidance in the tangled course of human events is in broad essentials the same.

In Shakespeare, as I have already indicated, the strongest religious suggestions are likely to occur in the great climactic moments when our imaginations are most alive and our emotions are most powerfully engaged. Consider the appalling scene where Cornwall is blinding the eyes of his host. In the sudden intervention by his servant we have one of the most stunning reversals in all drama, and one of the most momentous in its consequences. At the time, the servant seems to fail entirely. He is treacherously slain, and Gloucester loses both his eyes. But the wound the servant gives his master will lead to the death of Cornwall and the destruction of the other four villainous characters. The death of Cornwall will make Regan the rival of Goneril in their common passion for Edmund. Goneril will entrust a message for Regan and a letter for Edmund to the trusty scoundrel Oswald. Regan, to curry favor with this confidant of her sister's, will promise a handsome reward for killing Gloucester. The result will be Oswald's death at Edgar's hands, and Oswald's last act of fidelity will place the letter in the hands first of Edmund's wronged brother, and then of Goneril's wronged husband. Hence Edmund will die by Edgar's hand, Regan by her sister's, and Goneril by her own, all within a few minutes of one another.

What prompts Cornwall's anonymous servant to make his astonishing attack on his master? To this honest man Gloucester is just another nobleman. Cornwall, on the other hand, is his own liege lord, whom he has followed since childhood. If the men of the seventeenth century could see the inspiration of heaven in the sudden but not very wonderful idea of searching a well, can we doubt how they would have viewed the amazing act of Cornwall's sworn follower, when he breaks the great law of subordination, violates his oath of allegiance, and bends "his sword to his great master"—only to protect a total stranger? In a modern play we could explain the brave servant's deed as human nature's instinctive response to an unnatural act. Some in Shakespeare's audience could have taken this view. But Albany's "This shows you are above, you justicers," makes the poet's meaning clear. The fact that, to us and to Gloucester, the servant is an anonymous stranger deepens the impression that his sole function is to be Heaven's instrument.

Aristotle has observed that the most powerful effects in a tragedy come at moments of "tragic wonder," when great events strike us as both probable and astonishing. In *Macbeth* and *Hamlet,* Shakespeare, appealing to the common beliefs about witchcraft and demonology, achieves the tragic wonder in some of his greatest scenes by bringing the Weird Sisters or the ghost of the great King Hamlet upon the stage. In *King Lear* he achieves a similar effect by appealing to some of the most familiar of religious beliefs. Where we today, if we disregard these beliefs, find improbabilities in *Lear* which, as Bradley complains, "far surpass those of the other tragedies in number and grossness,"[24] Shakespeare's audiences must have been awed and astonished at the truth with which he depicted the ways of God to men.

In this paper I have tried to show that the dark view of man which we find in *King Lear* is normal in Elizabethan Christianity. Writers as typical as the Jesuit leader Robert Parsons, his Protestant editor, and the liberal Puritan Henry Smith all give powerful expression to the traditional Christian pessimism about our human nature and the probable destiny of most of us. Even the serene and large-minded Hooker is deeply aware of the tragic facts. But there is always hope. In the sudden turns of events, which to so many modern readers of *King Lear* suggest the rule of blind chance or blind fate, or even of a cosmic "malevolence which is invincible and unassailable,"[25] Elizabethan Christians of every faith were trained to see the inscrutable but deeply reassuring ways of a wise, just, and merciful providence. The catastrophic ruin that so suddenly destroys each evil character is only one part of the great scheme of the tragedy. But so plain is the Christian meaning here that we may expect to find it to be even more significant in the events that move us far more deeply— the purification of Lear and Gloucester through suffering, and the death of Cordelia.

The Ending of King Lear

By Nicholas Brooke

The problem of the ending of *King Lear* is most clearly posed in a notorious fact of theatrical history: for nearly a hundred and fifty years—from the first performance of Tate's version of the play in 1681 to Kean's presentation in 1823—the play was performed with a happy ending: Cordelia always, and usually Lear as well, remained alive. Nowadays, we all say, such a perversion of Shakespeare's greatest tragedy is unthinkable. The smoke of complacent incense goes up to the play's last action, and it seems to me must always tend, more or less, to obscure its nature. I said "complacent," for the assumption is that we know better than the eighteenth century. This assumption does not just mean that modern commentators know better than a sentimental theater audience, because many (though not all) of the best critics felt, like Johnson, that the audiences were right: "In the present case the publick has decided," wrote Johnson,[1] indicating one of his rare moments of solidarity with the "publick." Addison indeed had protested that "as it [*King Lear*] is reformed according to the chimerical notion of poetical justice, in my humble opinion it has lost half its beauty."[2] Dennis, according to Johnson, insinuated that Addison decried poetical justice to secure the favorable reception of his own *Cato*— and as in Mr. Spectator's "humble opinion" we hear the unctuous tones of Pope's Atticus, we may be inclined to believe Dennis. But then, Addison chose to write *Cato*, and his belief in the beauty of poetical injustice may therefore have been sincere, however unsupported here by argument. Johnson's position is not completely opposite, for the author of *Rasselas* could not support a *belief* in poetical justice: "A play in which the wicked prosper, and the virtuous miscarry, may doubtless be good, because it is a just representation of the common events of human life." And so Johnson's defense has to be in other terms than Dennis's, and he goes on, "But since all reasonable beings naturally love justice, I cannot easily be persuaded, that the observation of justice makes a play worse." This leads to the famous conclusion: "If my sensations could add any thing to the general suffrage, I might relate, that I was many years ago so shocked by *Cordelia*'s death, that I know not whether I ever endured to read again the last scenes of the play till I undertook to revise them as an editor."

I want to make two comments on this: first, that Johnson refers to Cordelia's death, not Lear's; and second, that he associates (without comment) the painfulness of her death with the whole theme of justice. The proposition that all reasonable beings naturally love justice is surely indisputable: the painfulness of seeing Cordelia dead was, for Johnson, a direct affront to that love of justice, and one for which the mere proposition "That's the way things happen" is not adequate justification.

Johnson's point seems to me a serious one, and I cannot find in any subsequent criticism which I have read an adequate answer to it: if the ending of *King Lear* is to be accepted, it must be as the shocking thing Johnson knew it to be. The disappearance of the happy ending may be traced through Hazlitt and Kean to Lamb: Hazlitt thought that "the concluding events are sad, painfully sad; but their pathos is extreme. The oppression of the feelings is relieved by the very interest we take in the misfortunes of others. . . ."[3] I am sure Hazlitt is right, but it is not a very elevating rightness; and it takes no account of that other set of oppressed feelings, our love of justice, for that oppression is not the misfortunes of others but of ourselves. If Johnson is right in believing that *that* feeling is involved in the final pain, then Hazlitt is beside the point; and so is Lamb, whom Hazlitt invoked as a greater authority than either Johnson or Schlegel:

A happy ending!—as if the living martyrdom that Lear had gone through,— the flaying of his feelings alive, did not make a fair dismissal from the stage of life the only decorous thing for him. If he is to live and be happy . . . why torment us with all this unnecessary sympathy?[4]

This is the judgment which echoes through all subsequent criticism as justification of Shakespeare's ending. But it has nothing to do with Johnson, nor even Addison: Lamb defends the death of Lear; Johnson attacked the death of Cordelia. And if one can say that Johnson seems to be overweighting a minor character, one must also say that Lamb has confused the *fact* of Lear's death with the manner in which it is achieved. For Lamb delivers a sense of Lear as already ninety-nine hundredths dead, and implies that the last living hundredth is so frail it has no capacity for energy or pleasure. That one might have thought true in Act IV; but in Act V Lear has displayed—astonishingly, but not incredibly—both: assured of Cordelia's love, he can contemplate happiness without illusions of freedom:

> *We two alone will sing like birds i' th' cage*   (V.iii.9)[5]

and he has also still the energy of anger and violence, neither purged away nor redeemed:

> *Howl, howl, howl!   O! you are men of stones:*
> *Had I your tongues and eyes, I'd use them so*
> *That heaven's vault should crack.*   (257–59)

and

> *I kill'd the slave that was a-hanging thee.*
> *Officer.   'Tis true, my lords, he did.*
> *Lear.   Did I not, fellow?*   (274–75)

What kills Lear is not simply his experience in the middle acts, but a new blow, the murder of Cordelia: if there is a logic in Lear's death, it is not *simply* the logic of exhaustion which Lamb propounds, and we are returned to Johnson's belief that it is rather the logic of common experience, of Truth to Nature— this is how things *do* happen—that is observed; and that *that* is too painful to contemplate.

Reposing on Lamb and underestimating Johnson, modern criticism has yet been uneasy. Deprived of Johnson's opposition between Truth and Beauty, committed in fact to Keats' equation, critic after critic has admired the relentless tragedy; and yet, feeling unable to rest simply with an emotional pattern, we have all tried to propose an intellectual pattern which shall match that emotional pattern—be one with it—and *yet* not be an affirmation of despair. No wonder it has proved difficult:

> *O! let him pass; he hates him*
> *That would upon the rack of this tough world*
> *Stretch him out longer.*   (313–15)

If Kent's judgment is true to the play—and of course it is—then it will be hard to justify a view of the play that finds in it a final affirmation of positive values; yet this is what nearly every critic I have read tries to persuade us he has done. And the movement gathers pace, seems to have become as characteristic of the twentieth century as Johnson's attitude was of the eighteenth. Here is a recent verdict, from Professor G. I. Duthie's Introduction to the New Shakespeare edition:[6]

> Gloucester has to suffer beyond his deserts, as has Lear—a common enough phenomenon amongst humanity: we sow the wind and reap the whirlwind. But, if tempted by the appalling sufferings of Lear and Gloucester to regard this as a "pessimistic" drama, we must bear in mind a second point. The gods are merciful. If, after all their agony, Lear and Gloucester died uneducated, unregenerate, then we should indeed have to speak of pessimism. But both, as they die, are wise, and redeemed. "Nothing is here for tears"—unless we weep for the means that conduce to the end, for the dreadful cost of the salutary outcome. We must do so; and the conclusion of the play has indeed a sober colouring. Yet the unassailable fact remains that the gods, in benignity, permit Lear and Gloucester to die in a state of spiritual health. Their sufferings are redemptive. There is no ultimate ground for pessimism here.

As for Cordelia's death, Professor Duthie has a short answer: "God moves in a mysterious way—he deals strangely with the Cordelias of this world. His methods are inscrutable. Shakespeare presents the whole picture—the mysterious as well as that which is plain. This, however, can mean 'pessimistic' drama only to those who cannot agree that the play is a Christian play" (p. li).

I have never been clear what constitutes a "Christian play." I should have supposed that label would involve some effort to justify God's ways to man, to make the mysterious less inscrutable. If so, Shakespeare's effort to write "a Christian play about a pagan world" (in J. C. Maxwell's oft-quoted phrase) proved self-defeating, for the pagans on the stage give no hint of the ultimate benignity of the gods: Lear saw no life in heaven for Cordelia, any more than on earth:

> *Thou'lt come no more,*
> *Never, never, never, never, never!*   (V.iii.307–8)

Nor does this look to me like "wisdom": it seems to be the collapse of language into bare iteration of an unredeemed negative. Is it a redeemed Lear who turns from this to the delusion that Cordelia lives, and, so deluded, dies at last?

And what of Gloucester's spiritual health when he died?

> ... *his flaw'd heart,*
> *Alack, too weak the conflict to support!*
> *'Twixt two extremes of passion, joy and grief,*
> *Burst smilingly.*   (V.iii.196–99)

One can be glad it was smilingly, but it is hardly spiritual health to die of the conflict 'twixt two extremes of passion.

In any case, one may diagnose that Professor Duthie is uncomfortable in his position, for he reverts again and again to the agony and the tears, until at last he paraphrases them away as "a sober colouring"; and then he is no longer speaking of the same thing that Kent, or Lamb, described.

That is the most cheerful view I know of the play: but it rests on the work of many other critics—its foundations appear to be respectable. What it does, I suggest, is to look harder at the fourth act than the fifth: for in Act IV we are shown redemption and regeneration—Gloucester at Dover falling down his molehill and agreeing to remember that

> *the clearest Gods, who make them honours*
> *Of men's impossibilities, have preserved thee.*   (IV.vi.73–74)

And Lear, coming off his wheel of fire to recognize Cordelia:

> *Pray you now, forget and forgive: I am old and foolish.*
>   (IV.vii.84)

That is, in effect, where Professor Duthie's play ends: it would be better for his case if the rest were silence.

Though no other account is as extreme as this, all seem to me to have the same characteristic, that they stop the play effectively somewhere short of what Johnson found intolerable. The methods vary: for Professor Danby,[7] intent on redemption, Lear is mad again when he says:

> *Thou'lt come no more,*
> *Never, never, never, never, never!*

which seems to me all too horribly and fatally sane. For Professor L. C.

Knights,[8] similarly intent, a doubt does arise, and calls for an addition to his earlier essay,[9] where he claims that "the mind, the imagination, so revealed is directed towards affirmation *in spite of everything*. Other readings of the play are possible, and have been made." But "For what takes place in *King Lear* we can find no other word than renewal." But we can, in the play, find another word:

> *Never, never, never, never, never!*

This is not the only tune: Professor Wilson Knight made part of my point years ago in *The Wheel of Fire:*[10] "For Lear there is no such joyful end. In face of the last scene any detailed comment of purgatorial expiation, of spiritual purification, is but a limp and tinkling irrelevance." True; but Wilson Knight then goes on into his own idea of "mystic love": "The primary persons in *Lear*, good and bad, die into love," which does not help. They mostly die of it, or in it, but *into* love is nowhere suggested at all. The impulse to escape the end into irrelevance is always there. D. G. James made this point emphatically, insisting, at length, that "the play's action is terrible in all conscience; but there is no crumb of Christian comfort in it."[11] Yet he proceeds through a series of very perceptive comments to the discovery that *Lear* does affirm a solution to Hamlet's dilemma, "Whether 'tis nobler in the mind to suffer . . . or to take arms": in *Lear* "Good . . . is made silent and patient" and " 'Ripeness is all.' This is the centre of Shakespeare's perception of life in his greatest play"; and so finally "She [Cordelia], and through her Shakespeare, had come to a sense of life, and therefore of death, in which the soul makes no demand either of life or death" (pp. 117–19). If either Cordelia or Shakespeare had come to this sense, I cannot follow them: I make the most passionate demands of life and death at the end of this play; that is witness of the tremendous vitality involved in it, as it is also the inescapable implication of the acute pain Johnson felt. To see that Lear can no longer wish to live is not to accept the conditions that have deprived him of that wish.

Yet even Bradley, who was more honest about his unease than any other critic, said much the same: "It is simply the feeling that what happens to such a being does not matter; all that matters is what she is."[12] It may not have mattered to Bradley, but it mattered to Lear; and it is what mattered to Lear that matters to us. Closer again to my point is John Holloway,[13] pointing to the "ironic turn in events, this constant intensifying of disaster at the moment when disaster seems to be over" (p. 90); and further, "If there is such an order [of Nature], it is an order which can accommodate seemingly limitless chaos and evil. The play is a confrontation of that, a refusal to avert one's gaze from that" (p. 92). But he goes on, "Its affirmation is as exalted, humane and life-affirming as affirmation can be, for it lies in a noble and unflinching steadiness, where flinching seems inevitable, in the insight of its creator." In a sense, this is true; but the stress on affirmation here has something of a handy-dandy air—a comforting word for a painful thing is itself a kind of flinching. And so, although Mr. Holloway insists that "good is far from enjoying a triumphant restoration," he can yet hear "at the close, some note less despairing": Lear "belongs" to union with Cordelia: "He deviated from it, and life itself brought him back. So with Gloucester . . . this idea of being brought back to rectitude is what the play ends with" (pp. 94–95). This would indeed be comforting, if it were true; but after his reunion with Cordelia, Lear's gleeful account of killing the hangman is, however exhilarating, hardly "rectitude"; and what life finally brings him back to as he dies, is delusion. For all his cautions, Mr. Holloway too seems to have stopped the play a little sooner than Shakespeare did; he too seems to feel that if it is to avoid the charges of despair, cynicism, and so forth, a tragedy must "affirm" a positive faith.

The record, then, is of a long series of strenuous efforts to circumvent the pain; and it is accompanied by a will to release large and encouraging affirmations once the pain is evaded. Bradley spoke of the Redemption of King Lear, and that, despite Wilson Knight and D. G. James, is the affirmation of Danby, L. C. Knights, and many others. It is what Johnson could not see, because he knew that redemption depends on an ultimate order implied in poetic justice, which he found rejected here. But Bradley did find such an order: "It implies that the tragic world, if taken as it is presented, with all its error, guilt, failure, woe and waste, is no final reality, but only a part of reality taken for the whole, and, when so taken, illusive. . . ." This has been enlarged upon by R. B. Heilman in *This Great Stage*,[14] the fullest and most perceptive study of *Lear* there has been: "For, throughout the verbal and dramatic patterns of the play, throughout the structural dualities, there is a consistent and continual intimation: in the cosmos there is a justice (whatever the injustice in fact), there is an order (whatever the chaos in fact), there is an underlying reality (whatever the deceptiveness of appearance)." Where this leads, Heilman does not say: but it must be to a belief that there is a mysterious Justice behind the injustice, that Johnson could after all have been cheered up.

I said that Duthie writes as though the play ended in Act IV; D. G. James found comfort (as do many others) in "Ripeness is all," which Edgar says while his father is still alive, in V.ii. This is a dangerous form of selective criticism:

why is *that* sentence a final affirmation, while almost no one accepts Edgar in the next scene telling Edmund about their father, now dead:

> *The Gods are just, and of our pleasant vices*
> *Make instruments to plague us.*   (V.iii.170–71)

Heilman's point is a more extreme instance of the same danger: "consistent and continual intimation" can only be inferred from consistent and continual affirmation: that is, a pattern of statements like Edgar's is accepted as meaning *something* whatever their context in character, situation, or counterstatements. This is to regard a play as being like a static picture; but it is not; it is a process, in which all statements, however convincing when made, are liable to modification or even contradiction in what follows. This is where Johnson was right to regard the end of the play as its only final statement: that provides the one fixed and final image, in this case an emblem which sums up all, Lear dying with the dead Cordelia in his arms. How that relates to earlier statements one can *only* know by following the process.

Johnson, I want to suggest, was right in believing that the play explicitly concerned itself with poetical justice. That, in more general terms, justice is a central theme, no one will question: the word reverberates through every Act and almost every scene—it is the direct concern of the most grotesque perversion of Lear's madness, the mock trial of his daughters; and in Act IV the whole movement of the play is, or seems to be, through regenerative experience toward a healing reward for the suffering Gloucester and Lear. In scene vi Edgar conducts his father through a little lecture-demonstration on how to see when blind, and duly points the moral:

>   *... therefore, thou happy father,*
>   *Think that the clearest Gods, who make them honours*
>   *Of men's impossibilities, have preserved thee.*
> *Gloucester.*   *I do remember now; henceforth I'll bear*
>   *Affliction till it do cry out itself*
>   *"Enough, enough," and die.*   (IV.vi.72–77)

Gloucester will *choose* endurance, not suicide; there *are* gods, and their ultimate justice is affirmed. The irony, that it was no gods but Edgar's little trick that saved Gloucester's life, will not escape us: but Edgar goes on:

> *Bear free and patient thoughts. But who comes here?*
> Enter Lear, fantastically dressed with wild flowers.   (80 f.)

He is more mad than ever we have seen him before—far beyond any acts of choice; and when his speech comes to coherence it is to deliver the most devastating indictment of justice:

> *What was thy cause?*
> *Adultery?*
> *Thou shalt not die: die for adultery! No:*
> *The wren goes to 't, and the small gilded fly*
> *Does lecher in my sight.*   (112–16)

The complacence engendered by Gloucester's reformation cannot stand what follows; though it is true that Lear's obsession is given as a condition of distorted vision—

> *Give me an ounce of civet, good apothecary,*
> *To sweeten my imagination*   (132–33)

—yet, even to Edgar, this is "Reason in madness," and unendurable:

> *I would not take this from report; it is,*
> *And my heart breaks at it.*   (142–43)

Lear's violence is breaking the rhythm of his verse—the metrical sense of order which once supported his tremendous rhetoric of revenge in thunder breaks down finally into

> *Then, kill, kill, kill, kill, kill, kill!*   (189)

The process which led through Gloucester's recognition of divine preservation by clearest gods has descended to an opposite extreme, and is immediately reversed again by the Gentleman's entry to take Lear to Cordelia:

> *Thou hast one daughter,*
> *Who redeems nature from the general curse*
> *Which twain have brought her to.*   (206–8)

The redemptive order is at work again, and Gloucester recovers from another despair he had not even voiced:

> *You ever-gentle Gods, take my breath from me:*
> *Let not my worser spirit tempt me again*
> *To die before you please!*
> *Edgar.*   *Well pray you, father.*   (218–20)

So it is a minor irony that as the play moves away from "kill, kill, kill," Edgar is forced to be a killer, of Oswald:

> *He's dead; I am only sorry*
> *He had no other deathsman.*   (259–60)

Poetical justice has been dealt out to Oswald; but, embarrassingly, the gods didn't do it themselves.

This, however, barely interrupts the movement of the play toward divine redemption: Cordelia leads off in scene vii with

> *O you kind Gods,*
> *Cure this great breach in his abused nature!*
> *Th' untuned and jarring senses, O! wind up*
> *Of this child-changed father.*   (IV.vii.14–17)

The resemblance to Edgar is obvious; yet there is a large difference: Cordelia makes no moral demands, asking only for a "cure"; and the musical harmony she aims at is a different thing from Edgar's invocation to penitence and humility; yet *she* gets what *he* wanted. The recapitulation of the storm that she provides, and Lear's waking speech upon a wheel of fire, are modulated into the minimal eloquence of

> *Pray, do not mock me:*
> *I am a very foolish fond old man,*

leading to

> *Do not laugh at me;*
> *For, as I am a man, I think this lady*
> *To be my child Cordelia.*

Cordelia.   *And so I am, I am.*

Lear.   . . . .

> *. . . your sisters*
> *Have, as I do remember, done me wrong:*
> *You have some cause, they have not.*

Cordelia.   *No cause, no cause.*   (59–75)

The pathos, as Hazlitt would say, is extreme: and so is something else: Cordelia's barely articulate love is the precise opposite of Lear's "kill, kill, kill"; and as much as that was conditioned by a soured imagination, so is this by a sweetened one. Much has been written (most by Heilman) about the play's concern with sight and blindness, nakedness and dressing-up; Edgar offered clear and patient thoughts as a moral vision for Gloucester, but he dressed it up in the rhetoric of gods. Here, the sense is decidedly of naked feeling—utterly convincing while also appallingly vulnerable. But though Lear does *see* Cordelia at last, her response is no clear-sighted truth: "No cause, no cause" is emotionally perfect, but it is far indeed from the truth: she had much cause. But we can hardly wish her to speak otherwise, nor possibly feel she "ought to." This is not "clear sight"; nor, if justice is a weighing of the scales, is it "just"; and, in its tremendous superfluity, it is not naked.

"Superfluity" is another of the play's key words: commentary too often fastens on Lear's and Gloucester's wish to make the rich shake the superflux to the poor and needy, in which Danby saw a reflection of sixteenth-century Protestant communism. But to understand the sense of this, we should remember Lear's

> *O! reason not the need; our basest beggars*
> *Are in the poorest thing superfluous:*
> *Allow not nature more than nature needs,*
> *Man's life is cheap as beast's.*   (II.iv.266–69)

The re-emergence—in Act IV very tenuous—of life and hope in Lear is not cheap: it rests on Cordelia's superfluity of affection; which is felt, surely, not as the suffering patience D. G. James discovered, but as a barely restrained impatience.

It is obvious that this scene completes an issue raised in I.i: there is nothing more for *justice* to do beyond this superfluity of humility and forgiveness. I do not want to raise the old argument as to whether Cordelia committed any fault in that scene; but I would point to a very marked contrast between then and now:

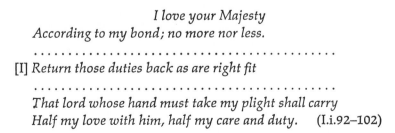

> *I love your Majesty*
> *According to my bond; no more nor less.*
> . . . .
> [I] *Return those duties back as are right fit*
> . . . .
> *That lord whose hand must take my plight shall carry*
> *Half my love with him, half my care and duty.*   (I.i.92–102)

Cordelia has our sympathy there, else we might notice the odd likeness of her words to Shylock's harping on his bond. "According to my bond; no more nor

less" is an attitude quite opposite to "no cause, no cause"; and in that superfluity of feeling, we do not feel any embarrassment for her husband that she
loves her father all: she could, without contradiction, love her husband all as
well; it does not go by balanced halves.

This affirmation, then, is essentially one of superfluity, and we may note
that where Edgar's gods were "clearest," Cordelia's are "kind"; but they are,
of course, still gods. Their existence here is affirmed by their kindness, as much
as in IV.ii Albany had found them proved by the death of Cornwall:

> This shows you are above,
> You justicers, that these our nether crimes
> So speedily can venge!   (IV.ii.78–80)

Nobody, I think, stops the play there, and claims its final affirmation of Je-
hovah; no more can we stop it in IV.vii with a final affirmation of Agape. The
process is one of continual ironic contrast, each limited affirmation modifying
the next experience, and being modified by it. Act V goes like a series of codas
—at several points *this* we feel could be the end; but there is always one more.
The beatific vision of IV.vii gives way to the jealous intrigues of Goneril and
Regan: the issue between the two worlds, good and evil, is poised on the battle,
to which Cordelia and Lear march in dumb show across the stage; a moment
later they are beaten—and the simple idea of complete regeneration is beaten
with them. So Gloucester feels:

> No further, sir; a man may rot even here.

Edgar is ready for him:

> What! in ill thoughts again? Men must endure
> Their going hence, even as their coming hither:
> Ripeness is all. Come on.
> Gloucester.   And that's true too.   (V.ii.8–11)

Edgar's utterance has the cadence of finality: this is the coda of a stoic play;
what exactly "Ripeness is all" means is much argued, but at least one may say
the phrase contrasts with "a man may rot even here"; the readiness for death
in Edgar's endurance includes a sense of perfected maturity. The sentence
sounds final, and I quoted more than one critic who took it to be so: yet the
complacence ("And that's true too") which Edgar thus engenders is immediately followed by

Enter . . . Edmund, Lear and Cordelia, prisoners

and to Cordelia's

> *Shall we not see these daughters and these sisters?*

Lear retorts

> *No, no, no, no! Come, let's away to prison;*
> *We two alone will sing like birds i' th' cage.*   (V.iii.7–9)

It is an image of perfect detachment: singing, with nothing to sing for. But it is worlds apart from Edgar's stoic endurance; and the frivolous lyrical games of repentance and laughter which Lear proposes are perfectly remote from ripeness. Yet Lear sees his gods as clearly as Edgar sees his:

> *Upon such sacrifices, my Cordelia,*
> *The Gods themselves throw incense. . . .*
> . . . .
> *The good years shall devour them, flesh and fell,*
> *Ere they shall make us weep.*   (20–25)

It is not the good years that devour them: it is (as Albany foresaw in V.ii) humanity preying on itself, for Goneril and Regan destroy each other. But interrupting that action, the readjustment of order traditional to tragedy is given in Edgar's single combat with Edmund, all trapped out in St. George's armor. Right triumphs, and another coda seems to be offered: the divine order of the universe is vindicated at last, and Edgar has another shot at saying the last word:

> *Let's exchange charity.*
> . . . .
> *The Gods are just, and of our pleasant vices*
> *Make instruments to plague us;*

—he is speaking of his father, and goes on—

> *The dark and vicious place where thee he got*
> *Cost him his eyes.*   (166–73)

This is as complete a cadence as "Ripeness is all"; but *this*—from the same speaker—is appalling: the measured affirmation of *justice* in these terms shocks everyone—its effect must be a rejection of these gods. Yet it is as perfect a reflection of the action as all the other affirmations of the gods; only, it moves us a stage further: to the recognition that divine order, if it exists, may be a horrible thing. The way is doubly prepared in the ironic process for us to accept that it does not exist—by the unacceptable "evidences," and by our no longer *wanting* its existence.

Edgar's description of Gloucester's death stands far removed either from this monstrous justice or from the comforting notion of ripeness:

> ... *his flaw'd heart,*
> *Alack, too weak the conflict to support!*
> *'Twixt two extremes of passion, joy and grief,*
> *Burst smilingly.*   (196–99)

Albany can still greet Goneril's and Regan's deaths as justice, but the sense of it as terrible, almost unwelcome, is given:

> *This judgement of the heavens, that makes us tremble,*
> *Touches us not with pity.*   (231–32)

The preparation is complete for the last action, which will make him tremble and touch him with more than pity:

> Re-enter Lear, with Cordelia dead in his arms.
> Lear.   *Howl, howl, howl!   O! you are men of stones:*
> ·
> *... She's gone for ever.*
> *I know when one is dead, and when one lives;*
> *She's dead as earth.*   (257–61)

This bare utterance is the final clear-sightedness: on this sacrifice no gods throw incense; nor were these instruments to plague us made from any pleasant vices of Cordelia's. There is no regeneration in symbols of natural growth to be made out of "She's dead as earth." Her death kills all life. To the moral chorus of Kent, Edgar, and Albany it is the end of the world:

> Kent.   *Is this the promis'd end?*
> Edgar.   *Or image of that horror?*
> Albany.   *Fall and cease.*   (263–64)

A strange elliptical phrase leaving only the words of finality from the implied invitation to the heavens to collapse. But the ironies are not over: from this dead fall, Lear *does* regenerate:

> *This feather stirs; she lives! if it be so,*
> *It is a chance which does redeem all sorrows*
> *That ever I have felt.*   (265–67)

It is not so; and nothing is redeemed. Lear's new-made self of IV.vii turns back into the old self, and we cannot do otherwise than welcome the return. The splendid rage of

> *Had I your tongues and eyes, I'd use them so*
> *That heaven's vault should crack*   (258–59)

—the boasting vitality of

> *I have seen the day, with my good biting falchion*
> *I would have made them skip*   (276–77)

—the half-mad blindness of his failure to recognize Kent, and, at last, the obsessive vision of the truth that breaks language down to reiterated negation:

> *And my poor fool is hang'd! No, no, no life!*
> *Why should a dog, a horse, a rat, have life,*
> *And thou no breath at all? Thou'lt come no more,*
> *Never, never, never, never, never!*   (305–8)

The movement of the play towards redemption in IV.vii is recapitulated here, but in reverse, to the opposite conclusion. There it was an emerging from madness; here it is a final retreat to madness:

> *Do you see this? Look on her, look, her lips,*
> *Look there, look there!*   [Dies   (310–11)

That really is the end, with no cadence, no affirmative conclusion, and even Edgar (or it may be Albany) is reduced to

> *Speak what we feel, not what we ought to say.*   (324)

The "ought" has entirely disappeared: the process of these last two Acts has continually set ideas of poetical justice, the avenging gods, against the perceptions of experience; and has not only made it impossible to retain *any* concept of an ordered universe, but has also promoted the reflection that any system of order results in very strange notions of justice. And in the end the subtlest and most tempting order of all is undone—the order of repentance, forgiveness, redemption and regeneration is reversed in unregenerate Lear's tottering broken-hearted into madness and death. To prattle of clear sight *here* is impertinent: clear sight was

> *She's dead as earth.*

Nothing grows from that.

Tragedy is said to be remorseless, though very few tragedies are. Yet Johnson was surely right to find this one unbearable—I would rather think myself capable of his pained repudiation than of Lamb's stoical acceptance. We are driven to see, not only the very human pain of Lear's end with Cordelia dead in his arms, but also the absolute negation of all forms of hope. Everything is here for tears. Nor can we say "The worst returns to laughter" unless we forget the earliest of the ironies that adjust Edgar's *sententiae*, that twenty lines later the sight of his blinded father had reduced him to realizing

> *the worst is not*
> *So long as we can say "This is the worst."*   (IV.i.27–28)

Yet perhaps, because it is the end, we *can* say "This is the worst," and allow the inevitable reaction to take place. This is the record of the critics I examined, after Johnson: one and all turn back from this completeness of tragic experience to reaffirm one or another of the inadequate structures of Order the play exposed. Bradley made his order outside the play, as was his habit, by reflecting on the emotional experience of reading it; and perhaps he was right to do so. Later critics—James, Knights, and especially Heilman—have felt obliged to find it in the play, and do so by fastening on one or another cadence without reference to the process of the play which invalidated it. These different critical abuses reflect different current practices, Bradley's emotionalism or the modern belief in static patterns. But behind them all is what seems to me strangest: the fulfillment of Matthew Arnold's prophecy: "Most of what now passes with us for religion and philosophy will be replaced by poetry." So it seems. Metaphysics, discredited in Arnold's time, soon faded from respectable philosophical academies: and here we have the spectacle of the literary critics metaphysicking for all they are worth. Eyes turned toward our ancient poets, we exhibit a longing for coherent systems regardless of whether we could believe in them ourselves. In poetry, it seems, it is enough to respond to an *idea* of system and feel comforted. But if we must have systems, it would surely be more honest in the face of *King Lear* to say, as T. S. Eliot said in *Ash Wednesday*,

> *Consequently I rejoice, having to construct something*
> *Upon which to rejoice.*

I have been careful here to say "we" and not "they," for in this matter one must ultimately declare oneself. The greatness of *King Lear* is in the perfect completeness of its negation, and in the superb energy with which it is enforced. Action and reaction are equal and opposite: that very energy, the sense of life in the presentation of death, is the source of all this impulse to affirm. But Bradley was surely right that the affirmation must come after the play; and to state it will always be wrong, always be a failure to hold to what this play really is. Yet I cannot, any more than anyone else, just stare at the end of the play and nod assent; to do that, and no more, would be to imagine one's own death. My notion—I can do no more than hint it here—is that the play insists on our adjusting to a state of universal disorder, of looking hard at *that*. But while there is no order, nor any wish for one, there are *values*, good as well as evil; but they can have no reference beyond themselves, no ultimate sanctions—they are quite superfluous, in fact. It is the very superfluity which alone is encouraging: without superfluity there would be no hope, only clear sight which is, at once, both necessary and impossible: "She's dead as earth." That naked knowledge must be clothed, though to clothe it is to be deluded—"no cause, no cause" was not true, it was superfluously loving. "Look on her . . . there, look there" was to look and see what was not. Hope springs eternal: it had better. "This," as Swift said, "is the sublime and refined point of felicity, called, the possession of being well deceived; the serene peaceful state, of being a fool among knaves." To recognize that, is to get about as close to *Lear* as most of us can manage. We need to understand the force of Johnson's repudiation, before we pretend to acceptance.

Shakespeare and the Toil of Grace

By Adrien Bonjour

One of the great advantages of a critical method hinged on the hidden meaning lies in the fascinating free play it affords for every sort of imaginative (and
imaginary) interpretation—whether of the first water, or faintly tinged with
wishful thinking, or stained all over with some strange obsession verging on
monomania. Leaving the smoke-stones in their sable caverns, and the gems of
purest ray to more authorized lapidaries, we shall here examine one of the
slight macles that sometimes happen to spot the clearest crystals.

The hidden meaning has thus been called to the rescue when baffling character problems (to use the old Schückingian terminology) seem to point decidedly to psychological deficiencies. It is then used as a sort of *tertium quid* allowing us to reconcile on a higher plane what was felt to be incompatible on
the ordinary level. One of the classical examples of the kind is the transfigura-
tion of Cleopatra. Leaving aside—for want of space and breath—Mr. Wilson
Knight's fine rhapsodies on *Antony and Cleopatra*, we shall turn for a while
to that brief and stringent interpretation of the play which the late Mr. Bethell
propounded at the close of the last war in a chapter of his still valuable study.[1]

In that twenty-page-long little essay, the author opposed Roman values and
Egyptian qualities. It is quite clear indeed that the contrast between "the practical reason, or worldly wisdom, with which are closely linked the notions of
restrictive morality and political order," as incarnated in Caesar, and "the life
of the spontaneous affections, with which are linked the notions of expansive
morality and esthetic order" (p. 124), as embodied in Cleopatra—in other
words, the lure of Egypt—is fundamental for an understanding of the play.
But though Mr. Bethell showed a fine and delicate appreciation of the organic

structure of the play and the intense poetry with which the whole drama is suffused, he spontaneously sided with the critics who find its psychology inconsistent. As he pointedly observed, "Regarding the play psychologically, one cannot reconcile the vicious, the vulgar, and the commonplace in Antony and Cleopatra, with the sublimity with which they are invested, especially as they face defeat and death" (p. 117). How is the deadlock to be avoided? The only way out, Mr. Bethell suggested, is to alter our critical approach radically: "Changes of character inexplicable by psychological determinism are readily explained if we perceive that Shakespeare is applying theological categories" (p. 129). Thus, high above the petty failure of psychology, it is theology that rises and provides us with the keys of Cleopatra's kingdom.

Yet, before we definitely let Cleopatra drop her sword Philippan to hang on the petticoats of divinity, we might do well, perhaps, to wonder whether psy · chology ought to be, like Hagar, so ruthlessly ruled out of the picture. The spectacular intrusion of theology has been both vigorously advocated and eloquently attacked, and does not rest so securely that we can dispense with speculating on the sort of ground—bedrock or quicksand—we are treading. Mystical interpretation was strongly upheld by Mr. Bethell, who pointed out that "the Elizabethan age was a theological age," and that

> Shakespeare's audience was accustomed to having the mystical significance of scriptural passages laid bare in their weekly sermons. . . . Now if the exotic and sensual *Song of Solomon* may be understood allegorically as the marriage of Christ and his Church . . . then it is not unlikely that the exotic and sensual *Antony and Cleopatra* might also yield its hidden meaning to an audience simultaneously aware of the two levels of story and significance.
>
> (Pp. 113–114)

But some skeptical critics did not find religious explanations so likely after all. "Pit and gallery a congregation!" Professor Stoll exclaimed with ever renewed amazement at the incredible freaks of those Imaginatives whom he had rather daub as Fantastics.[2] If Professor Stoll was perhaps a little too drastic in his dismissal, it must be owned that Mr. Bethell's syllogism was far from convincing if not actually fallacious. The purpose or, better, the *raison d'être* of the Bible is fundamentally different from that of poetic drama; and what is fitting in the one case does not necessarily suit the other. Suppose the Song of Solomon had been found completely detached from its biblical context, together with a few amorous poems written in the same vein. No one but the most stubborn and fanatic preacher would ever dream of seeing in it a representation of the marriage of Christ and his Church. The existence of the Song within the Bible had somehow to be accounted for on grounds other than its poetic beauty and sensuous imagery. Hence the esoteric interpretation superimposed on it, as it were from the outside, much later than the composition of the poem, and without any real internal necessity.

But who among Shakespeare's audience would actually have felt the need of applying that method in the case of a play like *Antony and Cleopatra*, a self-sufficient work of art if ever there was one? How easy and gratuitous that kind of interpretation is can be proved in the case of, say, Disney's *Snow White*. In the final revival of the heroine we can indeed see a compelling suggestion of immortality. The sorceress who poisoned her—and mark how the artist shrouded her in black garb to intimate satanic forces at work, opposed to the whiteness of snow, as a symbol of primeval purity and innocence—offered her, of all fruits, an apple. Even a schoolboy could see beyond the level of the story and be aware of the significance of the myth! The serpent's fruit—and remember its luscious and enticing appearance—was to drive her out of the Eden of her innocence right into the realm of sin and its corollary, the curse of death. But the arrival of the lover and the miraculous reawakening of Snow White from her sleep of death is of course an allegory of Christ overcoming the curse through the power of divine love, and thereby winning back eternity for the soul of man. That Snow White herself should rise exactly as she was, with "not so much perdition as an hair," is just another way of stating the resurrection of the body. Each of the seven dwarfs, moreover—and notice the theological importance of the number—has strong biblical connotations. Whether Walt Disney deliberately intended to stress the mystical significance of the old folk tale that he was so successfully reviving is immaterial: there it is nonetheless and, half-consciously perhaps, the artist did pictorially what Shakespeare had done dramatically, more than three centuries before, in the final scene of the *Winter's Tale*.

In fact, we should beware of the tendency to approach Shakespeare's text as did those Puritan preachers mentioned by Mr. William Empson, who extracted "the whole of their theology by logical analysis of any text they might happen to expound."[3] Let me hasten to declare that I am not suggesting for a moment that this is what Mr. Bethell has done. His eagerness to resort to the theological criterion in *Antony and Cleopatra*, however, made him perhaps a little too prone to be reconciled to the supposed failure of psychology. For we have reasons to assert that this failure is in a large measure imaginary, that it was invoked as a consequence of a lack of insight on the part of some traditional critics, that there is nothing psychologically irreconcilable between, say, the deliciously wanton wench with a teenager's boisterous heart of the early scenes and the tragic queen with her touching simplicity, nay sublimity, when she is in the shadow of imminent death. In short, the depth of the psychology is perfectly suited to the grandeur of the theme and the greatness of the poetry and, consequently, appeal to theological categories is quite unnecessary. For one thing, let us recall Mr. Stewart's study of Cleopatra's character. Here we discover a brilliant demonstration of the limits of an obsolete surface psychology with its "formal mode of regarding character derived less from nature than from fictions that have come to be felt as true merely because they are socially expedient, and have consequently come to be embodied in common literary convention."[4] No doubt "there are more things in heaven and earth than were dreamt of in the philosophy and psychology of the nineteenth century."[5] And Mr. Stewart is certainly right when trying to get at a profounder truth "from an actual correlation between high dramatic poetry and insight into substantial human nature."[6] Why should a rich sensuality in a woman blessed with a wide erotic experience necessarily prevent her from ever attaining such depths in love as render a human being capable of the highest sacrifice? Should a sublimely moving gesture be the sole privilege and monopoly of the strictly virtuous or the mystically etherealized woman?

Moreover, the current picture of Cleopatra as a "mixture of hoyden and strumpet" is patently misleading. It was Shakespeare's design to contrast the public image of Cleopatra with a more meaningful one. That is, there were those who were utterly unable to see in her love anything but gypsy's lust, a power used to turn her lover into a strumpet's fool. But the real Cleopatra of the play is endowed from the very beginning—and by sheer poetic hyperbole— with the Chaucerian freshness, the girlish spontaneity, the bouncing vitality, the feminine shrewdness, the fantasy and delightful *brio* so typical of Shakespeare's most attractive young women in love, from Rosalind to Perdita. Is not indeed that deliberate contrast, in the first act, already a prefiguration of the final scene? "Cleopatra as she is call'd in Rome" leads in a way to "boy my greatness / I' th' posture of a whore,"[7] while the mandragora that Cleopatra wants to drink in order to sleep out the great gap of time her Antony is away announces more dismal poison to bridge a greater gap.

Now this contrast is a representative aspect of the antinomy between the world of passion and the world of action, of the clash between the demands of deep passionate love and the stern imperatives of political and military action —the central theme of the play. Antony is torn between the opposite poles, the main lesson of his tragedy seeming to suggest that a man cannot in the long run be successful both as a great, passionate lover and as a mighty military and political ruler. This Cleopatra feels intuitively. She knows how the Roman world judges her love, how unable it is to understand it, distorting her as it does into a lascivious puppet. She also knows and fears the attraction of this same world, of what might be called the imperial message, and the lure it represents for her lover whose Roman blood rebels against a total dedication to love. To Cleopatra this pole of attraction is the enemy trying to tear her curled Antony away from her. And she is right enough: the appeal of worldly affairs works like a springe to catch her lover. Hence her exultation when, for one brief, precious moment, Antony returns unscathed:

> O infinite virtue, comest thou smiling from
> The world's great snare uncaught?[8]

From the Roman viewpoint, on the contrary, it is Cleopatra's beauty and love which act like a charm to lure Antony away from his worldly preoccupations and his manly duties. And up to a certain point this is right too. Nowhere is the contrast more striking than in Caesar's final tribute to Cleopatra's beauty:

> . . . she looks like sleep,
> As she would catch another Antony
> In her strong toil of grace.[9]

Cleopatra's strong toil of grace is, in Caesar's mouth, the exact counterpart of what she herself called the world's great snare, and the parallelism of the metaphors almost appears as a symbol for the two great conflicting forces of the play.

Is it really necessary to read therein, with Mr. Bethell, "one way of poetically stating the resurrection of the body?" And must we assume with him that "perhaps here, as elsewhere, the word 'grace' may have a tinge of theological significance?"[10] If the world's great snare is a dangerous delusion from Cleopatra's viewpoint, so is the Queen's strong toil of grace from Caesar's viewpoint: surely Mr. Bethell did not mean us to understand that the tinge of theological significance in the word "grace" was also a snare and a delusion? Or must we appeal to multiconsciousness to take the word at the same time with two opposite connotations?

If it can be said that to a certain extent both Caesar and Cleopatra are right—and this is no mean part of the tragedy—on one point at least the world of Caesar was wrong: it lamentably failed to grasp the depth and spiritual stature of Cleopatra's love. That is why her suicide cheats it of the triumph it needed to assert its own values and superiority. Her death after the high Roman fashion proves her to be ultimately as stoic in adversity as the great heroes of the Roman world who, Brutus-like, bore too great minds to grace with captive presence their enemy's chariot wheels. As Caesar himself is bound to acknowledge,

> *Bravest at the last,*
> *She levelled at our purposes, and being royal*
> *Took her own way.*[11]

In a manner her noble act raises her above the world of Caesar, since to her own Egyptian values she now adds the crown of Roman virtues—hence the emphasis on her diadem.

The fact, moreover, that from a certain point of view both Caesar and Cleopatra are right does not mean that Shakespeare has endeavored to strike an exact balance between Roman and Egyptian values. For one thing, as was recently emphasized by Professor L. C. Knights, "What Shakespeare infused into the love story as he found it in Plutarch was an immense energy, a sense of life so heightened that it can claim to represent an absolute value. . . . This energy communicates itself to all that comes within the field of force that radiates from the lovers, and within which their relationship is defined."[12] But the way in which the Roman mode of life is conveyed is singularly devoid of that kind of poetic intensity.[13] There are in fact very good reasons to assert with Mr. Schanzer that "towards its end the play becomes much less concerned with the presentation of the choice between two opposed modes of life and increasingly with the glorification of the choice Antony has made." This choice, it is clear, can be fully understood only in the light of the lovers' actual relationship. And here it seems to me that Mr. Schanzer's interpretation, in his study of *Antony and Cleopatra,* is particularly valuable, based as it is on the astonishing series of parallels drawn between the two lovers throughout the whole drama.[14]

These numerous echoes indeed all tend to make us grasp "the extraordinary likeness, the near-identity of Antony and Cleopatra, in feeling, in imagination, in tastes, in their responses to people and events, and in their modes of expressing these responses. The total effect of all this is to make us see their relationship as something much more than a sensual infatuation, more even than an exalted passion." This relationship fully explains Cleopatra's despair and pathetic grief at Antony's loss, which makes this dull world for her, in his absence, no better than a sty. This grief can be tempered only by her "eternal longings," her sentiment that she will meet him again in death. But in spite of this transcendent intimation—a poetic image of her final spirituality—her death is heartbreaking enough; and poor, sweet Charmian's "O, break! O, break!" at the sight of her dying mistress, whom she is at once to follow, is a token of the poignancy of Cleopatra's death. The hereafter ultimately remains a mystery, what Cleopatra herself, once her resolve is taken, calls "the secret house of death."[15]

That is why in the last resort, despite the raptures of the theologians who would turn it into a hymn to the resurrection of the body, the end of *Antony and Cleopatra* is, and remains, a tragedy. The drama is stirring and awe-inspiring enough in its poetic grandeur. Cleopatra therefore hardly needs the benediction of orthodox theology to tell the world, robbed of her jewel, that it is not worth leavetaking and, in a gesture both simple and sublime, to die "a lass unparallel'd."[16]

But theology is an exacting mistress. She keeps her votaries alarmingly alert and only too prone to stretch the greatest works of Shakespeare on her Procrustean bed. She has a knack of popping up in the most unexpected places as if casually conjured up by the Aarón touch of a mysterious ubiquity. And even when she lies dormant, like her fair sister Egypt in her sleep, she would fain catch another critical Antony in her strong toil of grace. But rather than deplore theology's presence in literature too seriously, let us smile it away cheerfully. For who knows if the radiant muse of Poetic Drama may not be tempted to open her garden (if not her bosom) somewhat more reluctantly to the strictly naturalistic quack than to your slightly erratic, but often inspired, Seraphic Doctor?

Shakespeare's Later Tragedies

By R. A. Foakes

In 1602 two plays were printed that had recently been staged with success by the Children of Paul's at their newly revived private theater, namely, John Marston's *Antonio and Mellida* and *Antonio's Revenge*. These figure in the histories of drama as the two parts of a revenge play contemporary with *Hamlet*, and heralding the later tragedies of Tourneur and Webster; but there is more to be said about them than this.[1] In order to appreciate them, we need to bear in mind that they were written to be acted by children, boys with piping voices from the choir school of St. Paul's Cathedral, before small audiences at an indoor theater. These audiences were drawn probably from the more sophisticated sections of the crowds who flocked to the public theaters, and from those who were able to pay rather more for their seats than was asked at the Globe. They had not seen children act for roughly a decade when the Paul's boys began to stage plays again late in 1599, to be followed by the Children of the Chapel at Blackfriars in 1600, and something about the plays, or the acting of the boys, or both, made them all the rage, as Shakespeare testifies in *Hamlet*.

One aspect of their novelty is indicated in Marston's deliberate use of his child actors to create a special effect; he fashioned plays packed with melodramatic surprises, and written in a style that frequently out-Herods Herod; and throughout the action he took care to remind his audience that they were watching boys in ranting parts that echo the manner of tragedies popular on the stages of the adult players. The Induction to *Antonio and Mellida* cites *The Spanish Tragedy* and *Tamburlaine*, inviting the audience to recall them; but Marston did not simply echo these plays, he exploited them, especially the former, for a new purpose. This can be seen, for instance, in his treatment of Piero, the ruthless villain of *Antonio's Revenge*, who enters in II.i to boast of the two murders he has just carried out, and to gloat over the tomb of Andrugio, one of his victims, as he plots further bloodshed. He cries,

> *I have but newly twone my arme in the curld locks*
> *Of snakie vengeance. Pale beetle-brow'd hate*
> *But newly bustles up. Sweet wrong, I clap thy thoughts.*
> *O let me hug my bosom, rub my breast,*
> *In hope of what may happe.*

He goes on to plot the death of Antonio, and ends his soliloquy with a call to his servant, Balurdo:

> *O! twill be rare, all unsuspected donne.*
> *I have bin nurst in blood, and still have suckt*
> *The steeme of reeking gore. Balurdo, ho?*

Balurdo, a singularly clownish servant for a villain, enters, as the stage direction states, "*with a beard, halfe of, halfe on,*" and complains,

> *When my beard is on, most noble prince, when my beard is*
> * on.*
> Piero.   *Why, what dost thou with a beard?*
> Balurdo. *In truth, one tolde me that my wit was balde. . . . I must*
> *be forced to conclude the tyring man hath not glewd on my*
> *beard halfe fast enough. Gods bores, it wil not stick*
> *to fal off.*

The tone of this is grotesque; it is difficult to take seriously the exaggeration of Piero's lines, especially when a choirboy is made to cry, "I have bin nurst in blood," and Balurdo's entry is simply comic, deflating the rant of the villain. The business with the beard refers to *The Spanish Tragedy*, where Balthazar, preparing for Hieronimo's play within the play, appears in half a beard; there it is natural for an actor to be putting on a beard for a part he is about to act, but Marston makes Balurdo do it directly in the main action of his play, so reminding us that we are watching actors fooling about, and not allowing us to become seriously involved.

This reveals a strong element of parody, of *The Spanish Tragedy* in particular, and of tragic rant in general. Some speeches in Kyd's play, notably Hieronimo's outbursts of grief, were imitated and parodied at this time in public theater plays, but Marston's parody is more extended, and more complicated, for it relates not just to this play, but to a whole species of tragedy, and depends also on the effect of boys strutting like adult actors, boys who, to paraphrase the words of Pandulfo in *Antonio's Revenge* (IV.ii.74), speak more than gods, yet are plainly less than men. Marston mocks, not so much one play, as the whole idea of heroic tragedy, as is evident at the opening of *Antonio and Mellida*, when his hero enters disguised as a woman, an Amazon—a new twist indeed, and reversing the normal convention of disguising the heroine as a man; the boy playing Antonio complains, ironically, in the Induction, "I a voice to play a lady! I shall nere doe it." In writing the second of his plays, *Antonio's Revenge*, Marston, as I interpret the evidence, imitated *Hamlet* as well as *The Spanish Tragedy*, and his mockery of the hero and villain represent a comment on a kind of tragedy that, for a sophisticated audience, was already rather old-fashioned—tragedy such as *Hamlet*, which continued to be the subject of jesting allusions in later children's plays, as in *Eastward Ho!* (1605), which has a footman named Hamlet, servant to a foolish Gertrude who sings a garbled version of Ophelia's song. In *Hamlet*, Rosencrantz says of the child actors,

> *These are now the fashion, and so berattle the common*
> *stages—so they call them—that many wearing rapiers*
> *are afraid of goose quills and dare scarce come thither.*
>
> (II.ii.337)

Marston was one who berattled the common stages with his mockery and parody, and helped to establish, and perhaps to turn Shakespeare's thoughts to, a new kind of tragedy.

I do not wish to suggest that a study of what Marston was doing in the Antonio plays *explains* Shakespeare's later tragedies, only that it helps toward understanding some aspects of them. Marston's writing in his first plays marks a new consciousness, a new spirit in the drama, one connected with the vogue for satire in the late 1590's, with the new comedy of humors, and with the first recorded use of the word "parody" in English, in Ben Jonson's *Every Man in his Humour*. Shakespeare, writing for the public theater and the adult Chamberlain's or King's Men, continued to produce heroic tragedies for a few years, though, at the same time, he composed *Troilus and Cressida* and *Measure for Measure*, which reflect something of the new spirit. When he turned, after *Macbeth*, to new tragic themes, in *Timon of Athens*, *Coriolanus*, and *Antony and Cleopatra*, it may be that he was, in his way, catching up with a new fashion on the stage.

This suggestion may seem a little strange, for it is hard to think of Shakespeare as following the example of others, and not as himself initiating movements and ideas, though there is little evidence that he was ever much of an innovator; also, it is difficult to think of these late plays except in terms of the four central tragedies. One modern view sees *King Lear* as the peak of Shakespeare's tragic development, and implies that after he wrote this, some sort of decline set in. Some exponents of this view are inclined to bring forward *Timon of Athens*, for the dating of which play there is not much direct evidence, and to argue that it preceded *Lear*, so making Timon's passionate outbursts in his misanthropy a prelude to Lear's storm speeches. Then, after the cosmic overtones and great poetry of *Lear*, there can be traced a narrower, more concentrated intensity in *Macbeth*, followed by a relaxation and loss of tragic urgency in *Coriolanus* and *Antony and Cleopatra*. The argument is not often expressed thus bluntly, but it has a respectable ancestry, was implicitly sanctioned by A. C. Bradley, lies behind the common references to *Hamlet, Othello, King Lear* and *Macbeth* as the "four great tragedies," and is fostered by the weight of concentration in modern criticism on *King Lear*. Also, it affords a ready though not necessarily a correct or adequate way of accounting for a common experience; for we all recognize that something different is happening in the later tragedies.

Another way of regarding these plays has sprung from the study of the tragic heroes in the earlier tragedies. Timon, Antony, and Coriolanus have all been interpreted as great, heroic souls, but there is no community of opinion about them, as there is about Othello or Hamlet. Antony in particular has been attacked as corrupt, morally weak, even infected with the deadly sins of sloth, gluttony, and lechery; and the difficulties of relating Timon and Coriolanus to earlier tragic heroes have given rise to an interpretation of these as "more satire than tragedy."[2] They have perhaps been seen most usefully as heroes of a new kind:

> Unlike the heroes of the middle tragic world, those of the last tragic world are deeply flawed. No one of them is a doer of duty, like Brutus or Hamlet, or an unselfish repenter for wrong done, like Othello or Lear. . . . Each of these heroes has faulty substance reaching to the very center of his character.[3]

Somehow they remain heroes in spite of this, at least in the sense of possessing dignity; in them "defects of human nature, including viciousness, need not always produce good results in order to dignify themselves, but can take on dignity through a quality in their very being."[4]

The common factor in these lines of argument, as in most modern criticism, is an approach that is basically moral, whether it springs primarily from a study of the themes, the poetry and its reverberations, or from a study of the character of the tragic hero; and it is an approach that has dominated, too, the criticism of Jacobean tragedy other than Shakespeare's. Discussion of this mutually affects and is affected by the criticism of Shakespeare's tragedies, as is exemplified in the titles of the two most recent books on the subject, *The Moral Vision of Jacobean Tragedy* and *Jacobean Tragedy: The Quest for Moral Order*.[5] The first of these, an intelligent and perceptive book, ends with a chapter on Shakespeare in which only the four "major" tragedies are discussed. The author regards Shakespeare as the master of the Jacobean dramatists, who wrote under his shadow and after *King Lear*, "the only Jacobean play large enough to confront and resolve the challenge which evil presents to man's belief in himself and his universe."[6] This challenge of evil seems to him to be the central issue of Jacobean tragedy, and he goes on to say:

> We find nothing in *Antony and Cleopatra* or *Coriolanus* which suggests that Shakespeare's view of the struggle for power changed after *Macbeth*; and despite its questionable shape *Timon of Athens* bears witness to Shakespeare's capacity for tragic emotion at the very time that he was about to embark on the late romances. I omit these later tragedies from discussion only because they seem to me quite removed from the "Jacobean" issues which link the earlier tragedies and dark comedies to the works of Shakespeare's contemporaries. They add to our knowledge of Shakespeare's mind and art, but they shed little light on the epistemological questions which lie at the heart of Jacobean tragedy. If we approach Shakespeare primarily by way of plot, we may conclude that *Othello* and *Macbeth* are the most "Jacobean" of his tragedies, because, like many of the plays of Tourneur, Webster, Middleton and Ford, they portray the disintegration of moral will and purpose. Great soldiers who become cowardly assassins, Othello and Macbeth are infinitely closer to such hero-villains as Byron, Vindice, Brachiano, De Flores and Giovanni than are Hamlet and Lear. But any broader view makes it apparent that *Hamlet* and *Lear* represent Shakespeare's deepest involvement in the tragic issues of the first Jacobean decade. Their larger, more philosophical actions and choric commentaries define the problem of moral decision and belief in an evil world and dramatize the tragic need of the idealizing mind to discover, accept, and relate itself to the realities of the universe.[7]

This is a useful summing-up of a view that seems to me misleading in spite of the measure of truth that it contains. It has grown out of the most impressive branch of recent orthodoxy in Shakespeare criticism, which supposes a "constant search for meanings that informs his work as a whole";[8] it reflects this attitude in its concern with themes and ideas, with "moral decision" and "epistemological questions," and it tends to emerge in a concern with the plays as defining moral problems, or, as Irving Ribner, the author of the second book cited above, puts it, in the argument that

> what all of these [i.e. Jacobean] writers of tragedy have in common is that their moral purposes are controlling factors in their plays, shaping character, plot and poetry so as to give expression to the presiding moral statement. This is generally true of Elizabethan and Jacobean tragedy.[9]

In my reading of the plays this matter of defining moral problems or making moral statements is not central; indeed, to think of Jacobean tragedy in this way is to make it appear much more homogeneous than it is, and also to reduce it to a series of tracts for the times, or statements about the human condition, then or now. If these plays make a "moral statement," they do so incidentally as part of the total experience they offer as works of art, and it falsifies them to give prominence to this one aspect. It is characteristic that both authors cited find little to say about Marston; the first finds the "ethical intention" of *Antonio's Revenge* "peripheral," and regards the play as a failed tragedy, while the second simply labels it "atrocious";[10] instead, they devote much space to Chapman or Jonson, who wrote ineffectual tragedies with a strong and stated moral aim.

To return to the long passage cited above from *The Moral Vision of Jacobean Tragedy*, it is not at all clear that *Hamlet* and *King Lear* "define the problem of moral decision and belief in an evil world"; the world that these plays image is one controlled by providence, by finally beneficent powers, and it might be better argued that they do something more difficult and profound in dealing with the problem of evil in a world that is potentially good. The villains, Claudius and Edmund, are shown to be committed to evil in what is an aberration from the norm represented in Hamlet or Edgar. Perhaps here Mr. Ornstein is allowing a confusion between the world in general (the "evil world" in which we live now?) and the world of the individual play, as it is created and circumscribed by the play's action and language. Such a confusion appears more obviously and more often in Mr. Ribner's *Jacobean Tragedy: The Quest for Moral Order*, as in his comment on Middleton's tragedies, "Middleton is concerned not so much with the complexities of human character as with the nature of evil in the world" (p. 124). A determination to find a general statement on the world at large is bound to hamper the critic from seeing what the world of the play is like.

In three of Shakespeare's middle tragedies the world of the play opposes good and evil figures, hero and villain, in such a way as to make us think of them as acting within a Christian humanist frame of reference, and to make us look for an ultimate triumph of good over evil. Even in *Macbeth*, the fourth of these plays, where "foul and fair" are at first confused, Malcolm restores health to a wasted kingdom, and, himself a saintly king, renews the rule of that "most sainted" Duncan whom Macbeth killed. By contrast, some Jacobean tragedies, like those of Webster, create a world in which evil is the norm, and good, as represented by Antonio and the Duchess of Malfi, who are hounded down like criminals, appears as an aberration. In other plays, like those of Middleton, the concepts "good" and "evil" have little strength or relevance in the world established by the action. Here that involvement of the universe which reflects with cosmic repercussions the sins of Lear, and that providence or fate which Hamlet knew was operating, however inscrutably, in the heavens, diminishes to something personal, to a psychological compulsion, or to the manipulation of one human being by another, as in a game of chess. So Beatrice-Joanna in *The Changeling* says, on the discovery of her guilt by her father,

> Beneath the stars, upon yon meteor,
> Ever hung my fate 'mongst things corruptible;
> I ne'er could pluck it from him.   (V.iii.155)

She is pointing to De Flores, who has indeed, as the play has shown, been her "fate"; and although there is in this play occasional talk of sin and guilt, we are not allowed to reflect too harshly on Beatrice, who thinks only in terms of honor, or simply to condemn De Flores, who triumphs in his death.[11]

A change is also evident in the figure of the hero as Jacobean tragedy develops. Marston's mockery of the romantic tragic hero and stock villain in the characters of Antonio and Piero may be seen as marking the beginning of the decay of such heroes as Hamlet and Othello, and such villains as Claudius and Iago. In Marston's later play, *The Malcontent*, Malevole, the hero, does little but rail, and Mendoza, the villain, attempts murder several times but never succeeds. Vindice, in *The Revenger's Tragedy*, combines in himself hero and villain; this play was roughly contemporary with *Macbeth*, in which, after the clear oppositions of Shakespeare's earlier tragedies, there is a blurring of moral areas, so that Macbeth cannot distinguish fair from foul, and himself becomes a hero-villain, finally damned. At about the same time, Chapman was writing *Bussy D'Ambois*, in which the hero arrogates to himself morality, law,

and justice, as if he could stand above society, and above Christian moral assertions:[12]

> When I am wrong'd, and that law fails to right me
> Let me be king myself (as man was made),
> And do a justice that exceeds the law.   (II.i.197)

Later on the hero tends to evaporate altogether; he dwindles into Charlemont
of *The Atheist's Tragedy*, who refuses to act when faced with a situation similar to that of Hamlet, or into Antonio in *The Duchess of Malfi*, who is incapable of action, and subordinate to the Duchess herself; and he vanishes in such
a figure as De Flores in *The Changeling*, who would have been simply a villain
in the framework of *Hamlet*. In the amoral atmosphere of Middleton's play,
the one virtuous figure, Alsemero, hardly exists as a character; De Flores takes
the center of the stage, enjoys Beatrice after committing murder for her sake,
and dies in triumph, rejoicing in a life's purpose fulfilled:

> . . . her honour's prize
> Was my reward; I thank life for nothing
> But that pleasure; it was so sweet to me
> That I have drunk up all, left none behind
> For any man to pledge me.   (V.iii.168)

To put it another way, these plays seem to be no longer concerned with, or
based on, a moral order in the way that Shakespeare's earlier tragedies are.
There is a sense, for instance, in which Hamlet is a very simple figure; we never
doubt *what* he is, for we know he is a good man opposing evil, and his moral
position is to that extent clear. What we find puzzling is his inactivity, not
what he is, but why he behaves as he does; it is not Hamlet, but Hamlet's problem, that troubles the critics. L. C. Knights puts it thus:

> Hamlet's question, the question that he is continually asking himself, is, How
> can I live? What shall I do to rid myself of this numbing sense of the mean-
> inglessness brought by the knowledge of corruption?[13]

The questions are sometimes formulated in other terms, and a variety of explanations of Hamlet's mystery has been provided by critics, but none doubts
what he is, or Othello, or Lear. In these plays the heroes come to terms finally
with a moral order that is basically Christian, and Iago's proposition, " 'Tis in
ourselves that we are thus or thus," is refuted in the larger knowledge that, as
Hamlet says, "There's a divinity that shapes our ends," in Othello's recognition:

> *This look of thine will hurl my soul from heaven,*
> *And fiends will snatch at it,* (V.ii.277)

and in Lear's sense that

> *Upon such sacrifices, my Cordelia,*
> *The gods themselves throw incense.* (V.iii.20)

Their frame of reference assumes a heaven over all, but in *The Changeling* De Flores triumphs in fulfilling Iago's claim, in being true to himself, which is all that matters; and though he is conscious of hell, he does not care, for it is the condition of everyone else to be there also:

> *De Flores.* *. . . now we are left in hell.*
> *Vermandero. We are all there, it circumscribes us here.* (V.iii.164)

The dwindling of the hero that can be traced from *Antonio's Revenge* onward affects Shakespeare, who exploits it characteristically in an unusual and dynamic way. In his later tragedies the protagonist or hero loses his ideal or typical aspect, and ceases to embody the values that the play sanctions, as do the heroes of *Hamlet, Othello,* and even, in large measure, of *King Lear,* in which play our attitude to Lear is established partly through the love for him of Cordelia and Kent. Macbeth is an equivocal figure, lost in his paradoxes, "Nothing is but what is not," and "I have thee not, and yet I see thee still"; we feel the pressure of evil within and upon him, and, as the play proceeds, the "deep damnation" he brings upon himself is displayed. This play marks a transition to a new kind of tragedy, new for Shakespeare that is, in which the protagonist is alienated from us in large measure from the beginning, and the moral oppositions of the earlier plays lose importance.

It is perhaps easier to think of Timon, than of Coriolanus or Antony, as simply "noble," and the Poet's allegory of Timon's condition at the beginning of the play may have been put there by Shakespeare to emphasize at once the protagonist's blindness.[14] The Poet's verses paint the goddess Fortune throned on a hill, drawing up Timon, and bestowing her grace on him, but go on to describe his fall:

> *When Fortune in her shift and change of mood*
> *Spurns down her late beloved, all his dependants,*
> *Which labour'd after him to the mountain's top,*
> *Even on their knees and hands, let him slip down,*
> *Not one accompanying his declining foot.* (I.i.87)

When Timon comes in, distributing largesse to all, he accepts the Poet's work, paying him for it, but not reading it. The Poet's moral is commonplace, as his friend the Painter emphasizes, but Timon will not regard it, will not acknowledge his debt to Fortune. The Poet had aimed to tell the truth, but is treated by Timon as a flatterer; and Timon himself gives truth to Apemantus' exchange with the Poet:

> Apemantus.   *Then thou liest. Look in thy last work, where thou*
> *hast feign'd him a worthy fellow.*
> Poet.   *That's not feign'd—he is so.*
> Apemantus.   *Yes, he is worthy of thee, and to pay thee for*
> *thy labour. He that loves to be flattered is worthy*
> *o' th' flatterer.*   (I.i.233)

Timon's bounty is noble in its generosity, yet it springs from a fault in him. He does not realize, as we do, that the men on whom he showers benefits are properly flatterers, and that he helps to make them what they are by his blindness to the reality and nature of others; they do not exist for him except as objects of his bounty, or projections of himself. In his self-love, he refuses to allow others to give, or even to repay; no, says Timon to Ventidius, who is anxious to return the money with which Timon redeemed him from prison,

> *You mistake my love;*
> *I gave it freely ever; and there's none*
> *Can truly say he gives if he receives.*
> *If our betters play at that game, we must not dare*
> *To imitate them: faults that are rich are fair.*   (I.ii.9)

Timon will not receive payment, as if to do so would be a "fault"; if Ventidius were proposing usury, repayment with interest, it might be a fault, but here the fault is Timon's, who will not permit others to be bountiful to him, as if he were a god dispensing gifts. Alternatively, he thinks of others as his semblables, and is unable to see them as persons in their own right. "I weigh my friend's affection with mine own," he says, in a phrase that marks his inability to look outside himself. His generosity is, finally, a kind of selfishness, and we see its obverse in his misanthropy, when he banishes himself from Athens to eat roots and curse humanity, no more isolated in the forest than he had been in the midst of his great feasts.

Alcibiades is presented even more critically. It is impossible to say who is right and who is wrong in his quarrel with the Senate of Athens, for the question whether his friend has murdered a man or not is seen as a legal matter only. And if we prefer Alcibiades here, we do so because we know the monumental corruption of the Senate, as revealed in their treatment of Timon; at worst, the friend's crime was one of passion, not the result of a settled meanness such as theirs. Alcibiades denounces them for thinking only of money, then readily accepts the gold Timon has found in the woods, when this is offered to him and his train of soldiers and harlots. Yet Alcibiades shows at last a generosity finer than that of Timon, for, when he has the hated city of Athens at his mercy, he determines only to punish the enemies of Timon and himself, and to restore "regular justice in your city's bounds," as he says to the Senators.

There is no hint that Alcibiades is a particularly good man; he is true to himself, to what he conceives to be a soldier's rights, and does not even return to attack Athens out of loyalty to Timon, but to satisfy his own honor. As he says at the end of the scene in which he is banished,

> 'Tis honour with most lands to be at odds;
> Soldiers should brook as little wrongs as gods.   (III.v.116)

Here, indeed, he speaks with an accent that might suit Coriolanus, another general who is banished and returns to fight against his own city.[15] In this play the soldier's nature is exposed to ruthless analysis. The spirit of Coriolanus, every inch his mother's son, is caught in her conversation with Valeria, who reports on the activities of young Marcius:

> *Valeria:* O' my word, the father's son! . . . has such a confirmed countenance! I saw him run after a gilded butterfly; and when he caught it he let it go again, and after it again, and over and over he comes, and up again, catch'd it again; or whether his fall enrag'd him, or how 'twas, he did so set his teeth and tear it. O, I warrant, how he mammock'd it!
> *Volumnia:* One on's father's moods.
> *Valeria:* Indeed, la, 'tis a noble child.   (I.iii.62–73)

This is a famous passage, but I do not think that the degree to which Valeria's final remark establishes the tone of Volumnia's comment has been noticed; Valeria's satisfaction reflects the staggering complacency of Volumnia, who is pleased to have her son, and her son's son, indulge in this kind of wanton rage and cruelty.

Such a spirit is fit for hand-to-hand war, and Coriolanus shows nobly in battle; but it is useless in peace. Shakespeare takes some care to differentiate the citizens, especially that intelligent First Citizen who, as "the great toe of this

assembly," stands up to Menenius; they are likable enough, if fickle and cowardly. The tribunes are a pair of politicians with an eye to getting on in the
world, and they are not averse to chicanery; yet we cannot find them despica-
ble, for the play does not allow this kind of judgment, and their pride and
duplicity no more than match the pride of Coriolanus and the duplicity of
Menenius. There is a kind of integrity in the refusal of Coriolanus to scheme,
like these. It is an unearned integrity, not a result of self-knowledge, an active
virtue, but merely an aspect of his nature; and it is related to an arrogance
which is purely selfish, a lack of contact with other human beings, which is
sharply revealed in two poignant moments in the first part of the play. One is
the moment after the battle at Corioli, when he begs the freedom of an old
acquaintance who has been taken prisoner; the gesture of friendliness is a
fruitless one, as he cannot even remember the name of his former host. Instead,
he puts the matter aside with the cry, "Have we no wine here?" Anyone might
forget a name, but here we have a rare glimpse of Coriolanus trying to do
someone a benefit, only to be defeated by his own qualities. For his failure to
remember the name is of a piece with his contempt for humanity in general;
he can think of the people only as "woollen vassals, *things* created / To buy
and sell with groats," or as bodies made for slaughter: "On fair ground I could
beat forty of them." Another revealing moment comes on his return in triumph
from Corioli, when he is welcomed by his mother, who stands with his wife,
Virgilia, to receive him. He kneels to his mother, and speaks first to her:

> Coriolanus.   *You have, I know, petition'd all the gods*
> *For my prosperity.*
> Volumnia.   *Nay, my good soldier, up;*
> *My gentle Marcius, worthy Caius, and*
> *By deed-achieving honour newly nam'd—*
> *What is it? Coriolanus must I call thee?*
> *But, O, thy wife!*
> Coriolanus.   *My gracious silence, hail!*
> *Wouldst thou have laugh'd had I come coffin'd home,*
> *That weep'st to see me triumph?*   (II.i.160)

Coriolanus and Volumnia talk the same language, of blood, honor, and battle,
and they can congratulate one another, share each other's triumph; but Virgilia has nothing to say. Only her tears speak through a silence that is most
eloquent, as she stands by him, an embodiment of what he cannot know, or
holds of no account, the common affections, tenderness, humility, peacefulness.

These moments of great dramatic force are revealing in a psychological, not a moral, sense; they bring out the inflexibility, the one-sidedness of Coriolanus. The tribunes recognize this, play on it, and easily drive him from Rome. He had denied their accusation that he was a traitor, but he now becomes one, joining with Aufidius to fight against country and family; and in his selfish concern with his own glory and honor, he can apparently contemplate burning mother, wife, and child in destroying Rome. It seems that war is all he knows, and it does not matter which side he fights on. Yet he does not do this out of wickedness, but out of insensitivity, and it takes his mother, kneeling to him as he had once kneeled to her, to stir in him the humanity he finds it easy to suppress, because it is so little a part of him. His withdrawal from Rome leads to his death, overwhelmed by Aufidius and his conspirators in an alien city, a traitor to both sides. He dies, in his own image, "like an eagle," boasting of his soldiership; yet he has also been, in his mother's image, a chicken:

> ... she, poor hen, fond of no second brood,
> Has cluck'd thee to the wars, and safely home,
> Loaden with honour. (V.iii.162)

The mature warrior, twenty-seven times wounded, three times crowned with the "oaken garland," inhabits the same body as an adolescent who flies into uncontrolled rage when called "traitor" or "boy," words which subtly hit home. The play is, in an important sense, a study of the clash between the two sides of a personality that is made whole only momentarily, as when he greets Virgilia, or, more poignantly still, when he finally yields to his mother, and "holds her by the hand, silent."[16]

Rome remains, the people, the tribunes, the patricians; Coriolanus lives and dies lonely, to himself. The people of Rome, commonplace, often corrupt, but engaging in their humanity, outlast the warrior who thought he could stand

> As if a man were author of himself,
> And knew no other kin. (V.iii.36)

In the third of the late tragedies, Antony and Cleopatra also stand as if they were authors of themselves, neglecting all else for love. This love is, on one level, a fine, even a majestic relationship; we feel its energy throughout the play, and its intensity, especially in their deaths, in Antony's "I come, my queen," and Cleopatra's "Husband, I come." Each commits suicide, Antony thinking she is dead, Cleopatra some time after Antony's death; each, dying, sheds other attributes to appear for the moment purified, all fire and air. At the same time, however, each dies, partly at least, to avoid being taken prisoner to Rome, and here, as always, there is much that is self-regarding about their love. It is a love that drives them apart as much as it brings them together, a love that is splendid as a vision, corrupting as an actuality. It turns Antony, in Philo's words, into a "strumpet's fool," or in the less bitter and more clear-eyed view of Octavius, into a boy, one who deserves

> to be chid
> As we rate boys who, being mature in knowledge,
> Pawn their experience to their present pleasure,
> And so rebel to judgment.   (I.iv.30)

In subduing himself to Cleopatra's whim, Antony shows, like Coriolanus, an adolescent side of his character, and in making his will lord of his reason, he drives his most faithful followers, including Enobarbus, to abandon him.

This is not to say that either Antony or Cleopatra is to be condemned. They are shown as adulterer and whore, it is true, and Antony's desertion of the virtuous Octavia is given full weight, as Maecenas describes it:

> Each heart in Rome does love and pity you;
> Only th' adulterous Antony, most large
> In his abominations, turns you off,
> And gives his potent regiment to a trull
> That noises it against us.   (III.vi.92)

In this scene, indeed, Octavius, who stands against Antony not just for respectability, but for law, order, and good government, and who is presented with a good deal of sympathy,[17] takes on for a moment the accents of Edgar or Kent, as he speaks to his sister:

> You are abus'd
> Beyond the mark of thought, and the high gods,
> To do you justice, make them ministers
> Of us and those that love you.   (III.vi.86)

The accent is appropriate, for Octavia, though scorned by Cleopatra because she is low of stature and gentle of voice, possesses, as Maecenas reports, "beauty, wisdom, modesty"; and, in the words of Enobarbus, she is of a "holy, cold and still conversation." He means that she is no match for Cleopatra's warmth and sexual energy (the word "conversation" had bawdy overtones), but in the terms of *King Lear*, Octavia has all the virtues; her qualities are precisely those of Cordelia. The difference is that in *Antony and Cleopatra* these virtues are not what the play sanctions. Octavia is a wan figure against the vitality of Cleopatra, and any comparison is likely to be, on the whole, to Cleopatra's advantage, however much Antony's image of her as a "triple-turn'd whore" may stick in mind; but it is a psychological, not a moral advantage.

In these plays the protagonists are distanced from us and presented critically. We are not allowed to feel for them as heroes after the pattern of Hamlet, as embodiment of what is noble and good. These plays are not concerned with oppositions between evil and good, with heroes and villains, or at least only in a subsidiary way. All values in them are relative, and Octavia's chastity is not a standard against which to measure Cleopatra's lechery. They show us men and women as they are rather than as they might be, engaged with one another in a world in which good and evil cannot be separated out, but are inextricably mixed. In the four central tragedies, the action is viewed against a pattern of universals, and the characters are generalized to some extent, insofar as they are defined in terms of good or evil; this can be seen in the degree to which some characters become symbolic or typical, Iago as evil incarnate, Malcolm and Edgar as good incarnate, Cordelia as grace incarnate. In Shakespeare's later tragedies the action does not come within the dispensation of the gods, of that divinity which shapes our ends, of heaven and hell; these have only an incidental function and importance. However, the later tragedies compensate for the distancing of the hero and the loss of moral urgency with a new realism, a more "dispassionate and scientific scrutiny of life."[18] They suggest an idea of a whole man, rather than of a greatly good man, a flexible rather than an absolute man. In this they relate to that new temper in Jacobean tragedy which led to plays like those of Middleton, in which personal worth is established in psychological rather than in moral terms; and it is in this way that they take their place in the development of Shakespeare's own work, and in the development of Jacobean drama as a whole.

The Fairy-Tale Element in The Taming of the Shrew

By E. M. W. Tillyard

That the induction and the main plot of *The Taming of the Shrew* go back to folk themes has long been known. Christopher Sly, picked up dead drunk, clothed in fine clothing, and made to wake up in a lordly setting corresponding to his clothes, has an ancestry going back to the *Arabian Nights*. Petruchio dealing with Katherina is only one of a long succession of wife-tamers. I shall have nothing to do with the first motif except later to point to an odd instance of its being combined with the second. But distinguishing between two different versions of the immemorial theme of the taming of the shrew, the second of which has been almost ignored, may help with an understanding of Shakespeare's play.

Petruchio's whirlwind wooing and subsequent cure of his newly wedded wife have usually been connected with the crudities of the fabliau tradition; and the latest study of Shakespeare's sources does not depart from this habit. Geoffrey Bullough writes as follows:

> The Petruchio-Katharina story . . . is a variant of the Shrew theme common in fabliaux from classical times. . . . Humorous discussions about mastery in marriage had enlivened the road to Canterbury in Chaucer, and the Jest Books of the Tudor age contained many stories of battle between the sexes. . . . French folk-literature was peculiarly rich in stories of this nature. Their interest often depends on the methods adopted by the husband or wife to win supremacy. In a crude specimen, *Sire Hain et Dame Anieuse*, the husband and wife actually fight for a pair of breeches until the husband knocks the wife into a tub of water and she has to beg for mercy. . . . Nearer to Shakespeare's theme are the tales in which the husband takes the initiative.[1]

And Bullough gives an example of the tales where the husband kills his domestic animals to show what happens to them when they are disobedient and what will happen to his bride if she offends in the same way. Among the resemblances, the one closest to Shakespeare is a Danish tale which not only gives this theme but includes the husband's teaching his wife to follow him in misnaming objects, and the wager on who has the most tractable wife. The story was first recounted by Svend Grundtvig and first related to the *Shrew* by Reinhold Köhler.[2] The characters are three sisters (as in the *Shrew*), who are all shrewish, and the worst of whom is tamed into a model wife as her sisters are not. It is a pity that Bullough did not include this tale in his analogues: analogues, for it can hardly rank as a source.

In all these tales it is the taming of the *wife* that is the main thing;[3] how the wife behaved before marriage is hardly touched on. But Shakespeare dwells as emphatically on the unapproachableness of the maiden as on the contrariness of the wife. It was through taking this truth into account that Peter Alexander conjectured that the Petruchio-Katherina story might be "a version of one of the great themes of literature, a comic treatment of the perilous maiden theme, where the lady is death to any suitor who woos her except the hero, in whose hands her apparent vices turn to virtues."[4] Alexander may be right, but I think Simrock takes us farther when he cites (I, 351–52) the legend of *König Drosselbart* or *King Thrushbeard*. But Simrock hardly develops his citation, on the ground that in this story the trials the shrewish wife is made to undergo duplicate those of the patient Griselda. I do not see what difference this makes, provided the resemblances to Shakespeare's play are close; and I find them close enough to wish to plead that more should be made of the story of King Thrushbeard as an analogue of *The Taming of the Shrew*.

The best-known version of the story is in the *Kinder- und Hausmärchen* of the brothers Grimm;[5] and here is a summary of it. A king had a daughter who was lovely but so proud that she would not look at any of her many suitors. In a last effort to get her married he organized a muster of all the eligible young men from a great distance round, lined them up according to their rank, and ordered his daughter to make her choice. With every suitor she had a fault to find; she singled out one of the kings for special rudeness, saying that his chin (which had a slight irregularity) was like a thrush's beak, whereupon her victim was nicknamed King Thrushbeard. Finally, she refused them all. Whereupon her father came to the end of his patience and swore that he would marry her to the first beggar who presented himself. A few days after, a fiddler in ragged clothes appeared at the king's palace, was admitted, and pleased the king with his music. For a reward the fiddler received the princess as his bride, and they were married then and there. At once he took her to his house, a hovel with no servants, and set her to do menial work. She did it badly and in the end her husband procured her a place in the kitchen of the palace of the land in which they lived. Here she did the humblest work and used to take home the scraps she picked up in the kitchen. One day a wedding was to be celebrated, and as she was standing at the door a finely dressed young man caught hold of her and dragged her into the hall where there was to be dancing. Here she dropped the pot in which she had hoarded some soup and scraps, and these, to her utter confusion, were scattered on the floor. As she tried to escape, the fine young man caught her, and she saw it was King Thrushbeard, who told her that her trials were ended: that he was the fiddler and that the wedding in course of celebration was theirs. All her trials had been to punish her proud spirit. She duly admitted her faults. Finally, she was clothed richly, her father and his court joined the celebrations, and all ended happily.

There are many versions of the story,[6] and these are spread over a large area, including Ireland. The version collected by the brothers Grimm differs from most of the others in making the king force his daughter to marry. Usually the rejected prince, arriving in disguise, attracts the girl by some charm, for instance an entrancing voice, or by some tempting object, which she must have at all costs. Often, the bride's humiliation is made worse by her husband's compelling her to steal and then seeing to it that she is caught. But all the versions have these differences from the wife-taming fabliau: they treat of the girl before as well as after marriage, and she is always a princess. They do not subject her to personal violence or sheer terror, but they cause her to be humbled, one might say educated, by a way of life the remotest possible from the one she has hitherto experienced and has finally abused. They present a sudden marriage uncelebrated at the time but celebrated with the utmost splendor after the girl has been tamed into repentance.

With respect to Shakespeare's *Taming of the Shrew,* scholars have been right in seeing traces of the fabliau treatment of the wife-taming theme. Katherina strikes Petruchio in the wooing scene, and even if he does not strike back he is coarse-mouthed to a degree. Further, the hawk-taming motive, so prominent in the scenes at Petruchio's country house, is in keeping with the violence of the fabliau treatment. Before any training was possible, a hawk's will had to be broken in a sheer head-on battle. There was no question of giving the bird a job. Nevertheless, if you take the whole play into account, its resemblances with *King Thrushbeard* are more than those with the fabliau. True,

Katherina is not a princess, but her shrewishness before marriage figures largely. Her lover appears at the wedding in rags, as the fiddler did when he came to get his bride; and if in so doing he did not disguise his identity at least he disguised his inner nature. Both King Thrushbeard and Petruchio take their brides to their homes (pretended or actual) immediately after the wedding ceremony. The tasks set the princess were educative as well as humiliating; and Petruchio, while proceeding to tame his hawk, pursues simultaneously a more kindly and educative method, trying to make Katherina see for herself the error of her ways. And finally the wedding, uncelebrated at the time, is celebrated in the last scene of the play, after the shrew has been tamed.

What with Chaucer and the Jest Books it is certain that Shakespeare knew the fabliau treatment of the shrewish wife. That he knew a version of the King Thrushbeard story cannot be proved; yet the resemblances between it and his play are so strong that it is likely he did. If, as is accepted, he used the Teutonic version of *Snow White* for parts of *Cymbeline*, there is not the least improbability about his knowing the other story.

I cannot pretend that by taking this new source into account we are better enabled to decide the literary nature of the *Taming of the Shrew*. That decision remains in doubt. A Mark van Doren finds the play quite satisfactory as a hearty farce, a Hardin Craig as a comedy where the farcical elements are remotely vestigial and need not trouble us. For myself I can neither ignore nor reconcile the two components—the farcical and comic—and am forced to conclude that the play fails insofar as it misses such a reconciliation. But however little bearing the sources may have on literary criticism, it is an interesting possibility that in framing his play Shakespeare resorted to both fabliau and fairy tale and that in his loyalty to both he was cheated of the unity at which surely he must have aimed.

Lastly I must point to a version of the King Thrushbeard story[7] that includes the theme of a person waking in alien surroundings and coming to think that the past has been a dream. It comes from Corsica and was collected by Julie Filippi. The beginning is on familiar lines but with the addition that the princess's pride caused her to be hated by her people. There is the usual muster of suitors, but the story differs from the norm in that the successful suitor is a late-comer reaching the palace after the rest have been dismissed. The princess likes him but is too proud to accept him without criticism. So she says she might have had him but for a twisted hair in his beard. Her father suggests that she can pull it out in fun after the wedding, but the suitor feigns meekness, goes down on his knees, and begs her to pull out the offending hair then and there. She pulls out a single hair at random and consents to the match. They are married at once but without the full religious ceremony.

Meanwhile the father and the husband of the bride have a private talk together and among other things fix the date of the church wedding, which is to take place in the bridegroom's country. Bride and bridegroom leave immediately and travel to the bridegroom's palace. The bride goes to sleep and in her sleep she is conveyed to a shepherd's hut where mean clothing is set out by her bedside. When she wakes she finds she is in a room along with sheep, dogs, and three white-bearded old men. She is terrified and asks where she is. In answer the youngest of the three, calling her daughter, expresses wonder that she no longer recognizes her home but dreams she is a king's daughter and a prince's wife. They all laugh when she protests, and her apparent father tells her to get up and go with her grandfather to take the beasts out into the fields, where he and her uncle will join them. She has to obey and before long gets used to the country life and really believes that her old life was a dream. After three months, when the church wedding was due, she is conveyed in her sleep to the palace and wakes up in rich surroundings and attended by four maids. At first she cannot believe in the new setting, and when the three old men come in and bow to her she calls them father, uncle, and grandfather. And so in a way they are, for that is their true relationship to her husband. Then her father appears, the wedding is celebrated, and the princess, now cured of her pride, becomes in due course a model queen.

I do not suggest that Shakespeare derived his own combination of the two themes used in his induction and main plot from a version of this Corsican story but think that the duplication is fortuitous. And yet there is just the chance I may be wrong. That Shakespeare knew some version of the King Thrushbeard story is probable; and in one detail at least the Corsican version is closer to Shakespeare than the others. Only in it does the proud girl want to marry the bridegroom for his own sake. Shakespeare does not tell us explicitly that Katherina wants from the first to marry Petruchio; but when it comes to the point, she does not oppose the betrothal, and when the bridegroom is late she gets into a passion of grief. Moreover, in the *Shrew* Kate in a soliloquy confesses she is ready to marry Ferando. There is nothing improbable in Shakespeare's transferring the appearance and reality theme from the princess in the Corsican story to the drunkard in his own induction. So I think there is just an off chance of derivation. But even if there were none, it is diverting to see the master dramatist and a humble teller of tales in wild Corsica hitting on the same conflation.

Ariel and the Outer Mystery

By Robert H. West

I

That *The Tempest* is mellow and serene is a critical commonplace, and hardly less so is that it has some of the qualities of a farewell. It seems to say that all lived happy ever after; but, as in most serious romance, the happy ending is an appropriate cap for the pleasing successes of the sympathetic characters rather than a suggestion that Ferdinand and Miranda lasted in their bliss much longer than Prospero, whose every third thought was to be upon his grave. The quality of the happy ending in *The Tempest* is not unlike that of "The Eve of St. Agnes":

> *And they are gone: aye ages long ago*
> *These lovers fled away into the storm.*

Shakespeare's lovers, too, and his king and his duke and all their retainers pass into the storm of time and are gone, long ago.

The Tempest is, in fact, a look into as fearful a face as life shows to a discerning man. Its disturbances of nature and of passion are so transient as to be illusory, and the calm that succeeds them is no more real. For constant behind the action is that which is neither storm nor calm, the eternal silence. It is background to the young yet muted love story, the bitter but frightless strain of treachery, and even to forgiveness, reconciliation, the new beginning, and all the rest of human goodness and success the play has to show. Without spoiling the court festivities of which it seems to have been a part, *The Tempest* conveys the poignance of man's insubstantial pageant.

In this anomalous display of human happiness against the shadow of mortality, Shakespeare is treating the mystery of felicity no less seriously than in the great tragedies he treats that of iniquity, and by some similar means. In *The Tempest* and the tragedies alike he touches human mystery with that of the nonhuman, of powers that come out of the silence around us. The ominous storm on Lear's heath and the dreadful coincidences of Desdemona's handkerchief seem the work of forces that, whether random or purposive, lie beyond the phenomenal and are manifest most indecisively to the senses and but guessingly to faith and reason. Related to these cosmic forces both dramatically and metaphysically are the apparition resembling King Hamlet and the beings that prophesy to Macbeth. Every living man, too, by his history of birth and his destiny of death has a part in this outer mystery. And every man's inner mysteries—his passions and his values, his good and his evil, his purposes obscurely shaped to his obscurely determined course—start with the outer and end in it. No wonder, then, if Shakespeare uses the outer mystery to accent the inner, and particularly the supernatural to set off the unknown in the natural. Rooted in a fathomless superhuman evil, the human evil of Macbeth and his lady itself grows fathomless; the hesitations of Hamlet turn largely upon his sense of the undiscovered country, a sense aroused in him and in us by the apparition like his father. And Ariel, in his own way also a part of the outer mystery, helps to remind us of the hollowness of our activities and the certainty of our end. In *The Tempest* Shakespeare puts beside the delight and achievements of the human characters the purer and more enduring delight and powers of Ariel. They seem a fact of supernature utterly discrepant with our frail state. The figure of Ariel suggests, perhaps, that in the scheme of things some glories may be mysteriously spontaneous, and unclouded by the prospect of an early end, but not those of man on earth. Ariel's supernatural pleasures throw into relief the transitory natural ones even of enraptured lovers.

Plainly great differences exist between the supernatural in the tragedies and that in *The Tempest*. In the tragedies the supernatural figures do not appear often or say much. They do nothing at all, or practically nothing; the action links them most tenuously to the human characters, and they are unprovided for in the endings. These plays no more tell what became of the ghost and the witches than they tell with certainty where they are from.[1] The ghost and the witches are in a sense indefinite, and their dramatic effect is not only of solemn mystery but of active terror, for they seem the face of superhuman frightfulness. In *The Tempest*, on the other hand, Ariel appears often, speaks much, and does nearly everything that is done. At the end he returns in delight to his own world. The dramatic effect is certainly not of active terror. Can it be of mystery?

In spite of Ariel's busy day with Prospero and his share in the pleasant provision for all deserving characters, he does belong to the outer mystery, and, like the ghost and the witches, expresses at once a sense of its presence and a deep reserve about its nature.

II

The first thing to notice is that Ariel is not Puck. Scholars have pointed out the fairy strain in the image we have of Ariel, but as Professor W. C. Curry and others have made clear, he appeals primarily to an intellectual rather than a folk tradition.[2] As the name of a spirit *Ariel* belongs not to folklore but to the elaborate literature of Cabalistic pneumatology, which Renaissance rituals and theories of magic had helped to bind into an uneasy syncretism with neo-Platonic and Christian pneumatologies. As a rational spirit ruling lesser spirits and controlling nature at the orders of a theurgist, Ariel appeals to Renaissance pneumatology as Puck appeals perhaps to folklore. The difference between pneumatology and folklore is not so much of subject matter as of tone and method. It is the difference between a naive account, unsystematically concerned with phenomena in the rude terms and local nomenclatures of the folk, and a sophisticated account that abstracts, assembles, compares, classifies, uses authority, and generally acts to earn pneumatology a place in systematic thought. However ill-starred such a study may seem to us, still it has even yet a kind of intellectual dignity that goes with serious speculations on profound subjects.

Now, *The Tempest* appeals to such speculations on the supernatural, and in it they override folklore as a sophisticated account usually will override the simplicities that it may be designed to explain. Renaissance pneumatology covers the data of folklore with the rationales of Scholastics or neo-Platonics or Cabalists or of some amalgam of them all and does it largely by making no distinction of species between fairies and daemons and no necessary difference between their activities.[3] In some of his characteristics Ariel may be fairylike, but this does not separate him from daemons or daemonology. We may see Ariel in the light of his time's rationalizations of the outer mystery, and of man's relation to it. In their own day these rationalizations were a dignifying force in the play and a vivifying one.

Recognition of the standing that pneumatology has in *The Tempest* calls for another and somewhat contrary recognition. Although *The Tempest* appeals to pneumatology, it does not ratify pneumatology; it invites us to account for Ariel in pneumatological terms, but it does not permit us to be positive that we have chosen the right ones. Such plays as Massinger's *Virgin Martyr* and Tourneur's *Atheist's Tragedy* may give grounds for an unarguable pneumatological interpretation of their respective angels and ghosts, but *The Tempest* provides no unequivocal key to Ariel. Perhaps because the assured pneumatologist necessarily loses some sense of supernatural mystery, Shakespeare maintains about Ariel the mixture of pneumatological reference and reticence that helps an audience to recognize him and at the same time to find him strange. This is a method that Shakespeare had followed in *Hamlet* and *Macbeth*. Scholars generally acknowledge that the dramatic "vitality" of the apparition in *Hamlet* comes largely from its correspondence to the apparitions of Elizabethan tale and the covering theory; it comes as largely, too, from the failure of a correspondence positive enough to make a whole cosmic scheme troop in the wake of such pneumatological detail as the play offers.[4] Faustus' Mephistophilis is most certainly a soul-hunting devil of the orthodox Scholastic pattern; his play makes it unquestionable. And with this positive pneumatological pattern comes the general scheme of Christian damnation and salvation. But the apparition like King Hamlet may be a ghost, it may be a devil; it may be from the Catholic purgatory or from a pagan purgatory. It is displayed with confusing features and, like apparitions in real life, left to the judgment of the beholder. Ariel shows the same sort of inconclusive correspondence to certain Jacobean ideas about spirits who answered to magic. Like the ghost, Ariel transmits to the audience the shock of recognition and accompanying sense of reality. Yet, like the ghost, Ariel does not fit pat to any single pneumatological scheme; rather he shows elements—and inconsistent ones—of several such schemes, so that he has not after all enough correspondence to any systematic exposition of spirits to damp the effect of a timeless unknown intruding into the phenomenal world.

Ariel's correspondences to pneumatology are plain enough. He is a "spirit" and so, Prospero seems to say, does not eat or sleep or have such senses as we have. He can go invisible, flame divided, take various forms, stir up the weather, cleave to human thoughts, and move with a speed greater than the wind's. Like air or water he is invulnerable to swords, yet he can feel pain, and he eats—or at least says he will suck where the bee sucks. He answers to the arcane powers of wand, book, and robe, and his name is well known in expositions of Cabalistic pneumatology. To the informed Jacobean playgoer these things would be marvelous or suggestive of marvels, but far from unheard of. As he recognized the notions of Lewes Lavater in *Hamlet* and of Reginald Scott and King James in *Macbeth*, so he would recognize those of Agrippa, Paracelsus, Michael Psellus, and their like in *The Tempest*. Still, the ghost and witches do not wholly fit any pneumatological description, and neither does Ariel.

Though the playgoer might well, for instance, be familiar with the name *Ariel*, both as in Isaiah and as that of a spirit in Cabalistical treatises, he would not know it (or if he would, commentators have yet to discover where) in any use that closely suggested Shakespeare's tricksy creature. Several sixteenth- and early seventeenth-century Christian writers on the Cabala mention Ariel, but always as the spirit of earth, not of air. The orthodox among them, more interested in exposing than in expounding the Cabala, intimate that he, like every other spirit that answers invocation, is a devil hunting souls. Those, on the other hand, who sponsor the Cabala, imply that Ariel is an angel and a great one serving God's providence. Cornelius Agrippa adds that *Ariel* is also the name of "an evil daemon."[5] The image of the supernatural in *The Tempest* does not suit closely with anything now known of the name *Ariel*, except that it belongs to a spirit listed in books about magic, to a being alien to man and largely mysterious to him.

Has Ariel a body? It would seem so; Prospero says he is of air, the cloven pine pained him, and he intends to suck where the bee sucks. The literalness of the pain, at least, is inescapable. He seems surely to have some kind of body, perhaps as described by various Platonistic and Calvinistic pneumatologists. Still, *The Tempest* does not always appear to ascribe body to the spirits Miranda knew. When Prospero discriminates for her between Ferdinand and a spirit, it is by distinctions that sound, superficially at least, like Thomistic not Platonistic ones. This gallant "eats, and sleeps, and hath such senses / As we have. . . ." The spirits that Miranda knew, then, did not eat or have senses? But if Ariel sucks, is it not to eat? If he knows physical pain and delights, has he not such senses as we have? These questions are standard ones in pneumatology, which answers them with variety and often with confidence.[6] In studying *The Tempest* perhaps we may ask them without quite being taxed with critical foolishness; at any rate, scholars have asked such questions. But the play does not answer positively and we cannot make it do so by scratching among the intimations that build up the dramatic image of mysterious Ariel. We simply will not find in *The Tempest* consistent correspondence to pneumatology.

From such ambiguous correspondence as does exist scholars conclude, nevertheless, that Ariel is, in general, rather by the Platonistic than the Thomistic pattern; he is an elemental of some sort.[7] How far, then, does he really fit contemporary descriptions of such creatures? Paracelsus and Michael Psellus, whose views are those most widely quoted in the sixteenth and seventeenth centuries, both aver that an elemental can go invisible and do various other feats, some of them like Ariel's. Like Ariel too the elemental has body which he must nourish, and he knows physical pain. But in Paracelsus' view an elemental is manlike in essential form, has sex, and yearns for sexual union with man to cure its soullessness.[8] The dramatic image of Ariel certainly includes no such yearning nor any sexiness. According to Psellus on daemons (a word not in *The Tempest*) all genera of them are hostile to man, their essential forms are by no means manlike nor their feeding beelike. Ariel's comment that swords "may as well / Wound the loud winds or . . . / Kill the still-closing waters" as him or his fellows echoes faintly a celebrated passage in Psellus that uses a similar obvious metaphor. But in Psellus the point of the passage is that daemons in spite of their ductile substance fear swords, for cuts pain them.[9] The dramatic image of Ariel is far wide of Psellus and Paracelsus.[10]

III

Mere pneumatological uncertainty does not in itself, of course, achieve the effect of dramatic mystery, but simply leaves the way open for it by preventing the audience from setting itself up in cosy familiarity with the supernatural. Shakespeare achieved the effect of mystery by displaying in the most subtle ways the differences between man and the powers above and around him, and the meagerness of the known links that man has with them. The apparition of King Hamlet is brief and painful; its words are cryptic and doubtful. And if this thing has indeed been man so short a while before, that only marks how foreign it now is to living man and all his world. In *Macbeth* the timeless, reasonless malice of the witches and the force of their prophecies, bound somehow to cosmic energization, are to men and their affairs like a flash of lightning in the night.

Now, as I have said, the presentation of Ariel is certainly not thus grim, obscure, and taciturn. Ariel is a prominent agent for control of the action; and he is in bondage to man, as the supernatural beings in *Macbeth* and *Hamlet* are not, through the coercive processes of ceremonial magic. He becomes familiar to us on the stage and has what may seem an ingratiating human personality. But that personality and its humanness are explicitly said to be illusory, and it shows emphatic differences from the human, differences chargeable to Ariel's species, not to his person. His link with man through magic, too, that brings him frequently to the stage was known to Jacobeans as tenuous and dangerous, and so the play shows it.

The clearest difference between Ariel and man is, of course, in his sensational feats, which include virtually the entire repertory of spirit feats except the disgusting ones like possession and copulation. The audience may remain calm. Given a spirit under duress of magic the Jacobean audience certainly was familiar enough with pneumatology to accept equably such labors as Ariel performs. But most of the human characters of the play do not duplicate the equanimity of the audience. They repeatedly exclaim in wonder and fear; and the skeptics among them are routed as handsomely as Horatio is in *Hamlet*. Ariel's feats keep constantly before us the great gap between man and spirit. "This is no mortal business, nor no sound / That earth owes." Ariel's powers are not surprising to the audience, but they are impressive.

A doubt of the nature of Prospero's magic and a concomitant doubt of the nature of Ariel are present in the play as constant undercurrent. Is Prospero confident that he fathoms spirits and that his control is real? He questions Ariel anxiously, instructs him most circumstantially, grows furious at a sign of restlessness, and calls him "malignant thing." Commentators have thought Prospero here harsh with Ariel as elsewhere with Miranda; some excuse Prospero because of the tensions of this crucial day. But what are these tensions? May Ariel be in fact a "malignant thing," as the orthodox held all spirits to be who answered invocation?[11] The phrase signifies Prospero's qualms and reminds the audience of its own uncertainty and of the essential incomprehensibility of spirits. We understand of them, says John Donne, "no more than doth a horse of us."

Prospero works hard. After Ferdinand and Miranda declare their love he says: "I'll to my book; / For yet ere supper time must I perform / Much business appertaining." Later he exclaims in a jubilation which implies relief that his "high charms work," and again that his "charms crack not," his "spirits obey," as though to his view his magical operation was a chancy affair. "Hush and be mute / Or else our spell is marred." To rule spirits or to know them is not naturally given to man, and reminders of it shade the dramatic sense we have of Prospero's success in managing the supernatural. Prospero prevails almost without resistance from his human enemies, and he praises his spirit servant; but still he is tense with an uncertainty that he alone among the characters can feel and that a modern audience probably appreciates much less than a Jacobean one did.

At last Prospero recites the successes of his "rough magic" and abjures it, burying his staff and drowning his book. Perhaps we may be confident at the end that his art was both effective and allowable; "it appears so by the story."

Still, Shakespeare's time asserted the practice of magic to be difficult at best, like any intricate and skillful management of delicately balanced, dynamic forces, and to convey even at its purest the dangerous vanity which we see Prospero finally abjure.[12]

The sense of the remoteness of Ariel from humanity and of the frailty of his links with it is most tellingly conveyed in his bearing toward his master matched against Prospero's toward him. Usually in the exaltation of success Prospero speaks affectionately to Ariel: "My brave spirit!" "My quaint Ariel!" ". . . well done, my bird . . . ," ". . . my dainty Ariel! I shall miss thee. . . ." To these tender expressions Ariel gives not the least response. He is respectful of Prospero's power and acknowledges it by making no "mistakings" and by repeatedly calling attention to the quality of his own work. But the nearest he comes to affection is "That's my noble master!" when assured of his liberty. His delight is chiefly in the approach of his freedom from Prospero, and more than once he reminds his saddened master of the agreed hour—and indirectly thus reminds the audience, too, of the specialness of his own glassy essence.[13]

Finally, indeed, Ariel does seem to border on sentiment. He who has re-ported the troubled castaways with complete detachment and gleefully man-aged them by arousing a terror of which he has not the least sense, notices them at last with what Prospero takes to be almost human feeling. Describing especially old Gonzalo's tears, Ariel concludes:

> Your charm so strongly works 'em,
> That if you now beheld them, your affections
> Would become tender. . . .
> Mine would, sir, were I human.

And so Prospero's do, for:

> Hast thou, which art but air, a touch, a feeling
> Of their afflictions, and shall not myself,
> One of their kind, that relish all as sharply,
> Passion as they, be kindlier moved than thou art?   (V.i.17 ff.)

It is an effective dramatic turn, and an ironic one, that Ariel's superiority to passion matched with passion's superiority to Ariel moved Prospero to take part with his nobler reason against his fury.

If this passage leaves the impression that Ariel fleetingly yearns for human-ity, it may leave equally the counterimpression that that yearning is indeed fleeting and is more in Prospero's sentiment—and in ours—than in Ariel.

There is a coolness in his observation of old Gonzalo's tears and of Prospero's tender inclination and in his comment on himself: ". . . were I human." He is not human. He is but air, and to suppose that he feels is a fallacy that the play notices though it does not insist on it. Man must go his own pathetic way as unattended by creaturely sympathy in animate supernature as in inanimate nature.

So by contrast as well as by similitude the outer mystery touches the inner. Remote though Ariel is from man, yet to Prospero, and in its different way to the audience, he resembles man and stands in the place of a man. For a moment, anyway, Prospero and the audience can credit him with human sympathy, and his happiness at the end is appropriate to the play's mellow conclusion. That far it is companionable to the happiness of the human character for whom he makes "calm seas, auspicious gales" to catch the royal fleet. But to this, Ariel's final task, succeeds the joy of native freedom unblemished by either the nostalgia or the misgivings that beset all men even in victory. With the best of human victory may mingle loss, for upon it, as upon defeat, lies the quietude of passion spent, a reminder of our end. Prospero hopes, he says, to see

> . . . the nuptial
> Of these our dear-belov'd solemnized;
> And thence retire me to my Milan, where
> Every third thought shall be my grave.   (V.i.309–12)

Meanwhile part of one night he'll waste with the story of his life upon this isle. As for the companion of his triumph: "Ariel, chick, . . . to the elements / Be free, and fare thou well."

Time-Beguiling Sport: Number Symbolism in Shakespeare's Venus and Adonis

By Christopher Butler and Alastair Fowler

Professor A. Kent Hieatt, in his study of Spenser's *Epithalamion*,[1] demonstrates a complex number symbolism controlling the structure of the poem. He shows for instance that the poem's twenty-four stanzas are divided, by a change in the refrain, into two groups which bear the same proportions as the hours of daylight and darkness on the longest day of the year, that of Spenser's wedding. The line total is also shown to be significant, since the "long lines" add up to 359, a representation of the "imperfect" apparent daily movement of the sun (one degree short of a full 360-degree revolution). The short final stanza or envoi of six lines brings the total to 365, a representation of the days in the year. Towards the end of his argument (p. 77), Hieatt wonders whether there may not be other Renaissance poems which are governed by a similar numerological decorum. And in fact research in progress[2] is beginning to show that such poems are quite numerous.

It is, however, startling to find among them a poem by Shakespeare. Numerological patterns are not perhaps so contrary to expectation in the works of a Benlowes, a Spenser, or even a Milton; but the current conception of Shakespeare does not encourage us to look for esoteric structures in his poetry. And yet, doesn't his Ovidian epigraph hint at the possibility of a meaning denied to the common reader?

> *Vilia miretur vulgus: mihi flavus Apollo*
> *Pocula Castalia plena ministret aqua.*　　　　(*Amores* I.xv)

> (*Let the vulgar throng admire worthless things;*
> *but to me may the golden-haired Apollo supply*
> *cups filled at the Castalian stream.*)

The curious frequency of the poem's mentions of specific numbers, and of indications of time, incline us to attempt to draw its "thousand honeyed secrets" from a numerological pattern, and in particular a temporal one.[3]

The myth of Venus and Adonis was commonly understood in the Renaissance as having a temporal or seasonal import. Sometimes Adonis was thought to symbolize the sun, sometimes seed; but almost always interpretation of the myth was concerned with its contrast of summer fulfillment and winter deprivation, and with the transition from one to the other at the equinox. The separation of Adonis from Venus, and his departure to the underworld, was interpreted as the entry of the sun into the lower or nocturnal hemisphere. This was conceived as occurring not with the beginning of the winter season proper, but at the precise moment of the autumnal equinox. That is to say, the cosmological interpretation of the myth posited a bisection of the year. George Sandys's commentary on the tenth book of Ovid's *Metamorphoses* provides a convenient popular statement of these ideas:

> Now *Adonis* was no other then the Sun, adored under that name by the *Phænicians*; as *Venus* by the name of *Astarten*: for the Naturalists call the upper Hemisphere of the Earth, in which we inhabit, *Venus*; as the lower *Proserpina*: Therefore they made the Goddesse to weepe, when the Sun retired from her to the sixe winter signes of the Zodiacke; shortning the daies, and depriving the earth of her delight and beauty: which againe he restores by his approach into *Aries. Adonis* is said to be slaine by a Bore, because that beast is the Image of the Winter; salvage, horrid, delighting in mire, and feeding on ackornes, a fruit which is proper to that season. So the Winter wounds, as it were, the Sunne to death, by deminishing his heate and lustre; whose losse is lamented by *Venus*, or the widdowed Earth, then covered with a vaile of clowds; Springs gushing from thence, the teares of her eies, in greater abundance; the fields presenting a sad aspect, as being deprived of their ornament. But when the Sun returnes to the Æquator, *Venus* recovers her alacrity; the trees invested with leaves, and the earth with her flowrie mantle: wherefore the ancient did dedicate the month of Aprill unto *Venus*.[4]

Shakespeare's *Venus and Adonis* is based upon a similar reading of the myth, to which it gives numerological expression by its adjustment to an exact set of numbers drawn from astronomy. The explicit action of the poem, the attempted seduction of Adonis by Venus, has behind it an implicit time scale. This is no mere static decorum, for the form of the poem participates in its thematic development, and displays a tragic movement from the solstitial to the equinoctial stages of the myth.

The traditional connection of the mythological Venus and Adonis with cosmic movements justifies us in exploring the symbolic value of the astronomical events narrated in the poem. In particular, its insistent identification of Adonis with the sun—he is Venus' "earthly sun" (l. 198) and when he leaves her she loses "the fair discovery of her way" (l. 828)—prompts us to trace the reported movements of the sun in relation to the plot. The simplest calculation of this order that can be performed is to determine the length of day and night in terms of lines of the poem. This is made easy for us, since Shakespeare has carefully noted the occurrence of midday and sunset on the first day of the poem's action, and of sunrise on the second day. We are not given, however, any account of the first sunrise—an omission which, as we shall see later, is not without significance—since the sun must have risen before the poem begins:

> Even as the sun with purple-colour'd face
> Had ta'en his last leave of the weeping morn,
> Rose-cheek'd Adonis hied him to the chase.[5]   (ll. 1–3)

This means that, in order to arrive at the metrical duration of the first day, we have to double the number of lines from noon to sunset.[6] The relevant places in the poem are:

> And Titan, tired in the mid-day heat,
> With burning eye did hotly overlook them ...   (ll. 177–78)

> "Look the world's comforter with weary gait
> His day's hot task hath ended in the west ..."   (ll. 529–30)

and, finally, sunrise on the second day of the poem:

> The sun ariseth in his majesty.   (l. 856)

Thus the first day occupies 706 lines, that is, 353 (ll. 178–530 inclusive) multiplied by two; and the subsequent night, 326 lines. The number of lines for a full day and night of twenty-four natural hours would therefore be 1032. Hence, dividing by twenty-four, we determine the measure for one hour: a modulus which turns out to be exactly forty-three.[7] Working from this modulus, we arrive at the durations in hours and minutes of the first day and night with which Shakespeare is concerned. These are: approximately sixteen hours, twenty-five minutes for day; and seven hours, thirty-five minutes for night.

Of course, this operation can be performed with *any* number larger than twenty-four; and any two parts of such a number, when divided by the appropriate modulus, will add to twenty-four. But, in this present case, the given numbers have a significance independent of the mathematical calculation. They are, as we shall see, known astronomical values: a fact that obliges us to regard them as intentional. It is notable (and consistent with the seasonal version of the Venus and Adonis myth) that the proportions of the poem's first day and night are commensurable with those of a solstitial, midsummer's day, in a northern temperate latitude.[8]

At the solstice, the difference between the periods of day and night, and therefore of the lengths of the temporal hours (that is, the hours arrived at by dividing each of these periods separately by twelve)[9] is extremely noticeable. The apparent amplitude of the temporal diurnal hour, at the summer solstice, and the corresponding brevity of the temporal nocturnal hour, are twice adverted to in the poem. When Venus promises Adonis that

> "A summer's day will seem an hour but short,
>   Being wasted in such time-beguiling sport,"   (ll. 23–24)

the rhetorical amplification depends on the comparatively great length of a summer's day, and the "hours" of such a day. Venus' kisses will make a long day seem "an hour: but short." On the other hand, during the solstitial night, the temporal hours have the opposite appearance. When Venus, separated from Adonis, sings her "heavy anthem"—

> Her song was tedious, and outwore the night,
>   For lovers' hours are long, though seeming short   (ll. 841–42)

—why are the hours described as "seeming short"? Only because the temporal nocturnal hours do in fact seem short in summer.[10]

The objection might conceivably be raised, at this point, that our argument is somewhat dependent upon its internal consistency. But the number 1032 as a measure of the full day occurs again—and in a line series completely independent of that discussed above. For the proportion of the poem representing Adonis' life consists of 1032 lines;[11] so that in one sense we can say that Adonis is alive during twenty-four hours. In view of the mythological identification of Adonis with the sun, this correspondence is easily understandable: the numerological trajectory of the actual sun is equivalent to that of the symbolic sun Adonis. Perception of this pattern increases the poignancy of Venus' outcry:

> "Wonder of time," quoth she, "this is my spite,
>   That thou being dead, the day should yet be light."
>   (ll. 1133–34)

These lines, which have no doubt been previously construed as mere hyperbole, are now seen to have been intended with a precise connotational meaning.

It remains to consider the given numbers 353 and 326 (denoting the semi-diurnal and nocturnal periods) which determined the length of the twenty-four hour day as 1032 lines.[12] These figures 353 and 326 are curiously "one short" of the lengths of the lunar synodic and sidereal years respectively.[13] Nor are these the only instances in the poem of numerological counts that fall short. The portion representing midday to sunset is fifty-nine stanzas, one short, that is, of the sixty minutes of an hour. Wasted in time-beguiling sport, a summer's day seems literally "an hour but short," even though it is in fact the longest possible day.[14] These failures to complete an expected measure are obviously to be related to the turning point of the poem's plot. For the latter is also a failure to reach fulfillment: Venus, unable to seduce Adonis, finds that even when she is in "the very lists of love" she has "to clip Elizium and to lack her joy."

Further, one can establish parallels in the action and structure of the poem which develop this effect of falling short. It is particularly marked in the case of the kisses, chronicled throughout the poem with odd persistence, and more than once connected explicitly with the passing of time:

> "Ten kisses short as one, one long as twenty.
>   A summer's day will seem an hour but short . . ." (ll. 22–23)
> "There shall not be one minute in an hour
>   Wherein I will not kiss my sweet love's flower." (ll. 1187–88)

We notice that in stanzas 8, 9, and 10, we have a first series of kisses, all of them given by Venus to Adonis. In stanza 8 she "stops his lips, / And kissing speaks"; in stanza 9 she "murders with a kiss"; and in stanza 10 she achieves no fewer than three kisses—"she kiss'd his brow, his cheek, his chin." This series of five kisses, moreover, is doubled; for "where she ends, she doth anew begin." Thus, up to the end of the first ten stanzas, Venus bestows in all ten kisses. We might expect, as did Venus, that the series of kisses would be answered by Adonis; but in the event he is reluctant to "pay this comptless debt" (l. 84), and "when her lips were ready for his pay, / He winks, and turns his lips another way" (ll. 89–90). This sequence of events in stanzas 8, 9, and 10 finds an exact antithesis in the similar sequence of events in stanzas 80, 90, and 100—stanzas whose numbers are multiples of the previous ones. Here, at the climax of the poem's action, Adonis is at last kissing Venus. In stanza 80 "He kisses her, and she by her good will / Will never rise, so he will kiss her still," and in stanza 90 "the honey fee of parting tender'd is." But in stanza 100, where we should expect the fulfillment and completion of the series, it does not come. Instead, Venus is refused:

> *Now is she in the very lists of love,*
> *Her champion mounted for the hot encounter.*
> *All is imaginary she doth prove;*
> *He will not manage her, although he mount her:*
> *That worse than Tantalus' is her annoy,*
> *To clip Elizium and to lack her joy.*   (ll. 595–600)

Thus, in the very center of the poem (conventionally a significant place, in numerical composition),[15] we find the same falling short as in the astronomical calculations. It seems only reasonable to suppose that the numerological structure of the poem is intended to provide an unequivocal comment on the symbolic meaning of the human events.[16]

A further numerological complex associated with the number of kisses bestowed in the poem is announced by Venus' early prediction of their duration. This prediction seems very strange in its context, unless it can be given some esoteric meaning:

> *"And yet not cloy thy lips with loath'd satiety,*
> *But rather famish them amid their plenty,*
> *Making them red, and pale, with fresh variety:*
> *Ten kisses short as one, one long as twenty.*
> *A summer's day will seem an hour but short,*
> *Being wasted in such time-beguiling sport."*   (ll. 19–24)

The line "ten kisses short as one, one long as twenty" makes sense, if taken quite literally and regarded as expressing a ratio of line-durations. The *ten* kisses given by Venus to Adonis up to the end of the first ten stanzas occupy the same space in the poem as the *one* kiss given by Adonis to Venus in stanza 90, which has taken ten stanzas to elicit. There is thus a literal enactment of the phrase "ten kisses short as one." (Similarly, Venus' first kiss to Adonis is in stanza 8, and Adonis' first kiss to Venus is in stanza 80: again a ratio of ten to one.)

The series of Venus' kisses which is completed in ten stanzas can also be considered as being completed in sixty lines. This points to the sixty minutes of an hour, a measure which is alluded to in Venus' later vow: "There shall not be one minute in an hour / Wherein I will not kiss my sweet love's flower." We notice that on a modulus of one line per minute, the whole poem falls just one stanza short of twenty hours. (Like the "copious stories" of all lovers, st. 141, it is "never done.") The same number twenty is also mentioned verbally with an astonishing frequency:[17] yet it is at first difficult to assign to it any precise numerological significance. Sometimes it occurs in situations with an emotive connotation of grief:

> *"Ay me," she cries, and twenty times, "Woe, woe,"*
> *And twenty echoes twenty times cry so.*   (ll. 833–34)

This is in agreement with the symbolic value attached to the number by the numerologist Pietro-Bongo, who says: "Numquam Vicenarium numerum adhibet, nisi ad res tristes, luctuosas, acerbas. . . ."[18] The character of the other numbers in the poem, however, leads us to expect the number twenty to have a temporal import.

That this is in fact so becomes clear as soon as we grasp the occasion of the poem. The clue to this is given by the dedication. For Southampton was exactly twenty years old in the year of the poem's first appearance, 1593. The conclusion seems inescapable that the number symbolism of *Venus and Adonis* is so adjusted as to refer to the age of Shakespeare's patron. Casting Southampton in the role of Adonis suggests many tantalizing questions with regard to the poem's content that are beyond the scope of the present paper. Certain results relevant to our present approach, however, are immediately obtained. For example, it becomes more intelligible why the poem should contain so many references to Adonis' age; why he should appeal to Venus, "Measure my strangeness with my unripe years" (l. 524), and why, in Venus' hyperbole, she should exclaim, ". . . the world hath ending with thy life." Moreover, not only are all the references to the number twenty more meaningful—

> *Were beauty under twenty locks kept fast,*
> *Yet love breaks through, and picks them all at last*
>
> (ll. 575–76)

—but also the length of the poem is itself explained. For the "complete" length of the poem is 1200 lines (that is, 20 x 60): a representation of twenty hours. Thus the very form of the poem sets forth the theme of time's brevity. A whole summer is compressed into a single day, and that long day into "an hour but short." Southampton's twenty summers seem but twenty hours.

The notion of a twenty-year period enables us to explain a number not previously dealt with, the total number of kisses bestowed throughout the poem. Such prominence is given to the kisses that they should have some symbolic force more exact than that arrived at above. In view of the planetary roles of the human characters, we should expect their kisses to refer to conjunctions of the planets Venus and Sol. And indeed we notice that the closeness of the human Venus and Adonis as they kiss is repeatedly stressed: "Incorporate then they seem, face grows to face"; "their lips together glued." Moreover, the most elaborately described kiss, that begun in stanza 90, occurs at sunset, one of the two occasions when Venus and the sun may appear in the sky together. Now it was well known in the Renaissance that the motion of the planet Venus appears as an oscillation from one side of the sun to the other; the complete period of the oscillation being about 1.6 years or 584 days. In elongation east of the sun Venus is seen as the evening star, while towards western elongation it is visible in the morning. (This fact, that the planet is sometimes a morning, and sometimes an evening, star seems covertly alluded to in the exclamation of Shakespeare's Venus:

> "O where am I?" quoth she, "in earth or heaven?
> Or in the ocean drench'd, or in the fire?
> What hour is this, or morn, or weary even?
> Do I delight to die, or life desire?")[19]   (ll. 493–96)

Between the elongations of Venus there lie the superior and inferior conjunctions with the sun; of which conjunctions the inferior, when Venus is two and a half times more brilliant than at the superior, is much the more noticeable. The interval between the inferior conjunctions is such that in the twenty years of Southampton's lifetime, represented in the poem, a total of twelve occurred. This total is in accord with the number of kisses exchanged between Venus and Adonis throughout the poem.

The *dénouement* of the myth of Venus and Adonis, as cosmologically interpreted, is the tragic destruction of Adonis by the boar of winter. We notice that at the corresponding point in the poem, when Venus discovers "the foul boar's conquest on her fair delight" (l. 1030), this event is immediately connected with the alternation of light and dark. The goddess's light-giving eyes "Like stars asham'd of day, themselves withdrew . . . / Into the deep dark cabins of her head" (ll. 1032–38) and were commanded by her troubled brain to "consort with ugly night" (l. 1041). Moreover, since the boar kills Adonis with a kiss, it may be regarded as supplanting Venus as his lover: the sun has been removed from proximity with Venus in the upper hemisphere to a dark vicinity with the boar in the lower. Various authorities advance various explanations as to why the boar should symbolize winter. Some give the trivial reason that the animal is at his best in that season; others, more obscurely, say that the beast's bristliness resembles the condition of nature in winter; while, according to a tradition that is given its fullest expression by Valeriano, the explanation is made to rest in the boar's love of darkness. Its downward-directed eyes, we are told, betray a hate and fear of light; and justify a further, moral allegorization of the polysemous animal, as lust. This last development of the myth is reflected in Adonis' unwittingly accurate prophecy:

> "But lust's effect is tempest after sun,
>   Love's gentle spring doth always fresh remain,
>   Lust's winter comes ere summer half be done."   (ll. 800–802)

In the normal seasonal order of things Adonis should be parted from Venus at the equinox. We should therefore expect some formal representation of an equinoctial state in the latter part of the poem. This in fact proves to be the case. For the metrical durations of the night and the second day of the poem (stanzas 89 to 144, and 144 to the end) turn out to be equal, as are the durations of day and night at the equinox. Thus the poem's structure dramatically telescopes the movement from the solstitial to the equinoctial situation. The statement "lust's winter comes, ere summer half be done" is mimed very precisely, since the poem's solstitial state is interrupted to become the equinox. Indeed, the first, midsummer day is incomplete. For, as we have seen, its sunrise is not included within the poem's frame. If that twenty-four hour period at the solstice were completed, no doubt summer *would* half be done; but before this can happen—"ere summer half be done"—the boar has intervened, the equinoctial point is passed, and winter has begun. It is natural to ask what the duration is, of this first, unfulfilled day. The answer adds yet another strand to the poem's complex texture of temporal symbolism. For Venus hails the sun on the second morning ("Oh thou clear god, and patron of all light") at line 860—just twenty hours from the beginning of the poem, on our forty-three-lines-per-hour modulus. Thus the midsummer hours of the first day briefly recapitulate the twenty years of Southampton's lifetime.

So far we have demonstrated certain numerical patterns occurring in the formal structure, which provide a counterpoint to the themes of the poem. There is also, however, a series of substantive numbers, occurring in the text itself. Most prominent among these are the large numbers referred to in a variety of contexts. The hyperboles that introduce the number twenty ("twenty hundred kisses"; "twenty thousand tongues") point to some relationship with the vigesimal patterns considered above: the formal representations of twenty-year and twenty-hour periods. In the last paragraph, we saw that the first, solstitial day was only twenty hours long. Now the large numbers mentioned in the text within this same portion of the poem—that is, before sunrise on the second day—are as follows:

"A thousand honey secrets shalt thou know."	1000
(l. 16)	
"No dog shall rouse thee, though a thousand bark."	1000
(l. 240)	
. . . a thousand ways he seeks	1000
To mend the hurt . . .	
(ll. 477–78)	
"A thousand kisses buys my heart from me."	1000
(l. 517)	
"What is ten hundred touches unto thee?"	1000
(l. 519)	
"Is twenty hundred kisses such a trouble?"	2000
(l. 522)	
"He cranks and crosses with a thousand doubles."	1000
(l. 682)	
"If love have lent you twenty thousand tongues . . ."	20,000
(l. 775)	
"Ay me," she cries, and twenty times, "Woe, woe,"	
And twenty echoes twenty times cry so.[20]	800
(ll. 833–34)	

By addition, we find that if the total of these figures is regarded as a temporal measure, it confirms the pattern already established on a formal basis. For the summation of the substantive series is 28,800, the number of minutes in twenty days. Here again the "little time" of Southampton's twenty summers is epitomized in a numerical metaphor.

If the foregoing analysis is correct, or if even a fraction of it is correct, we must assume that interpretation of *Venus and Adonis* has scarcely begun. Any overall reading of the poem must now take as its starting point the number symbolism we have attempted to reconstruct. For the numerological form points to astronomical and mythological spheres of reference, in terms of which alone the poem's intended meaning may be understood. In spite of Shakespeare's undeniably ironic handling of conventional Ovidian situations, the deceptively simple human events adumbrate their philosophical and cosmological counterparts more fully and seriously than has yet been suspected. He seems to manifest, in this poem at least, the same preoccupation with the processes of time which is observable in certain of his contemporaries. *Epithalamion* might almost have been written in emulation of *Venus and Adonis* in an attempt to "overgo" Shakespeare in the field of subtle temporal numerology.

Sonnets 127-154

By Brents Stirling

Most editors and critics of Shakespeare agree that the sonnet series 127–54 is distinct from other groups and that its problem of disarrangement, if any, is a separate one. But of those who find the sonnet order disturbed, very few are hopeful of restoring it. The difficulty is not that possibilities are lacking, but that they abound: so long as the conventional standard of loose or 'plausible'[1] linkage is accepted, one rearranger vies with another and, except for contenders who may be mad, the competition is about equal. Restoration fails from sheer opportunity. Thus, although granting that Thorpe's 1609 sonnet order (Q) is faulty, students of the text are willing to let well enough alone. I reopen the question only because I think that important evidence has been overlooked.

We should be more aware that the series provides its own standard of linkage. The existing text includes combinations so pointed, so unmistakable, that they may imply a Shakespeare who joined sonnets clearly and emphatically or not at all. Although these linked elements of 127–54 rarely exceed two sonnets in length, they make up in quality for their lack of extension: instead of vague

thematic agreement they offer a sharp unity of subject matter, and they supplement this with phrasal echo. They often contain a syntactical 'run-on' between sonnets. Some are pairs, two sonnets functioning as one (e.g. 135-36),
and some are transitional units (e.g. 141-42). I shall call these respectively
'clear Q pairs' and 'clear Q sequences.'

Individually, such combinations are well recognized; what I wish to note is
their frequency and normative quality. There are six clear Q pairs: 131-32,
133-34, 135-36, 139-40, 149-50, and 153-54. And at minimum, there are four
clear Q sequences: 132-33 bridging two of the pairs (see the "heart"–"groan"
link between 131-32 and 133.1); 141-42 with a last line–first line link; 143-44
(to be discussed later); and 151-52. Perhaps 147-48 should be added. With allowance for overlapping, these clear pairs and sequences account for at least
eighteen of twenty-eight sonnets in the series.

Thus, even in their doubtful 1609 order the last twenty-eight sonnets offer
ten examples of close linkage. A reader who can take time to compare them
with examples of loose or merely 'plausible' interconnection will find, I think,
that they are in a class by themselves. These Q units are the undeniable ones;
no rearranger with a conscience could disrupt any of them, although he might
well join one with another. I adopt them here as the standard for a tentative
restoration of the sonnet order. This means that the Q series will be altered
only when the change restores a linkage of the cogent kind found in our clear
pairs or sequences, and it also means that no clear unit will be split. Some Q
links of the loose and potentially accidental sort will be broken, but only when
they conflict with a restoration that the adopted standard seems to require.
Otherwise, I shall let them stand. Yet when retained, the loose links do not
qualify as evidence, for a rearranger may not alternately use them and reject
them. Nor may the orthodox editor, for that matter; if he holds that vague
connection supports so many rearrangements that it supports none, then he
may not use it to justify the text of 1609. For no one can say that the 1609
series is not itself a rearrangement, whether intentional or accidental. It has no
external authority and its internal authority is limited to 'clear' combinations
that cannot be questioned.

I do not ask readers to assume that the standard of linkage derived from
clear Q units prevails in other Elizabethan sonnet arrangements, or to agree—
at this point—that it should extend further than it does in Shakespeare's terminal series. I shall simply apply it in a limited reordering of sonnets 127-54, and
we shall see what happens.

What are some possible restorations that meet this standard? The first is a relatively uncontroversial one easily checked with a copy of the Sonnets at hand. It is suggested by parallels between 143 and 135–36—the "Will" sonnets, long thought to be closely related. These are often lumped together in a fragment of three without concern for other sonnets. But note that 143 and 144 are joined in a clear Q sequence; in both sonnets the poet pursues the woman who pursues another man. Note also that the sequential effect is enhanced if the order is transposed to 144, 143. Indeed, 144 appears to begin a group, and if we allow it for that reason to precede 143 we have a time-honored device: an introductory sonnet directly followed by an epic simile which amplifies it. (See, for example, Shakespeare's authentic pair, 117–18.) With unusual specification sonnets 135–36, the "Will" pair, continue the theme and phrasing of 143. So they should follow the reversed unit 144–43; but should the group end with this recombination? The clear pair 133–34, with its triangle of poet, friend, and mistress, is uniquely related to 144, which has introduced the poet and his "two loves," the man and the woman. Sonnets 133–34 also continue the "Will" note of 143, 135–36 (see 134.2). So one's impulse is to form a series of 144, 143, 135–36, 133–34; but this would break a clear linkage in Q—the "heart"–"groan" note which bridges the pairs 131–32 and 133–34 (see 131–32 and 133.1). According to our standard, therefore, the restored order should run 144, 143, 135–36, 131–32, 133–34. The new group can now be tested by reading, and an added check will show that within limits of 'clear' linkage none of the reordered sonnets fits elsewhere in the 127–54 series.[2]

This rearrangement is in a pattern that will become familiar. No clear Q pair or sequence has been broken,[3] although one (143, 144) has been transposed in order, with a gain of internal unity. Two new relationships appear—that of 143 with 135–36, and of 144 (as introductory sonnet) with the group as a whole. And the new connections maintain a standard established by the ten clear Q units. Finally, in forming the new group, sets of two consecutive sonnets (135–36 and 143, 144) have been moved intact, a reordering which implies that the disarrangement in Q is a disarrangement by twos. Of this, more later.

Next, we may consider a change in the sonnet order that will restore two broken pairs and a broken sequence. The pairs to be restored are 137>141 and 152>147;[4] the sequence is 141–42>149–50. Evidence for the new links will appear in a quotation of the first nine sonnets of a group, but before considering this evidence we should sense the direction in which it leads. After noting the intact Q twos in a restoration of 144, 143 / 135–36 / 131–32 / 133–34, it will be interesting to find that a second restoration brings together like units. The pattern will become:

```
                        137  ⎫
                             ⎬  restored pair
clear Q sequence  ⎧     141  ⎭⎫
                  ⎨     142   ⎬ restored sequence
clear Q pair      ⎧     149   ⎭
                  ⎨     150  ⎫
                             ⎬
clear Q sequence  ⎧     151  ⎭
                  ⎨     152  ⎫
                             ⎬  restored pair
Q sequence        ⎧     147  ⎭
                  ⎨     148
```

Except for sonnet 137, to be explained later, here once more is the scheme of interlocking Q pairs and twos found in the first restored group.

Again, if the rearrangement is to be convincing, it must begin with new links of the quality found in clear Q units. Next, it must not break any existing link; if, for example, sonnets 142 and 149 are to be joined, the new sequence must be 141–42>149–50. And the four sonnets brought together must be compatible. As these conditions are met, a 'control' will appear and the sonnet order will become increasingly independent of free choice. Then a final test will be possible. As new links are determined, pairs or sequences may or may not fall together in a structurally and thematically unified series. If they do, the restored order, already subject to effective testing, will be considerably strengthened. Presently we shall see that nine sonnets, joined for various reasons, turn into a surprisingly cohesive series on a common theme: enslavement to sensuality with the poet's eyes and heart as "perjured" agents of betrayal.

All of these claims naturally need demonstration, which would be very awkward in discursive form; thus clarity will be gained and space actually saved by full quotation which appears below. The quoted series stems mainly from restoration of two pairs. So, as a first step, examine it with attention to 137> 141 and 152>147. In each of these restored pairs note, in addition to other links, the phrasal echo between one concluding couplet and the other. Since this device is found in five of the six clear Q pairs,[5] it is plain that in 127–54 Shakespeare used it consistently. When separated sonnets show the couplet echo along with other qualities found in pairs, the evidence for linking them becomes strong.[6]

Now we may consider the nine sonnets in series. Throughout, a broad thematic unity will be clear enough, but there are pointed relationships that can be missed on a first reading. These I describe in a running commentary which is supplemented by occasional underlining of text and by cross-reference in the left-hand margin. Q numbers are preserved only to identify sonnets.[7] The text is in modern form.[8]

[137]

Thou blind fool, Love, what dost thou to mine eyes,
That they behold, and see not what they see?
They know what beauty is, see where it lies,
Yet what the best is take the worst to be.
If eyes, corrupt by over-partial looks, 5
Be anchor'd in the bay where all men ride,
Why of eyes' falsehood hast thou forged hooks,
Whereto the judgement of my heart is tied?
Why should my heart think that a several plot
Which my heart knows the wide world's common place? 10
Or mine eyes seeing this, say this is not,
To put fair truth upon so foul a face?
    In things right true my heart and eyes have erred,
    And to this false plague are they now transferred.

[141]

In faith, I do not love thee with mine eyes,
For they in thee a thousand errors note;
But 'tis my heart that loves what they despise,
Who, in despite of view, is pleased to dote;
Nor are mine ears with thy tongue's tune delighted; 5
Nor tender feeling, to base touches prone,
Nor taste, nor smell, desire to be invited
To any sensual feast with thee alone:
But my five wits nor my five senses can
Dissuade one foolish heart from serving thee, 10
Who leaves unsway'd the likeness of a man,
Thy proud heart's slave and vassal wretch to be:
137.13–14 ⎡ Only my plague thus far I count my gain,
       ⎣ That she that makes me sin awards me pain.

[142]

141.14 ⎡Love is my sin, and thy dear virtue hate,
       ⎣Hate of my sin, grounded on sinful loving:
O, but with mine compare thou thine own state,
And thou shalt find it merits not reproving;
Or, if it do, not from those lips of thine, 5
That have profaned their scarlet ornaments
And seal'd false bonds of love as oft as mine,
Robb'd others' beds' revenues of their rents.
Be it lawful I love thee, as thou lovest those
Whom thine eyes woo as mine importune thee: 10
Root pity in thy heart, that when it grows,
Thy pity may deserve to pitied be.
    If thou dost seek to have what thou dost hide,
    By self-example mayst thou be denied!

137>141

A restored pair. 141 directly qualifies 137 ("In faith, I do not . . ."). 137 has arraigned both eyes and heart; 141 clears the eyes of guilt and places blame on the heart alone. The echo of couplets ("plague") between the two sonnets is unmistakable. "Plague" in this sense is not used elsewhere.

137>141–42>149–50

A restored sequence. The couplet of 149 recalls the opening two lines of 142 ("hate on" supplementing "hate"). As 149 develops 142, 150 pointedly develops 141 (eye *vs.* heart) and reasserts (line 4) the 'perjury' note begun in 142. In the sequence highly specific ideas are repeated and significant phrasal echoes occur.

Sonnets 137, 141, and 150 are plainly meant to function together. Their wide separation in Q prevents this; the restored sequence permits it and also retains the three sonnets in necessary logical order (141 following from 137 and 150 from 141).

[149]

Canst thou, O cruel! say I love thee not,
When I against myself with thee partake?
Do I not think on thee, when I forgot
Am of myself, all tyrant, for thy sake?
Who hateth thee that I do call my friend?   5
On whom frown'st thou that I do fawn upon?
Nay, if thou lour'st on me do I not spend
Revenge upon myself with present moan?

141.3–10   What merit do I in myself respect,
            That is so proud thy service to despise,   10
137.4; 141.3   When all my best doth worship thy defect,
            Commanded by the motion of thine eyes?
142.1–2   But, love, hate on, for now I know thy mind;
            Those that can see thou lovest, and I am blind.

[150]

141.1–3;   O, from what power hast thou this powerful might
149.11   With insufficiency my heart to sway,
            To make me give the lie to my true sight,
            And swear that brightness doth not grace the day?
            Whence hast thou this becoming of things ill,   5
            That in the very refuse of thy deeds
            There is such strength and warrantise of skill,
137.4; 149.11   That, in my mind, thy worst all best exceeds?
            Who taught thee how to make me love thee more,
            The more I hear and see just cause of hate?   10
            O, though I love what others do abhor,
142.1–3   With others thou shouldst not abhor my state:
            If thy unworthiness raised love in me,
            More worthy I to be beloved of thee.

[151]

Love is too young to know what conscience is;
Yet who knows not conscience is born of love?
Then, gentle cheater, urge not my amiss,
Lest guilty of my faults thy sweet self prove:
For, thou betraying me, I do betray   5
My nobler part to my gross body's treason;
My soul doth tell my body that he may
Triumph in love; flesh stays no farther reason,
But rising at thy name doth point out thee
As his triumphant prize. Proud of this pride,   10
He is contented thy poor drudge to be,
To stand in thy affairs, fall by thy side.
    No want of conscience hold it that I call
    Her 'love' for whose dear love I rise and fall.

149–50, 151–52

This Q sequence, kept intact, continues the restored sequence. 151 renews the central idea of 142, mutual guilt, also suggested in 150 (lines 11–12). 152 caps this with two phrasal echoes of 142 ("bed-vow," "new hate") as it continues the note of shared guilt from 151.

Phrasal echoes include repetition of the special sense of "dear" (151.14; 142.1).

152 makes dominant the 'perjury' note begun in 142 and, like 150, joins it (lines 11–14) with the 'eye' theme of previous sonnets. (I restore the Q reading "perjured eye" in place of the usual emendation "perjured I.")

[152]

In loving thee thou know'st I am forsworn,
But thou art twice forsworn, to me love swearing;
142.8   In act thy bed-vow broke, and new faith torn,
142.1–2; 149.13   In vowing new hate after new love bearing.
But why of two oaths' breach do I accuse thee,   5
When I break twenty? I am perjured most;
For all my vows are oaths but to misuse thee,
And all my honest faith in thee is lost:
For I have sworn deep oaths of thy deep kindness,
Oaths of thy love, thy truth, thy constancy;   10
And to enlighten thee, gave eyes to blindness,
Or made them swear against the thing they see;
    For I have sworn thee fair; more perjured eye,
    To swear against the truth so foul a lie!

[147]

137.14;   My love is as a fever, longing still
141.13   For that which longer nurseth the disease;
Feeding on that which doth preserve the ill,
The uncertain sickly appetite to please.
My reason, the physician to my love,   5
Angry that his prescriptions are not kept,
Hath left me, and I desperate now approve
Desire is death, which physic did except.
Past cure I am, now reason is past care,
And frantic-mad with evermore unrest;   10
My thoughts and my discourse as madmen's are,
At random from the truth vainly express'd;
152.13–14   For I have sworn thee fair, and thought thee bright,
Who art as black as hell, as dark as night.

[148]

137.1   O me, what eyes hath Love put in my head,
150.3   Which have no correspondence with true sight!
147.5–7   Or, if they have, where is my judgement fled,
That censures falsely what they see aright?
147.13–14   If that be fair whereon my false eyes dote,   5
What means the world to say it is not so?
If it be not, then love doth well denote
152.13   Love's eye is not so true as all men's: no,
How can it? O, how can Love's eye be true,
That is so vex'd with watching and with tears?   10
No marvel then, though I mistake my view;
The sun itself sees not till heaven clears.
    O cunning Love! with tears thou keep'st me blind,
137; 141; 150   Lest eyes well-seeing thy foul faults should find.

152>147

A restored pair. Note the obvious echo of couplets on the fair-foul, fair-black perjury ("For I have sworn thee fair . . .").

147, 148

The Q sequence is kept intact. 147 begins the terminal theme of Reason's abdication in favor of perjured judgment that declares foul or black to be fair. 148 concludes this (line 3), and connects it again with the blindness theme of earlier sonnets.

Note the likely eye-aye-no pun in 148.8, with its echo of 152.13. The line may be read ". . . not so true as all men's no."

The end sonnet, 148, is rhetorically parallel with the beginning sonnet, 137. And it finally answers the question that 137 asks. 137 introduces every specific note of the series; 148, in parallel style, 'resolves the issue.'

A likely objection to this sonnet arrangement is that it separates 148 and 149, which appear to be connected by couplets on the poet's blindness. But there is little else joining the two, and the blindness note appears in other sonnets. I have not considered 148–49 a 'clear pair' because it lacks the multiple and syntactical unity of combinations like 149–50. Nevertheless, several editors have found the sequence 148, 149, 150 a persuasive one. If one feels strongly that it should be retained, there is an alternative rearrangement: 137, 141–42, 151–52, 147–48, 149–50. The alternative order preserves many relationships found in the quoted series, and also resembles it in maintaining a combination of intact twos from Q. It has difficulties not shared by the quoted series, but they need not be discussed here. My purpose is not to 'settle' the sonnet order in detail but to identify the content of original groups or shorter units, and to relate their disarrangement to a consistent theory governing the 1609 text. Thus, if variant restorations bring the same sonnets into a group and imply the same theory of text disturbance, differences between them of sonnet order are not material at this time.

The kind of evidence supporting the series just quoted calls for completing it with sonnets 129 and 146. They express—and conclude—a theme already apparent; neither fits elsewhere; and 146 is the perfect 'envoy' sonnet for the new group. But what of the 'pattern of intact twos' which addition of 129 and 146 appears to break? This question will be answered, significantly perhaps, at a later point. Meanwhile, I offer the two added sonnets with notations that emphasize echoes, especially of sonnet 147.

[129]

	The expense of spirit in a waste of shame
152.3	Is lust in action; and till action, lust
142.7; 150.4; 152; 147.13	Is perjured, murderous, bloody, full of blame,
	Savage, extreme, rude, cruel, not to trust;
	Enjoy'd no sooner but despised straight; 5
147.9	⎡Past reason hunted; and no sooner had,
	⎣Past reason hated, as a swallowed bait,
147.10–12	⎡On purpose laid to make the taker mad:
	⎣Mad in pursuit, and in possession so;
	Had, having, and in quest to have, extreme; 10
	A bliss in proof, and proved, a very woe;
	Before, a joy proposed; behind, a dream.
	All this the world well knows; yet none knows well
	To shun the heaven that leads men to this hell.

[146]

Poor soul, the centre of my sinful earth,
151.6   . . . . . .⁹ these rebel powers that thee array,
Why dost thou pine within and suffer dearth,
Painting thy outward walls so costly gay?
Why so large cost, having so short a lease,   5
Dost thou upon thy fading mansion spend?
Shall worms, inheritors of this excess,
Eat up thy charge? is this thy body's end?
Then, soul, live thou upon thy servant's loss,
And let that pine to aggravate thy store;   10
Buy terms divine in selling hours of dross;
Within be fed, without be rich no more:
147.3–4, 8   So shalt thou feed on Death, that feeds on men,
And Death once dead, there's no more dying then.

Thus far, nineteen sonnets of the 127–54 series have been rearranged in two groups. What of the remaining nine: 127, 128, 130, 138, 139, 140, 145, 153, and 154? The last two form a clear Q pair isolated from the rest by almost all editors. Sonnets 139–40 also make up a clear pair with a claim to independence. I think that the order should be reversed to 140, 139, but since the reversal does not affect the larger scheme of restoration, I merely recommend it in passing.[10] Sonnets 127 and 130 (in either of two possible orders) are commonly thought related. I can find no internal evidence linking 128, 138,[11] or 145 with other sonnets, and therefore regard them as independent 'singles.'

Here, then, is the full plan of rearrangement.

I My Mistress' Eyes (three independent pairs on a related theme)
    A. 140, 139.   B. 153, 154.   C. 130, 127 (possibly collateral with II)
II Poet, Friend, and Mistress
    144, 143, 135, 136, 131, 132, 133, 134
    (A possible restriction of this group is discussed on pages 152–53.)
III Perjury of Eye and Heart
    137, 141, 142, 149, 150, 151, 152, 147, 148, 129, 146
    (Alternative possibility: 137, 141, 142, 151, 152, 147, 148, 149, 150, 129, 146. See page 144.)
Three Independent Sonnets: 128, 138, 145

This attempt at restoration is based on a standard of evidence derived from Q itself, from its 'clear' elements (left intact) which imply that rearranged sequences must show a special kind of unity. It is by no means unlikely that an occasional link in the chain is accidental, but I find it hard to believe that chance governs the composite result. I must repeat, however, that the result is meant to be provisional—to invite attention not to a settled sonnet order but to a method of procedure.

Does the reconstructed sonnet order (including its variants) imply a coherent theory of manuscript history, one that will explain the disarrangement found in Q? If we allow the table of rearrangement to stand for Shakespeare's text, we find that Q has failed to retain the longer sequences, Groups II and III, but has preserved ten of the original two-sonnet units. Thus, with very few exceptions it has been possible to restore groups by fitting together intact units of two from the 1609 series. That the doubtful Q text should lend itself to re-arrangement of this kind suggests that behind the 1609 printing lay a manuscript in which sonnets were inscribed two to a leaf. Disruption of sequence in this manuscript could occur by displacement of leaves, but the displacement could not affect sonnets on the same leaf. In other words, original units of two would be preserved, but longer sequences could be disturbed. This hypothesis is consistent, moreover, with occasional clear pairs or twos which Q seems to have reversed (140, 139; 144, 143). If sonnets were inscribed two to a leaf, recto-verso, a leaf accidentally turned over would keep the two sonnets together but transpose the authentic order.

The hypothesis also squares with a peculiar relationship between surviving elements of two and the Q scheme of numbers. Since the numbering 127–54 is a continuation of 1–126, we can be sure that it was not added to the text until Thorpe's copy was assembled in the mass, perhaps at the time of printing. As for the twenty-eight sonnets, 127–54, assume now that the 1609 printer's copy (or a manuscript behind it) was a series of fourteen leaves containing two sonnets each. The number pattern imposed in Q would then have become 127–28 for sonnets from the first manuscript leaf, 129–30 for those from the second, and thus to 153–54 for the two sonnets from the last leaf. In short, if the last twenty-eight sonnets were inscribed two to a leaf on fourteen leaves, the two sonnets on any single leaf would have received in Q a pair of consecutive numbers running odd-even (e.g. 141–42, not 140–41). So far we have only an assumption and a conclusion from it. But we have evidence from Q itself that many undeniable units of two survive within a generally questionable text. See the clear pairs and sequences listed on page 135. If manuscript leaves, now identified by odd-even Q numbering, are responsible for this survival,[12] then (1) authentic twos preserved in a doubtful portion of the text should have the odd-even number order representing leaves that preserved them, and (2) other

sonnets in the doubtful text area should form twos ('leaves') of the same numerical pattern. This is what we find. One disjointed series is composed of the
first six sonnets: 127–28, 129–30, <u>131–32</u>. The clear, or preserved pair (underlined) shows the odd-even number order, and the remaining four sonnets,
when cast into twos, or leaves, also show it. Another disjointed series exhibits
the pattern (authentic but dislocated twos again are underlined): 137–38, <u>139–
40</u>, 141–42, <u>143–44</u>, 145–46, <u>147–48</u>. The remaining doubtful sequence contains the last four sonnets: <u>151–52</u>, <u>153–54</u>. The series is discontinuous, but the
authentic twos surviving within it are in the familiar number order.

Thus I infer, as a working principle, that in the series 127–54 each odd-numbered sonnet and its even-numbered successor represent the content of a single
manuscript leaf. Use of the table on page 145 will show that ten leaves identified
in this way correspond with ten two-sonnet units of the rearrangement. The
leaves are 139–40(I–A) / 153–54(I–B) / 131–32 / 133–34 / 135–36 / 143–44 (all
representing II), and 141–42 / 147–48 / 149–50 / 151–52 (all representing
III). Two leaves (139–40 and 143–44) reverse the sonnet order in the table, but
they still represent units of two in the attempted restoration. Thus, to the extent of ten two-sonnet units, our restored or 'original' sonnet order could have
been disarranged into the 1609 order simply by displacement of manuscript
leaves (including a turning-over to verso-recto of leaves that then became represented in Q by sonnets 139–40 and 143–44).[13]

But the hypothetical manuscript has fourteen leaves, not ten, and the additional four do not correspond with two-sonnet units in the restoration table.
These anomalous leaves (again identified by odd-even Q numbers) are 127–28
/ 129–30 / 137–38 / 145–46. Since they fail to represent intact twos of the
restored series, how can they fit an explanation of its disarrangement by leaf
displacement?

If it seems that our hypothetical manuscript is in trouble, the difficulty may
end in reassurance. Of eight sonnets in the four anomalous leaves three (129,
137, 146) are from Group III of the restored sequence, two (127, 130) are from
I–C, and three (128, 138, 145) are the independent sonnets that internal evidence places apart from any restored group or shorter unit. This suggests that
the anomalous leaves result from a copying of Group III after I–C and the
three independent sonnets had been mixed with it. Here a reader may properly
suspect patchwork on the manuscript hypothesis. Ten of its 'leaves' correspond
with units of two in the restoration table, but four do not. Shouldn't we infer
from this either that the hypothesis must be changed fundamentally or that
the restored groups should be modified to fit it? I shall try to answer the question. First, the restored groups (page 145) must rest on internal or 'literary' evi-

dence and may not be changed to suit a manuscript theory unless the internal evidence permits. Otherwise we have circularity. Second, our manuscript hypothesis can support the restored groups by explaining their two-sonnet fragments found in Q; but this is not all that the hypothesis must explain. The internal evidence points not only to several restored groups but to three miscellaneous 'singles' (128, 138, 145). How did the singles enter Q and how did they happen to be numbered as they are? Further, how did sonnets 129 and 146 become separated from Group III and from each other? And how was I–C split so that one of its sonnets now follows 129 and the other precedes 128? In substance, if it is to explain *all* of the disarrangement in Q our hypothesis must be enlarged so that it answers these questions. This can be done with no alteration of the reconstructed manuscript; we need assume only that it was a copy made after I–C and the miscellaneous singles were mingled with Group III[14]— the sort of thing so frequently responsible for corruption in derived texts. I shall try to reconstruct the process, but for clarity's sake shall avoid nonsignificant alternatives or complications.

Reference is again to the table on page 145. In the mingling prior to copying, the independent 138 became lodged before the opening sonnet of Group III. The 'envoy' sonnet (146) became separated from the rest of Group III, allowing for an interpolation between 129 and 146 of I–C (130>127) plus the two extraneous sonnets 128 and 145. The mixed sequence thus became: 138, the first ten sonnets of III, and then 130, 127, 128, 145, 146. A scribe copying this in manuscript leaves of two sonnets each, recto-verso, would have produced a leaf and sonnet order running (according to numbers later used in Q): 138, 137 / 141, 142 / 149, 150 / 151, 152 / 147, 148 / 129, 130 / 127, 128 / 145, 146. In brief, he would have rendered the mixed sequence into a manuscript form that now fits our theory of Q disarrangement. Since I–A, I–B, and II of the restored sequence already agree with the hypothesis, we thus have all twenty-eight sonnets in a manuscript from which the 1609 sonnet order can be derived by assuming a disarrangement of loose leaves each containing two sonnets inscribed recto-verso. The disarrangement includes an accidental turning over of three leaves that thus became identifiable in Q by the sonnets numbered 137–38, 139–40, and 143–44.

Enlargement of the hypothesis to account for anomalous leaves does not raise internal difficulties. In a reconstructed mingling of Group III, the pair I–C, and the three independent sonnets, it would be embarrassing if, for example, III had to be broken at various points to allow for random insertion of misplaced sonnets. But no such confusion arises; instead there is a 'normal' process of addition and combination. Note again the assumed order, prior to copying, of mixed elements (those foreign to Group III are bracketed): [138], 137, 141, 142, 149, 150, 151, 152, 147, 148, 129, [130, 127], [128], [145], 146. The extraneous 138 enters the series not in the middle but at the beginning—a likely place for an added sonnet. The only splitting of Group III is a separation from it of its 'envoy' (146), and since this sonnet is the eleventh and concluding one of the group, it could have been on a readily detachable end-leaf. Separation from III of 146 leaves 129 ending the group, and at that point—again a likely place for added elements—the pair 130>127 appears intact. After it come the two independent sonnets 128 and 145 which, although unconnected, are similar in nature and could readily have been inserted together. Then appears 146, the separated end-sonnet of III.

In outline, then, the hypothetical text history of sonnets 127–54 has four stages: (1) existence of the original groups and independent pairs in their first manuscripts, in which sonnets may or may not have appeared two-to-a-leaf; (2) a mingling of I–C, III, and the independent sonnets in the manner described; (3) a copying of these mingled elements onto manuscript leaves each having two sonnets inscribed recto-verso, a copying that must also have included I–A, I–B, and II, unless they were originally in the two-to-a-leaf form; (4) the end-result: a manuscript of fourteen leaves containing two sonnets each, one recto and one verso—a manuscript directly or indirectly behind Q, from which the 1609 sonnet order was derived through disarrangement (including occasional reversal) of the leaves. Like the restored groups, these four stages of manuscript history must be inexact or incomplete in some details, but it does not matter at present so long as basic principles of disarrangement and restoration remain unaffected.

In spite of consistency shown by the manuscript hypothesis, is the final disarrangement (stage 4) implausible? At the time of copying (stage 3), is it not likely that the sonnets received numbers (not those of Q), or that the manuscript leaves or pages were numbered, or that the leaves were bound in proper order? Under any of these conditions a subsequent disarrangement of leaves resulting in the Q order might be thought improbable. Yet, in a copying that produced at most fourteen manuscript leaves, fulfillment of any of the three conditions is doubtful. And under editorial standards of the time it is far from certain that numbering of sonnets, leaves, or pages would have led to a careful reassembly of displaced elements before printing. In the printing-house, moreover, unbinding, partitioning, and partial disarrangement of a manuscript were distinct possibilities. Add to these uncertainties a known willingness of collectors and publishers to tamper with a sonnet order (they were the first 're-arrangers'),[15] and a disturbed sequence after final copying of the manuscript becomes not only possible but likely; with one proviso: any two sonnets on a single leaf of our hypothetical manuscript would remain together unless separated in editing or printing.

The manuscript hypothesis accounts, of course, for the preservation in Q of so many undeniable units of two sonnets each and for the consistent odd-even Q numbering imposed on these preserved but often dislocated twos. It likewise accounts for the disruption by twos in Q of longer sequences restored here by literary evidence. But in addition to explaining this 'systematic' disarrangement in the 1609 text it accounts for seemingly random displacement—the appearance of a grim sonnet on lust (129) between the dainty, affected 128 and 130, and the sequential absurdity of a pretty sonnet like 145 followed by the *de profundis* note of 146. Such anomalies are explained by the mingling of sonnets, followed by copying, that produced manuscript leaves 127, 128 / 129, 130 / and 145, 146.

Although the reconstructed manuscript underlying sonnets 127–54 may be deductively plausible, it would be reassuring if we could know whether any manuscripts substantially like it played a part in Elizabethan sonnet history. Space allows for two significant examples. In Harleian MS. 7553, Constable's seventeen 'Spiritual Sonnets' appear on ff. 32–40, two to a leaf, recto-verso, with apparent exception of the final sonnet on an end-leaf by itself. There is no numbering, although the sonnets have titles which appear to be in ink different from that used in the text.[16] Except for the presence of these titles the manuscript is exactly in the form of our hypothetical manuscript for sonnets 127–54.

Three different arrangements of twenty-one Constable sonnets (unrelated to the 'Spiritual Sonnets' of Harleian MS. 7553) offer an interesting problem which can be solved, I think, only by assuming an earlier manuscript source of the kind inferred here for the Shakespeare series. In content, the Harington manuscript, the 1592 *Diana*, and the first twenty-one sonnets of the 1594 *Diana* are substantially the same except for the sonnet order.[17] The sonnets from 1 to 10 in the Harington sequence are the sonnets that 1592 presents as 1, 3, 5, 7, 11, 13, 15, 17, 19, 21 (Harington omits number 9 of the 1592 order). The sonnets from 11 to 21 in Harington are those appearing in 1592 as 2, 4, 6, 8, 10, 12, 14, 16, 18, 22, 20. The 1594 sequence is similar to the Harington; in terms of the 1592 sonnets, it runs 1, 3, 5, 7, 9, 11, 13, 15, 17, and a substitution for 19; then follow 8, 2, 4, 10, 12, 14, 16, 18, 20, 22, 6. So far as the twenty-one sonnets are concerned, the Harington manuscript and the 1592 and 1594 editions apparently stem from the same source. Kenneth Muir (*NQ*, CXCIX, 424–25) explains the strangely separate grouping, in Harington and 1594, of the 1592 odds and evens by assuming an original manuscript with the sonnets arranged in two parallel columns. The copyist responsible for 1592 read this text crosswise, and in transcribing it proceeded from each sonnet in the left column to the opposite one in the right column. The Harington copyist worked down the left column, finished it, and then transcribed the right column. (Mr. Muir's account allows for deviations which cannot be discussed here). Thus, in sonnet content Harington's 1, 2, 3, 4 . . . duplicate 1592's 1, 3, 5, 7 . . . ; Harington's 11, 12, 13, 14 . . . reproduce 1592's 2, 4, 6, 8 . . . .

One difficulty with Mr. Muir's theory is that it requires either an original manuscript page of remarkable length—one that could contain columns of eleven sonnets each[18]—or else a copyist (for Harington) who for two or more consecutive pages could follow the left column only, and then double back to transcribe the right column from the same pages. I offer a different explanation: an original manuscript in eleven loose leaves with the sonnets, in the 1592 order, running two to the leaf, recto-verso. This, of course, is the kind of manuscript I have inferred for Shakespeare's series 127–54. The 1592 copyist accurately followed its order from page to page, but the Harington scribe worked from leaf to leaf, first copying all the recto sonnets (odd numbers in the 1592 order). As he finished each sonnet he discarded the original manuscript leaf recto side up, thus completing a pile with 11^r on top. Then he turned the pile over and addressed himself in the same way to the verso sides (2, 4, 6, etc.— even numbers in the 1592 arrangement). In this process, the Harington copyist skipped the ninth sonnet (5^r)[19] and transcribed his last two sonnets in reverse order. If the 1594 copyist or compositor worked from the same original manuscript, he followed a similar course, although he produced a rearrangement, accidentally and otherwise,[20] as he moved through the verso sequence; (note the differences between Harington and 1594 in their rendition of the 1592 even numbers).

This explanation of a memorable confusion implies, of course, that 1592 correctly reproduces the original manuscript order, while Harington and 1594 do not.[21] Why should the latter two contain the same error? If the original manuscript had numbered leaves, the numbers (from 1 to 11) would have been on the recto sides only and could have implied not the leaf order but the sonnet order. Hence a rendering by Harington and 1594 of the recto sonnets first. It is worth noting that, except for the Harington copyist's missing the sonnet on 5^r, both his arrangement and 1594 reproduce the assumed recto order but depart accidentally or intentionally from the verso order, the one that would have been without leaf numbers.

The nature of Harleian MS. 7553 (Constable's 'Spiritual Sonnets') and my explanation, if valid, of sequential variants in three other Constable texts suggest that the manuscript form attributed to sonnets 127–54 was not unusual. A practice of inscribing sonnets two to a leaf, recto-verso, is borne out by the Harleian manuscript, and an assumed original manuscript of the same kind accounts for the *Diana* confusion without complication. An assumption that can do this and can also explain sequential difficulties in sonnets 127–54 may prove useful. Perhaps it can help us to understand anomalies in other sonnet sequences, including Shakespeare's 1–126.

There is a final question. To what extent do the pattern of surviving twos in Q, the restored sonnet order, and the manuscript hypothesis support one another? Since the last two derive from the first, and since the first stems from a subjective impression of the 1609 text, are not all three simply different ways of expressing the same intuition? Is the argument circular?

The presence of intact but scattered twos in sonnets 127–54 can be surmised only by appealing to the Q text, but this does not make the intuition a matter of whim or convenience. A reader may test it for himself: can he regard the six surviving 'clear pairs' and the four 'clear sequences' (page 135) as accidentally coherent units? If not, can he then view as accidental the close ties between separated sonnets like 143 and 135–36? Or, can he grant that a poet given to the tight linkage, with couplet echo, of pairs that survive in Q would have allowed several intervening sonnets to spoil the parallel thought and phrasing, including couplet echo, in 137>141 or 152>147? If the answer to such questions is the one I think probable, respect for the text commits us to certain rearrangements, but at the same time holds us to the preservation of clear twos. If these conditions are accepted, a shifting of sonnets in units of two follows as a working principle, to be applied wherever the internal evidence permits.

But it is a working hypothesis only. It yields interesting results; yet these in turn must be judged by their own internal evidence. And even in its instrumental function the idea of surviving twos has limits. If conflicting group restorations meet its requirements, the pattern of twos will not help to decide in favor of one or the other. Should Group II, for example, stand as restored on page 159, or should 131–32 be removed and the remainder arranged as 135–36, 143, 144, 133–34? Literary evidence may favor the first emended order, but the pattern of twos supports either. This is also true of restored Group III and its variant (page 144). Hence the principle of Q disarrangement by intact twos is hardly a control which eliminates all but the one, the true, sonnet order. A scheme promising such magic would be embarrassing. Even so, a reordering of the last twenty-eight sonnets begins to lose some of its distressing uncertainty. A strict standard of restored linkage and a requirement that no clear unit of two be broken drastically limit new combinations of the loose or intuitive kind. Ironically, when we accept this limitation there are unlooked-for results. Highly unified groups of sonnets begin to take form.

In summary, the internal evidence of Q implies a survival of intact twos; then, as the implication is experimentally used to control rearrangement it 'works' by helping to shape new groups that justify themselves by internal evidence. And this evidence meets the standard set originally by clear Q units. Whatever the circularity here, it is not tautology.

But what of the manuscript hypothesis? Without it there would be serious difficulty: although internal evidence implies that Q retained many units of two from a disarranged original text, it is quite necessary to explain how this could happen; otherwise the internal evidence simply leaves us with a physical improbability. What kind of original text could plausibly survive in a derived text as a system of intact but disarranged twos? Is there a normal manuscript form that would make such an apparently strange result not only possible but probable? The manuscript hypothesis answers this question satisfactorily and agrees, moreover, with evidence drawn from the Constable manuscripts and editions.

"A Lover's Complaint": A Reconsideration

By Kenneth Muir

I

"A Lover's Complaint," published in Shakespeare's *Sonnets* (1609), has been comparatively neglected by the critics. Some, indeed, have assumed that Shakespeare was probably not responsible for the poem. These include Hazlitt, Lee, Saintsbury, Kittredge, Parrott, C. S. Lewis, and also, apparently, Rollins. Robertson ascribed it to Chapman,[1] and Murry concurred in this ascription.[2] J. W. Mackail, in what is otherwise the best essay on the poem, suggested that it was written by the Rival Poet of the Sonnets.[3] Those who have thought that Shakespeare was the author have been somewhat perfunctory in their comments. Malone called it a "beautiful poem, in every part of which the hand of Shakespeare is visible." Swinburne remarked that "it contains two of the most exquisitely Shakespearean verses ever vouchsafed to us by Shakespeare, and two of the most execrably euphuistic or dysphuistic lines ever inflicted on us by man." Samuel Butler considered it to be a "wonderful poem." John Dover Wilson regarded it as a deliberate parody by Shakespeare of Chapman. George Rylands speaks of it as "that little-appreciated Elizabethan masterpiece," declaring that it "shows an advance on the lyrical *Venus and Adonis* and the rhetorical *Lucrece*."[4]

The best case against Shakespeare's authorship of the poem is Mackail's. He argues (p. 63) that its vocabulary is non-Shakespearian; that "the style and evolution of the poem"

> must be set down as not characteristically Shakespearian, and in some respects as characteristically un-Shakespearian. A certain laboriousness, a certain cramped, gritty, discontinuous quality, affects it subtly but vitally throughout.

The author, unlike Shakespeare, fumbles at the beginning of the poem, and "its preciosity, its strained rhetoric, its parade of learned words" would suit the Rival Poet as characterized by Shakespeare.

Very little has been written about the poem during the last thirty years, and it may therefore be worth while to reopen the question of the authorship of the poem, to examine the validity of the arguments put forward by Mackail and Robertson, and to attempt a reassessment of the poem, irrespective of its authorship.

The vocabulary of the poem is certainly unusual, though the parade of learned words is no more obvious than in *Troilus and Cressida*. There are more than fifty words in the poem which are not found elsewhere in Shakespeare's works.[5] Fifteen of these are compound epithets: some of these are compounds of noun and participle (e.g., *heaven-hued, maiden-tongued, skill-contending, heart-wished*); others are compounds of two adjectives, or of adjectives with participles (e.g., *comely-distant, deep-green, deep-brained, sad-tuned, strong-bonded*). Another group of words is formed by the addition of prefixes (e.g., *encrimsoned, enswathed, impleached, unapproved, unshorn, enpatron*); others are formed by the addition of suffixes (e.g., *phraseless, termless, fastly, weepingly, acture, extincture*); others again are verbs coined from nouns or adjectives (e.g., *sheaved, sistering, lover'd, pensiv'd, livery*); some are comparatively common words which Shakespeare did not happen to use again (e.g., *beaded*—if this is the correct reading—*blusterer, consecrations, maund, laundering*); and a few are the ink-horn terms which are most frequent in *Troilus and Cressida* (e.g., *annexions, congest, fluxive*). Some of these words are apparently coinages: at least the Oxford Dictionary does not give prior instances of their use. These include *acture, encrimsoned, enswathed, impleached, unapproved, unexperient, invised,[6] annexions, lovered* and *laundering*.

The presence of so many "un-Shakespearian" words is not, however, a decisive argument against his authorship; for all Shakespeare's plays contain words he did not use more than once, some of which he probably coined for the immediate purpose. The words listed above are similar to words used by Shakespeare: *annexment* and *enacture* in *Hamlet, pleached* in *Much Ado about Nothing, crimsoned* in *Julius Caesar*; and if *sister* as a verb occurs only in a possibly non-Shakespearian part of *Pericles*, he used *husband* as a verb in *King Lear*. There are, moreover, a number of words in "A Lover's Complaint" used once only in Shakespeare's other works: *cautel* in *Hamlet, dialogue* as a verb in *Timon of Athens, pelleted* in *Antony and Cleopatra, commix* in *Cymbeline* and *reword* in *Hamlet*. Clearly the unusual words in "A Lover's Complaint" are of the kind which Shakespeare would coin or borrow.

Since Hart's studies in Shakespeare's vocabulary,[7] it has been accepted by most critics who have given the matter their attention that the presence of words not used elsewhere by Shakespeare cannot be used to disprove his authorship of a play. In his later plays, at least, he used a previously unused word every ten or fourteen lines on an average, and a word new to our literature (on the evidence of *O.E.D.*) every eighteen to twenty-eight lines. In works of which Shakespeare was the part author—*Edward III* and *The Two Noble Kinsmen*—he used new words about twice as frequently as his collaborators.[8] There are 329 lines in "A Lover's Complaint," so that one would expect to find in it at least twenty-three, and possibly as many as thirty-three, words not previously used by Shakespeare, and about fifteen words which are not known to have appeared in print before. As the poem is short, it would be unwise to lay much stress on the exact figures. In fact the number of unused words, and of words used with a different meaning, is considerably more than thirty-three, but the newly coined words number about fourteen. As the poem has been dated as early as 1585, and as late as 1603, precision is impossible in either case.

These figures do not, of course, prove that Shakespeare wrote the poem; but at least they throw doubt on the view that because of its vocabulary he could not have written it.

If we turn from vocabulary to wider questions of style, there may seem, at first sight, to be more substance in Mackail's arguments. No one could deny that there are very weak lines and clumsy expressions in the poem. Mackail cites as examples of feebleness:

> *Whereon the thought might think sometime it saw . . .*   (10)

> *What's sweet to do, to do will aptly find . . .*   (88)

> *For on his visage was in little drawn*
> *What largeness thinks in Paradise was sawn.*[9]   (90)

Although such lines are manifestly weak, they are not weaker than numerous lines in Shakespeare's acknowledged works; and even if the lines were too bad for Shakespeare, there are others too good for some unknown poetaster, and, perhaps, too good even for Chapman. As Mackail admits (p. 62):

> There are more than a few passages in the poem which are like Shakespeare at his best, and of which one would say at first sight that no one but Shakespeare could have written them, so wonderfully do they combine his effortless power and his incomparable sweetness.

Although Mackail disagrees, it is surely easier to believe that Shakespeare wrote a poem with a number of feeble lines—some explicable by textual corruption or lack of revision—than that some other poet, having steeped himself in Shakespeare's poems and sonnets, succeeded at times in equaling his models.

Sir Edmund Chambers goes so far as to admit that Robertson's arguments for Chapman's authorship of the poem are "more plausible than some of his ascriptions to that writer."[10] This, however, is not saying very much. Robertson relies a good deal on Mackail's essay, and he fastens on the suggestion that the poem was written by the Rival Poet. He seeks to show that the words used in the poem have the same meaning and accentuation as when they are used by Chapman, but not as when used elsewhere by Shakespeare. His first example is *authorized*:

> His rudeness so with his authoriz'd youth . . .   (104)

> Authoriz'd by her grandam.   (Macbeth III.iv.65)

> Authorizing thy trespass with compare . . .   (Sonnet 35)

He suggests unwarrantably that the accentuation of the word in *Macbeth* is different from that in the other lines, though in all three the accent is on the second syllable; and, somewhat embarrassed by the sonnet accentuation, he suggests that this sonnet is either not Shakespeare's, or else written by Shakespeare in imitation of Chapman. His second example is:

> He had the dialect and different skill . . .   (125)

> In her youth
> There is a prone and speechless dialect
> Such as move men.   (M.M. I.ii.188)

In both passages, as Robertson admits, the meaning of *dialect* is "persuasive skill," so that the Chapman parallels he gives are largely irrelevant.

More significant are the words which occur both in "A Lover's Complaint" and in Chapman's works, but not elsewhere in Shakespeare's. Chapman does use *maund*, *affectedly*, *sawn*, *forbod*, *pallid*, and *charmed* (in the sense of "exercising charm"); but we may observe that *maund* is not rare, that *affectedly* is a word that any poet might have coined from *affected*, that *sawn* is not used by Chapman in the sense of "sown" but only in the modern sense, that *forbod* is used in *Lucrece* (though most editors emend to *forbade*), that *pallid* is used by Spenser, and that in any case it is not certain that the *palyd* of the first edition means *pallid*. Robertson gives other examples, but they can mostly be ignored. Some words used in "A Lover's Complaint" can be interpreted in a different way; others listed by Robertson are used by Shakespeare as well as by Chapman; many are not precisely paralleled in Chapman's works—*acture*, for example, being nearer to Shakespeare's *enacture* than to Chapman's *facture*; and one word, *invise*, occurs only in "The Contention of Phillis and Flora," a poem which is no longer ascribed to Chapman.

But the strongest argument against Robertson is that by using the same methods he brings himself to believe that Chapman collaborated with Shakespeare in at least thirteen of his acknowledged plays. If we refuse to accept the argument that Chapman had a hand in *Troilus and Cressida* and *Julius Caesar*, our low opinion of "A Lover's Complaint" should not permit us to acquiesce in Robertson's ascription of the poem to Chapman.

II

Every one of Shakespeare's works has internal links with others. If, for example, *Troilus and Cressida* had been published anonymously, it would have been easy to demonstrate Shakespeare's authorship by its links with *Lucrece* and the Sonnets, with *Romeo and Juliet* and *Hamlet*. Even plays to which Shakespeare contributed a few scenes only—*Sir Thomas More* and *The Two Noble Kinsmen*—have multiple links with his known works. If, therefore, Shakespeare wrote "A Lover's Complaint," we should expect to find parallels in it with his known works. Editors have pointed out a number of these but without, apparently, realizing their full significance. The following parallels may be offered as examples.

The forsaken lover is described in the first stanza as

> *Storming her world with sorrow's wind and rain.*

In the storm scene of *King Lear*, the Gentleman tells Kent that the King

> *Strives in his little world of man to out-storm*[11]
> *The to-and-fro conflicting wind and rain.*

This parallel may, indeed, be regarded as suspect because its validity partly depends on a plausible emendation. More significant is the parallel between the third stanza and a passage in *Antony and Cleopatra:*

> *Oft did she heave her napkin to her eyne,*
> *Which on it had conceited characters,*
> *Laund'ring the silken figures in the brine*
> *That seasoned woe had pelleted in tears.*

So Cleopatra, replying to Antony's accusation that she is cold-hearted toward him (III.xiii.158), exclaims:

> *Ah, dear, if I be so,*
> *From my cold heart let heaven engender hail,*
> *And poison it in the source, and the first stone*
> *Drop in my neck; as it determines, so*
> *Dissolve my life! The next Cæsarion smite!*
> *Till by degrees the memory of my womb,*
> *Together with my brave Egyptians all,*
> *By the discandying of this pelleted storm,*
> *Lie graveless . . .*

Shakespeare does not use the word *pelleted* except in these two passages. In the poem, the tears are the pellets of sorrow; in the play, Cleopatra's frozen tears, turned to hail, are the pellets of her grief. Steevens says that *pellet* was "the ancient culinary term for a *forced meat ball*," and it was also an heraldic term. The heraldic associations are certainly not present in Cleopatra's speech. Hailstones may properly be spoken of as a "pelleted storm"—a storm of pellets—but it looks as though the more complicated imagery of *Antony and Cleopatra* was suggested by the lines of the poem, linked, perhaps, with the later lines:

> *That not a heart which in his level came*
> *Could scape the hail of his all-hurting aim.*

The play was performed before the poem was printed, so that Shakespeare must have had access to the manuscript. It may be added that on at least four occasions he uses the idea of salt tears acting as seasoning:

> *Seasoning the earth with show'rs of silver brine*   (*Luc.* 796)

> *With eye-offending brine. All this to season*
> *A brother's dead love.*   (*T.N.* I.i.30–31)

> *How much salt water thrown away in waste,*
> *To season love!*   (R.J. II.iii.72)

> *'Tis the best brine a maiden can season her praise in.*
>   (A.W. I.i.55)

The most interesting parallels, however, are with *Hamlet*. Both Laertes and Polonius warn Ophelia against Hamlet, whose attentions, they assume, are as dishonorable as those of the handsome seducer of "A Lover's Complaint." Hamlet was the "observed of all observers," as the seducer was

> *one by nature's outwards so commended*
> *That maidens' eyes stuck over all his face.*   (80)

Laertes tells his sister that Hamlet may love her now,

> *And now no soil nor cautel doth besmirch*
> *The virtue of his will.*   (I.iii.15)

It has been suggested that Shakespeare borrowed the word "cautel" from Henry Swinburne's *Briefe Treatise of Testaments and Last Willes*;[12] but the word is also used in "A Lover's Complaint," though not elsewhere in Shakespeare's works. Laertes warns Ophelia that she may suffer loss of honor

> *If with too credent ear you list his songs,*
> *Or lose your heart, or your chaste treasure open*
> *To his unmaster'd importunity.*   (I.iii.30–31)

This is precisely what happens to the heroine of "A Lover's Complaint." The seducer urges her to lend

> *soft audience to my sweet design,*
> *And credent soul to that strong-bonded oath.*   (278)

Shakespeare uses the word "credent" on two other occasions,[13] and in each case he associates it with fornication or adultery. Ophelia tells her father that Hamlet has "made many tenders of his affection" and "given countenance to his speech" with "almost all the holy vows of heaven." Polonius retorts that "when the blood burns," the "soul lends the tongue vows." So in "A Lover's Complaint," the seducer shows the girl the presents he has received from his former victims:

> *Lo, all these trophies of affections hot,*
> *Of pensiv'd and subdu'd desires the tender.*   (218–19)

Earlier in the poem, he urges the maid not to be afraid of his "holy vows" (179). Polonius finally tells Ophelia not to believe Hamlet's vows:

> for they are brokers,
> Not of that dye which their investments show,
> But mere implorators of unholy suits,
> Breathing like sanctified and pious bonds[14]
> The better to beguile.   (I.iii.127–31)

So the forsaken lover was aware beforehand of the seducer's evil reputation:

> For further I could say "This man's untrue,"
> And knew the patterns of his foul beguiling;
> Heard where his plants in others' orchards grew;
> Saw how deceits were gilded in his smiling;
> Knew vows were ever brokers to defiling;
> Thought characters and words merely but art,
> And bastards of his foul adulterate heart.   (169 ff.)

The seducer afterward tells of the nun, "or sister *sanctified*," who had fallen in love with him; and he urges the maiden to believe his "strong-*bonded*" oath (279). Ophelia, finally, is urged by Hamlet to get to a nunnery, which recalls the most spectacular of the seducer's conquests; and she is dragged to a muddy death. The heroine of the poem throws her presents in the stream, "Bidding them find their sepulcres in mud."

Although the word *broker* was frequently used as a synonym for pimp,[15] and although the subject of seduction would almost inevitably involve the use of some of the words common to the two passages, the links between them would appear to be strong enough for us to assume that one passage was influenced by the other. Several explanations are theoretically possible:

(1) Shakespeare might have read "A Lover's Complaint" in manuscript before he wrote *Hamlet*—that is, between 1593 and 1601.

(2) Both Shakespeare and the author of the poem might have been influenced by a corresponding scene in the Ur-*Hamlet* (if there was one).

(3) The author of the poem might have written it after the publication of *Hamlet,* and before the entering of the *Sonnets* in May, 1609.

(4) "A Lover's Complaint" might have been written by a friend of Shakespeare's, who had access to his manuscripts.

(5) Both works may have been written by Shakespeare.

Any of these explanations is possible, but only the last is at all probable.[16]

III

The publication of the poem with an authentic text of the Sonnets—a text which may, indeed, be printed from Shakespeare's manuscript,[17] though not, presumably, with his permission—is strong *prima facie* evidence for his authorship of the poem. Although Sir Sidney Lee thought that the publication was comparable with that of *A Passionate Pilgrim*, and although Mackail believed that some of the sonnets were spurious, it is obvious that even if we were doubtful about the authorship of a few of the later sonnets, the collection was not an anthology by various hands. Lee had some hard things to say about the careless printing, though many of the alleged misprints look more like a conscientious following of authorial spelling.[18] As the volume was already of a respectable size without additional matter, the publisher had no need to pad it out with a poem by another writer; and the name "William Shake-speare" is repeated after the title "A Louers complaint." It must be assumed, therefore, without strong evidence to the contrary, that the poem was indeed by Shakespeare; and this is the assumption that is made in the remainder of this essay.[19]

As the poem is written in the seven-line stanza of *Lucrece*, it should probably be dated after *Venus and Adonis* and not, as some have surmised, as early as 1585; and as *Lucrece* was apparently the "grave labour" promised in the dedication to the earlier poem, "A Lover's Complaint" was probably written after *Lucrece*. It has some links with the Sonnets and more significant links with plays written after 1600 than with those written before. It is possible, therefore, that it was written about the turn of the century. Some have dated it after 1601 because of supposed echoes of Holland's Pliny;[20] but the parallels are not necessarily with the translation, so that they cannot be used to date the poem. Perhaps it represents a first draft which Shakespeare intended to revise —one would expect the reverend man of stanza 9 to offer the lady good advice after her story—or which he regarded as too slight to publish by itself. He was sufficiently busy between 1601 and 1609 for him to have had little leisure for nondramatic poetry; and he must have realized that the poem was small beer compared with *Hamlet* or *King Lear*. When he published *Venus and Adonis* he could speak of it as the first heir of his invention, his earlier plays being as yet unpublished, and not regarded as serious literature; but, a decade later, he was recognized as the best dramatist of his time, and he had less need to publish nondramatic poetry.

By the time the Sonnets were published, the vogue for sonneteering, started by Sidney, was already over. Drayton added a few sonnets to his collection after 1605, and one or two younger poets continued to write in the idiom of the past age; but parody, overproduction, and Donne's new style had combined to make the love-sonnet unfashionable. In the same way, "A Lover's Complaint" belonged to a class of poem which had been popular in the 'nineties and even before. Some "complaints," including those in *The Mirror for Magistrates*, are put into the mouths of historical figures. Lodge's "Complaint of Elstred" (1593) and Daniel's "Complaint of Rosamond" (1592) are of this kind—the latter being in the same stanza form as "A Lover's Complaint," and both being published with sonnet sequences. Other complaints are spoken by mythological or allegorical characters—for instance, *The Lamentation of Troy for the Death of Hector* (1594), and Barnfield's "The Complaint of Chastitie" (1594) and "The Complaint of Poetrie" (1598).

Shakespeare's poem is unusual in that it is concerned with a fictional character in a modern, though pastoral, setting. The first eight stanzas describe the behavior of the deserted woman, as observed by the poet from a hill. She is asked by "a reverend man that graz'd his cattle nigh," who had formerly lived in the city, "the grounds and motives of her woe." The remainder of the poem consists of the woman's story of how she was seduced, and during this tale we are not reminded at all of the initial observer, and only once of the aged man. Within the story is a long speech of the seducer, filling fifteen stanzas. Knowing that the woman is aware of his promiscuity, he cheerfully admits his conduct, but (like Juan in *Man and Superman*) he excuses himself by claiming that he was solicited by the woman in each case, that he was never before in love, and that he was guilty of "errors of the blood, none of the mind." He shows the valuable presents he has received from his lovers and offers them to the first woman, as he claims, that he has really loved. He argues, oddly, that his former lovers are anxious that she should capitulate, not because they wish her to be as frail as they themselves have been, but because they want to be happy in his happiness. But the woman is not won by his arguments. She had fallen in love with him before he began to woo, and she is overcome not by his words but by his tears which made her pity him and believe his "holy vows." She confesses at the end of the poem that he was so beautiful, and so good an actor, that his tears and blushes

> *Would yet again betray the fore-betrayed,*
> *And new pervert a reconciled maid.*

The underlying theme of the poem was a favorite one of Shakespeare's, the difficulty of distinguishing between appearance and reality. The heroine of the poem knows the seducer's evil reputation, but this knowledge does not save her. The theme is expressed, as in *Much Ado about Nothing*, by clothing imagery.[21] The seducer's chin was like "unshorn velvet"; his rudeness

> *Did livery falseness in a pride of truth;*   (105)

and, in the penultimate stanza,

> *Thus merely with the garment of a grace*
> *The naked and concealed fiend he cover'd,*
> *That th' unexperient gave the tempter place,*
> *Which, like a cherubin, above them hover'd.*

Here the seducer is compared to a fiend, as Satan, under the distorting influence of sexual desire, appeared to be a cherub. The effect of this double image, linked by the ambiguous *tempter*, is to associate the seducer and Satan, so that the woman in her fall becomes a second Eve.

The largest group of images, however, is taken from war, and these express the battle between the sexes. The aim of the villain-hero is to make the woman surrender without marriage; the conscious aim of the heroine is to preserve her chastity, and, unconsciously, to conquer the man by persuading him to marry her, his former conquests adding to the glory of her victory. Her straw hat— "a platted hive of straw"—"fortified her visage from the sun." Her eyes

> *their carriage ride*
> *As they did batt'ry to the spheres intend.*   (22)

She shielded her honor "with safest distance." Stories of the man's licentiousness were a protection to her:

> *Experience for me many bulwarks builded.*   (152)

She compares her honor to a besieged city:

> *And long upon these terms I held my city,*
> *Till thus he gan besiege me.*   (176)

The seducer compares the pearls and rubies given him by his victims to their grief and blushes:

> *Effects of terror and dear modesty,*
> *Encamp'd in hearts, but fighting outwardly.*   (202)

The woman who becomes a nun,

> *The scars of battle scapeth by the flight.* (244)

The man tells the heroine, in reference to his previous victims:

> *I strong o'er them, and you o'er me being strong,*
> *Must for your victory us all congest.* (257)

The man boasts that his parts assailed the nun's eyes, or else that her eyes, attracted by his beauty, assailed her heart. The man assures the heroine that "Love's arms are peace"; he tells her that his very victims urge her

> *To leave the batt'ry that you make 'gainst mine.* (277)

Finally, the heroine declares that

> *not a heart which in his level came*
> *Could scape the hail of his all-hurting aim.* (309)

There are indications, however, that the seducer is not entirely hypocritical, and that he, like the heroine, is in some sense a victim. His account of the nun's passion for him, though designed to weaken the heroine's resistance, expresses what seems to be a genuine wonder at the power of love, which overturns morality and religion:

> *Religious love put out Religion's eye . . .*
>
> *My parts had power to charm a sacred nun,*
> *Who disciplin'd, ay, dieted in grace,*
> *Believ'd her eyes, when they t'assail begun,*
> *All vows and consecrations giving place.*
> *O most potential love! vow, bond, nor space*
> *In thee hath neither sting, knot, nor confine,*
> *For thou art all, and all things else are thine.*
>
> *When thou impressest, what are precepts worth*
> *Of stale example? When thou wilt inflame*
> *How coldly those impediments stand forth,*
> *Of wealth, of filial fear, law, kindred, fame!*
> *Love's arms are peace, 'gainst rule, 'gainst sense, 'gainst*
>   *shame,*
> *And sweetens, in the suffering pangs it bears,*
> *The aloes of all forces, shocks and fears.* (250 ff.)

The last three lines of this stanza are an example of the kind of weakness which has made critics reluctant to admit Shakespeare's responsibility for the poem. It seems probable that it represents a first, or at least an early, draft. Shakespeare had abandoned the forceful clarity of *Venus and Adonis* and *Lucrece,* and he was striving, not always successfully, toward the complexity of his mature dramatic verse.

Yet the number of such confused passages is small, and they are far outweighed by the numerous brilliant lines and well composed stanzas:

> *. . . but spite of heaven's fell rage,*
> *Some beauty peep'd through lattice of sear'd age*   (13)

> *Laund'ring the silken figures in the brine,*
> *That season'd woe had pelleted in tears.*   (17)

> *But ah! who ever shun'd by precedent*
> *The destin'd ill she must her self assay,*
> *Or forc'd examples 'gainst her own content*
> *To put the by-past perils in her way?*   (155)

> *Oh, father, what a hell of witchcraft lies*
> *In the small orb of one particular tear!*   (288)

> *He preach'd pure maid, and prais'd cold chastity.*   (315)

It is difficult to agree with Mr. Rylands that the poem is a masterpiece, even though it has masterly things in it. But the comparative failures of a great poet are often of singular interest. In "A Lover's Complaint" Shakespeare was hampered at times by the stanza form—perhaps because he had abandoned rhyme for some years, except for particular dramatic purposes. He was hampered, too, we may suspect, by the genre of the complaint, in which we see everything through one character's eyes. Above all, his unrivaled linguistic daring was temporarily out of control, perhaps under the influence of bad models—Chapman, Marston, and Markham. A fear of tameness—and a number of lines are flat indeed—led him sometimes into the opposite vice of rhetorical inflation. The poem is inferior in most ways to Shakespeare's other narrative poems, and it is inferior to the best of the sonnets; but it is not without its own special flavor, and it adds something to the total impression we have of Shakespeare as a poet.

Shakespeare and the Trivium

By Hardin Craig

The trouble began with Ben Jonson's left-handed and possibly self-defensive compliment to Shakespeare in line 31 of "To the memory of my beloved, the AUTHOR MR. WILLIAM SHAKESPEARE: and what he hath left us," in the First Folio of 1623: "And though thou hadst small *Latine,* and lesse *Greeke.*" This has been taken, and still is, as a direct statement that Shakespeare knew little Latin and still less Greek. What Jonson meant, however, was that in spite of Shakespeare's deficiency in knowledge of the classical languages, he had surpassed the great authors of Greece and Rome. This is clear enough even if Jonson when he wrote suggested, as he may have done, that he himself was proficient in these tongues. In any case, his famous line gave rise to a lasting belief that Shakespeare was unschooled.

Jonson's disagreement with Shakespeare about neoclassicism is of course well known[1]—from *Timber,* Fuller's *Worthies* and elsewhere—but that is not the issue. Milton in *L'Allegro,* lines 131–34, suggests an idealistic "naturalistic" explanation of Shakespeare's greatness, which Dryden develops into mysticism. Milton says,

> Or sweetest Shakespeare, Fancy's child,
> Warble his native wood-notes wild.

Dryden says that Shakespeare was "naturally learned" and uses the word "magick" several times. Both Milton and Dryden apparently thought that

Shakespeare owed nothing to books. There are other variants, the most attractive of which is perhaps the open defense of Shakespeare reported most interestingly by Rowe in "Some Account of the Life of Mr. William Shakespeare" prefixed to his edition of Shakespeare.[2] Hales declared before a group of quite distinguished persons about 1633,

> That if Mr. *Shakespear* had not read the Antients, he had likewise not stollen any thing from 'em; . . . and that if he [Ben Jonson, who was present] would produce any one Topick finely treated by any of them, he would undertake to shew something upon the same Subject at least as well written by *Shakespear.*

H. Ramsay in *Jonsonus Virbius* (1639) plainly states that Shakespeare could "scarce understand" Latin. Leonard Digges, in verses prefixed to Shakespeare's poems in 1640, brings up the inevitable issue between nature and art and attributes to Shakespeare "Art without Art unparaleled as yet." Shakespeare, he says, got nothing from "Greekes nor Latines." And so on with others.[3]

The belief that Shakespeare was unschooled lived on vigorously until our time, possibly still lives. Scholars knew, however, that Shakespeare was a man of broad and extensive learning. Many books and articles were written that made this clear, one would think, to any person of intelligence. The popular belief was a great nuisance, and, as an error accepted as truth, it lent support to wrong theories and rendered difficult a concept of Shakespeare in line with nature and common sense. The whole matter needed a thorough clean-up, and this it received at the hands of Professor T. W. Baldwin in *William Shakspere's Small Latine & Lesse Greeke.*[4] It is a work of great and accurate learning and is, from the point of view of inductive reasoning, a masterly work that takes the form of determination of cause from effect. The context for abstraction on which the author bases his conclusion is simply overwhelming—hundreds of evidences that Shakespeare attended a standard grammar school of the reign of Queen Elizabeth. The criteria, explicable on that assumption and on that assumption only, are made up not only of the familiar Latin authors of the grammar school—Ovid, Virgil, Horace, Juvenal, Persius—but also of special editions and textbooks. Evidences of the special simpler texts of the lower school, the attention to Latin speaking, and also incidental features of the atmosphere and administration of grammar schools are in abundance.

To be sure, there have been preserved no records of attendance at the King's Free Grammar School at Stratford-upon-Avon for the period when William Shakespeare was of school age, but the signs in his works of his having attended such a school are completely satisfying to any person capable of reading and honest thinking. So convincing is Professor Baldwin's argument that Shakespeare attended an Elizabethan grammar school that I have been convinced negatively that he did not attend a university. The works of such writers as Sidney, Spenser, Hooker and others, who went to Oxford or Cambridge, afford indications that universities also made their marks on their students. This is a set of signs that Shakespeare seems to lack. The establishment of the fact that Shakespeare's learned culture was primarily that of the grammar school makes me wish to make a small contribution to our knowledge of Shakespeare's education; it will be interpretative rather than immediately factual.

What does it mean to have been educated in a grammar school? In view of the relation in our age between secondary schools and universities, it seems to mean little; but historically one may say that the roles are reversed, since the grammar school has had, and might in fundamental matters still have, more value to civilization than the university, since education in grammar schools, if carried far enough, might be said to be culturally adequate. Universities as regards learned culture in the broad and effective sense have been professional and social institutions. Only now and then have they been in a true sense educational institutions. This is true in general in our country and in our time, although learned culture has also deteriorated in secondary schools.

The historical picture of the grammar school is very different. Let us begin at the beginning. There are three great principles of education that were discovered, but not formulated, by Plato.[5] They may have been in some sense formulated in Aristotle's time, since he wrote treatises on poetics, rhetoric, ethics, and politics, and extensive works on logic. But we have no records of the use of these three principles as a school curriculum in ancient Greece, although grammar was certainly taught in typical form by the use of Homer.

In quite modern terms we may define the first of these three principles as the awakening of intelligence and understanding and of decision as to appropriate action. The first step is knowledge of words and their meanings, or what is now called symbolization. Following sense perception thus acquired, the next step is what is called by Whitehead concrescence. Locke called it reflection. This is now recognized as an automatic and unconscious process of cognition in the fourth dimension. It results in conduct or sense of truth. In plain language, this is reading, understanding, judging, and creative action. This is what the ancients called grammar. Nothing could be more developmental and more educative from childhood to old age. Grammar was the first of the "trivial" subjects.

The second was what might be called persuasion. That term will do as well as another to designate a duty that lies on every man and woman born into the world, especially on every mother and father, every minister of a gospel, every statesman, and every teacher of every kind. It includes all of us who are normal human beings. Our fate depends on the perpetuation of our institutions—our rights, our religion, and our race. Every virtue in the list has to be learned by every generation, practiced, and recommended, or we are lost. To make progress we have to do still more. This is what the ancients called rhetoric.

The third principle is that of order, truth, construction, system, self-control. It seems, so far as civilized life is concerned, to be an absolute essential. It appears also as law and is generally believed to permeate nature, indeed to be an expressive aspect of nature. Most of us believe that ignorance of natural law or its violation has been the chief obstacle to cultural growth and is so still. The doctrine of evolution has helped us to think that it is really not necessary for us to make messes of our individual lives, our society, and our government. This third Platonic principle was called logic, but was a far broader subject than what the word now means or suggests.

At some time after the Peripatetic period, probably in the Hellenistic period at Antioch, Athens, or Alexandria, these three subjects—grammar, rhetoric, and logic—appeared as the curriculum of a school. To limit them to childhood was perhaps the worst mistake ever made in the field of education, a field simply littered with errors and blunders, although it may be that in the two thousand years that ensued, this relegation to childhood and youth may have saved the great subjects of the trivium from obliteration. The agent of transmission of the trivium from the ancient world to the Middle Ages was *De Nuptiis Philologiae et Mercurii* by Martianus Capella, a Roman born in Carthage in the fifth or fourth century A.D.—the extent of our information. *De Nuptiis* is a long allegorical work in verse and prose dull enough to suit early medieval taste. It includes not only the trivium but the quadrivium, thus completing the Seven Liberal Arts by the addition of four subjects regarded as mathematical—arithmetic, geometry, astronomy, and music. When the quadrivium was invented is not known. It was thought that Capella followed Marcus Terentius Varro, who lived from about 116 to 27 B.C. This might have been immediately true, but Varro was an encyclopedist, the reputed author of 620 books; and whatever he wrote was *ipso facto* not his own. There is a better idea that would account in some measure for the survival of the Seven Liberal Arts.

Everything considered, it seems probable that the Seven Liberal Arts were established as the curriculum of the grammar school in its final and enduring form in Rome, a curriculum which was there given an organization of such vitality that it lasted for about two thousand years; indeed, it did not lose its entity until the twentieth century in our own country.[6] There is no doubt that the Latin grammar school covered the needs of its pupils in practical fashion. There was, for example, provision for moral instruction that seems to have lived on. The situation between Greek and Latin was perfect for bringing out the educational advantages of what was called grammar, and that may be the reason the schools were called grammar schools. Greek discharged for Latin during the third, second, and first centuries B.C. exactly the same function that Latin discharged for vernacular languages in the Middle Ages, the Renaissance, and the modern world until about 1900 A.D. That is, the Roman boy was faced with Greek to be translated into Latin, construed into meaning in that tongue. With this discipline came knowledge of and interest in simple Greek classics, which the student became able to explain. Consequently, he formed opinions, and later was impelled to create something of his own. There was a way of achieving this creation, a process called mimesis, which it may be safely said few modern scholars understand. This was the cultural process in classical humanistic study, has been so in the two thousand years that have intervened, and will continue to be, as far as we know, forever.

The trivium formed, generally speaking, the curriculum of the grammar school, but it suffered some deterioration, especially rhetoric, which sometimes became merely figures of speech. Logic often became merely dialectic or disputation. But grammar, so natural was it, held its own pretty well. In the twelfth century trivial subjects were to some extent restored, and fortunately also in the Renaissance. This brings us to the education of Shakespeare.

We are again under obligation to T. W. Baldwin for an account of an almost miraculous revivification of the grammar school curriculum in England (I, 75–84). It came about in Colet's founding of St. Paul's School with the advice of the great Erasmus, possibly the only man alive who knew enough and understood enough to make such a restoration possible. Eton and Winchester were not too badly out of line, but even they were affected, shall we say, by the new humanism. English grammar schools attained, as Baldwin shows, a definitive form under Edward VI; and under Queen Elizabeth there was a still further extension of the old curriculum. The movement toward uniformity in cathedral schools, well advanced before the end of King Henry VIII's reign, was carried to a definitive stage under Edward VI. In this connection Baldwin's study of the education of Prince Edward and of Princess Elizabeth (I, 185–284) is most illuminating.

One is struck not only with the detailed and rigorous method of the grammar school but with the overwhelming quantity. The texts used in the Lower School were Lily's Latin grammar, *Sententiae Pueriles*, and the *Disticha* of Dionysius Cato, these followed by Aesop and, strangely enough, by Terence, Mantuan, and Palingenius. There is no evidence of abbreviated selections such as seem to have been used in classics read in contemporary university classes, and the only conjecture that seems plausible is that the Latin language was so well learned that these works were as accessible as English. Nevertheless, the burden seems to be very great if sixteenth-century boys were like modern boys. This matter of the ground covered in Elizabethan grammar schools is still more surprising in the Upper Grammar school—Ovid, Virgil, Horace, Juvenal, Persius, and a possible array of other Latin poets, such as Lucan, Silius Italicus, Martial, Catullus, and Seneca; meantime, also Greek, rhetoric, ethics. One has the uneasy feeling that there is a quantitative aspect to a renascence, so that it may be that, if we are ever to have one, our students in schools and colleges will have to work five or ten times harder than they do now.

To get a concept of Shakespeare's education we shall have to go still further. Rhetoric seems to have been well studied. Baldwin (II, 1–238) makes a point of the reading of the pseudo-Ciceronian *Ad Herennium* and of the rhetoric of Susenbrotus, as also of the *Copia* of Erasmus and of Quintilian, without whom there could have been no complete comprehension of the true function of rhetoric. Baldwin also stresses the use of Cicero's *Topica*, which served as a sort of bridge between logic and rhetoric. As to logic itself, it was certainly present in the grammar school course, but it may have been set aside usually as a university study.[7]

The trivium, as we have seen, was presented as three subjects of study, three aspects of one process of mental action. There might have been more or fewer subjects. The nature of these has been explained but not the fact that grammar, rhetoric, and logic are not coordinate. Grammar is propaedeutic and fundamental, so that it happens that the metaphysics of rhetoric and logic as well as other subjects that concern the whole environment are those of grammar. Since, however, grammar from the beginning was a procedure through and by means of literature, it may be thought of as the great humanistic field, this for many reasons easily understood. The point is, Locke saw that thought operates on sense perception plus what happens in the mind over and above sensation and perception. This Locke called reflection.[8] He proceeds at great length in his determination of the nature of this higher process, but we shall find it clearer to resort to A. N. Whitehead, who posits a simpler explanation in what he calls concrescence. Perhaps the following brief statement will serve:

> Thus to arrive at the philosophic generalization which is the notion of a final actuality conceived in the guise of a generalization of an act of experience, an apparent redundancy of terms is required. The words correct each other. We require 'together,' 'creativity,' 'concrescence,' 'prehension,' 'feeling,' 'subjective form,' 'data,' 'actuality,' 'becoming,' 'process.'[9]

In this brief and very general list Whitehead is providing for a vast and varied composition of this activity of the higher brain, so that not all elements mentioned here may be necessary in each "concrescence" or in the conclusion of the process. He would say that "concrescence" is an operation of the whole mind, with no so-called faculties required. In grammatical exercise this would usually be a simple appreciation of truth, beauty, or goodness unaffected by any motive of self-interest or partisanship. If the complex of concrescence, for example, is affected by purpose, a prehension in the form of feeling, the mental act may be in the area of "rhetoric"; if by data, subjective form, or, let us say, a prehension of social or personal uneasiness, the mental activity will be in the field of logic, and so on. Subjects vary greatly, but there is only one process, which in typical form is grammar.

It happens that in the first field, that great area originally called grammar, the subject itself begins with the indispensable step called symbolization—there being no book learning without words and the alphabet—goes on with the features of sense perception and concrescence from the simplest primer to the most advanced level of learning. As it proceeds grammar reveals the environment and becomes inevitably acquainted with the problems of living. The ideal of grammar was and is thus the particular basis of all education and the builder of what we may call humanism. It thus functions in a double way: as the principia of all thinking and the special road to human culture, the most important of all subjects, since it is the introduction to all learned culture. It provides both growth of mind and the gateway to all learning. Grammar was and might be still an education in itself, and this is at least true, that it is still in control of literacy.

Shakespeare evidently had the brightest of minds and his acquisitions, mainly in literature, were nothing short of miraculous. There are about 1750 echoes or reflections in Shakespeare's plays, largely from Latin literature, of his studies in grammar school. These are neither ornaments nor thefts, but are, for the most part, organically used in the expression of his own dramatic or literary purposes. They are not what he got from the grammar school; they are what the grammar school taught or inspired him to do on his own, and are thus a perfect example of the educative process as it used to be and might be still, a skillful artistic triumph of mind and of persuasion and order.

Some simple illustrations will make these matters clear. They could be drawn from any play of Shakespeare or from poems or sonnets, a fact that makes one satisfied with the canon of his works. We shall choose them from *King John*. One general remark is, however, called for. Shakespeare was a master of the concrete and could make it tell its story without summation or explanation, so that his concrescences often remain unexplained—not always. A perfect case in point is the Queen's description of the death of Ophelia in *Hamlet* (IV.vii.167–84). The late Professor Una Ellis-Fermor saw in this passage an interesting feature of Shakespeare's art, namely, an evocative pressure on reader or hearer that increased interest and enjoyment by inducing participation.[10] We select as such an example of unexplained concrescence Prince Arthur's plea to Hubert from *King John* (IV.i.40–70).

King John has captured his nephew Arthur, true heir to the English throne, has put him in prison, and intends to blind him and put him to death. King John has overborne the scruples of the essentially merciful and honest Hubert —this by means of a power of seduction not unintelligible to us, but of an intensity that is hard for us to understand. To imagine the lifelong poverty and obscurity of the ordinary medieval man will help us to do so.

Hubert, to be followed by executioners, enters the prison where the little boy spends his lonely hours. Arthur is glad to see him. "Good morrow, Hubert," he says. He looks at Hubert and sees with his sharp child's eyes that Hubert is pale. Hubert is the only world he has, so that Arthur is affectionate and grateful to the soldier. Hubert hands him the cruel order, and he reads it. "Must you with hot irons burn out both mine eyes?"—and you will note that like a child he thinks it would be well if he might have one eye left. Then with the direct perspicacity of childhood he goes to the heart of the matter, "And will you?" he says, and Hubert replies, "And I will." Then follows this marvelous concrescence from the brain of a child:

> *Have you the heart? When your head did but ache,*
> *I knit my handkercher about your brows,*
> *The best I had, a princess wrought it me,*
> *And I did never ask it you again:*
> *And with my hand at midnight held your head,*

And like the watchful minutes to the hour,
Still and anon cheer'd up the heavy time,
Saying, "What lack you?" and "Where lies your grief?"
Or "What good love may I perform for you?"
Many a poor man's son would have lien still
And ne'er have spoke a loving word to you;
But you at your sick service had a prince.
Nay, you may think my love was crafty love
And call it cunning. Do an if you will;
If heaven be pleased that you must use me ill,
Why then you must. Will you put out mine eyes,
These eyes that never did nor never shall
So much as frown on you.

The doctrine of plenitude ignored the imperfections of childhood. Arthur speaks in a language much too mature for his age. As a little prince, he had heard talk about the exalted station of royalty. This he repeats, but the very nature of childhood shines through. Arthur remembers the handkerchief, which he says a princess had wrought for him, and like a child he remembers that he never got it back and never asked for its return. Arthur remembers his own "sick service" to Hubert and points out that most little boys would have slept soundly through the whole episode. One does not know why these little people are such bargainers, but they seem to be. Arthur says his was not "crafty love" nor "cunning," but this is an area of adult life. He cannot prove his point and makes the quick surrender of helpless childhood. In the words, "Will you put out mine eyes?" one hears the scream of the young in the presence of danger and fear. Hubert breaks down, as who would not? and Arthur sees salvation in Hubert's countenance.

O, now you look like Hubert! all this while
You were disguised.

As one moves from passages simply and magnificently revelatory of the human such as this—the sorrows of Constance for example—into the social, the tendency for which *King John* is noted, one finds no change in mental process or its relation to the concrete, but one does find purpose, persuasion, compulsion. One finds oneself in the region of rhetoric as anciently conceived. Consider, for an example, the following speech by Cardinal Pandulph to King Philip of France (III.i.253–61):

All form is formless, order orderless,
Save what is opposite to England's love.
Therefore to arms! be champion of our Church,
Or let the Church, our mother, breathe her curse,
A mother's curse, on her revolting son.
France, thou mayst hold a serpent by the tongue,
A chafed lion by the mortal paw,
A fasting tiger safer by the tooth,
Than keep in peace that hand which thou dost hold.

Finally, there is one other aspect of the mental process illustrated in *King John* that may be worth thinking over. It is Philip the Bastard's famous speech at the end of the play:

O, let us pay the time but needful woe,
Since it hath been beforehand with our griefs.
This England never did, nor never shall,
Lie at the proud foot of a conqueror,
But when it first did help to wound itself.
Now these her princes are come home again,
Come the three corners of the world in arms,
And we shall shock them. Nought shall make us rue,
If England to itself do rest but true.

This is a generalization of the broadest type, on all that has happened in the play and also of all that English experience of sedition had to say. It expresses a universal belief in Shakespeare's England. There has been a disposition to regard such universals as the product of supernatural intrusion. The passage seems to me, however, to bear the marks of normal concrescence and to be an evidence that the human mind is capable of exalted ratiocination whether it thinks so or not.

The Great Rival: Shakespeare and the Classical Dramatists

By T. J. B. Spencer

It is not easy nowadays for us to understand the feelings of humility with which the writers of the sixteenth century viewed the literature of Antiquity. There was so little in their own languages which approached the qualities of the great Classics—the sophistication, clarity, confidence, and polish, which all could feel and applaud in Cicero, Terence, Virgil, Pliny, Seneca, Ovid, and a dozen others. How easy it was to have a simple standard of criticism!—what the Ancients did was right; any other method was wrong; if you followed closely the practices of the Greek and Latin writers, you might be able to produce good literature; if you did not, you would certainly produce bad literature. The use of the vernacular had to be *vindicated*. Du Bellay writes his *Deffence* of the French tongue. Daniel exclaims defiantly: "All our understandings are not to be built by the square of *Greece* and *Italie*. We are the children of nature as well as they."

The comparison between Shakespeare and the classical dramatists began early; quite early in Shakespeare's lifetime. He was 34 when, in 1598, there was published that curious book *Palladis Tamia, or Wit's Treasury* by Francis Meres.

> As *Plautus* and *Seneca* are accounted the best for Comedy and Tragedy among the Latines; so *Shakespeare* among the English is the most excellent in both kinds for the stage.[1]

It was a magnificent compliment to a young writer; and at that time most of Shakespeare's best plays were not yet written. Meres mentioned (for comedy) *The Two Gentlemen of Verona, The Comedy of Errors, Love's Labour's Lost, A Midsummer-Night's Dream, The Merchant of Venice;* and (for tragedy) *Richard II, Richard III, Henry IV, King John, Titus Andronicus,* and *Romeo and Juliet.* He included the historical plays of Shakespeare among his tragedies —a natural thing for a classically educated person to do, who, even if he did not remember the *Persae,* knew the *Octavia,* one of the tragedies attributed to Seneca.

In the panegyrical poem that Ben Jonson wrote after Shakespeare's death, printed among the prefatory poems before the Folio of 1623, he proudly emphasized the rivalry. Jonson says that, though Shakespeare had "small Latin and less Greek," he would make comparison between him and not only his English contemporaries, but the ancient tragedians and comedians, too:

> *. . . call forth thund'ring Æschilus,*
> *Euripides, and Sophocles to us,*
> Pacuvius, Accius, *him of* Cordova *dead,*
> *To life againe, to heare thy Buskin tread,*
> *And shake a Stage: Or, when thy Sockes were on,*
> *Leave thee alone, for the comparison*
> *Of all, that insolent* Greece, *or haughtie* Rome
> *Sent forth, or since did from their ashes come.*
> *Triumph, my* Britaine, *thou hast one to showe,*
> *To whom all Scenes of* Europe *homage owe.*

These are strong words; all the stronger, because Ben Jonson constantly expressed, elsewhere, his prejudice in favor of Greek and Roman literature as the standard of excellence.

We may, of course, question the sincerity and common sense of Jonson's comparisons in these lines. We can stand for the comparison with Seneca, certainly. But it is hard to include the Greek tragedians, too little known at that time and hardly available enough to make the comparison intelligent. And as for Accius and Pacuvius, there could be few criticisms more pointless than to ask anybody to call forth their meager fragments, those ghostly writers, mere names in biographical dictionaries. Perhaps it was only Ben Jonson's fun.

Although the challenge had been thus thrown down by Ben Jonson—one who is notorious for taking a rather rigid classicizing view of literature—yet it was difficult for criticism to take it up: to assess the merits of Shakespeare in comparison with the ancient dramatists—let alone to explore the merits of ancient dramatists in comparison with Shakespeare. The Latin drama, which was inevitably the basis for literary judgment, was not merely a classical drama, a dead drama (as it is, practically speaking, nowadays). The plays of Plautus and Terence were performed in academic surroundings and were an influence upon neo-Latin plays throughout Europe. Shakespeare's rivalry was with a living rival, not a long-dead one.

Yet the Shakespearean drama was obviously so different; and, as literary self-consciousness increased in the seventeenth and eighteenth centuries, there seemed to be many indications that Shakespeare was lacking in that artistic responsibility so manifest in the admired Greeks and Romans. The practice of the English theater was closely connected with the necessity of entertaining ordinary people. "Those who live to please must please to live." From this starting point, the English drama had taken its prevailing tone, unlike the drama in France, where patronage was heavy enough to accustom audiences to a kind of play contrived fairly closely on the pattern of the better-known plays of the Greek and Latin dramatists. In England, however, the play and the "dramatic poem" have always been sharply defined. The prevailing attitude of the playwrights, working for a playhouse which must remain solvent, has not been one of reverence for the classical dramatists. The question for them was, regardless of the *form*: Are they useful? What can be borrowed from them? Nowadays it may be possible to discern, or convincingly argue for the existence of, Senecan and Terentian influences upon Elizabethan plays and even upon Shakespeare. To an experienced critic of the seventeenth or eighteenth century it was obvious that the *form* of Shakespeare's plays, both comedy and tragedy, was different from that of the Greeks and Romans; and we need not be surprised to find that comparisons were difficult to make, or that classic status was difficult to award. Some of the best critics seem at their worst when trying to make a comparative estimate of Shakespeare and the Ancients.

By the time of Dr. Johnson, certainly, Shakespeare had already achieved something of the position of a Classic. In his preface to his edition in 1765 Johnson wrote:

The Poet, of whose works I have undertaken the revision, may now begin to assume the dignity of an ancient, and claim the privilege of established fame and prescriptive veneration.

But it must be admitted that Shakespeare was still only gradually and painfully establishing himself as a classic. Many and vigorous were the rejections of his classic status by seventeenth- and eighteenth-century men of letters. Milton's allusions had not been encouraging; not merely the familiar lines in *L'Allegro*, but also his praise of Shakespeare in the second Folio:

> ... *to th' shame of slow-endeavouring art*
> *Thy easie numbers flow.*

And on April 1, 1748, the Earl of Chesterfield wrote a letter to his natural son on the advantages of education and on the benefits of keeping the best company; he illustrated his remarks by pointing out that

> if Shakespeare's genius had been cultivated, those beauties, which we so justly admire in him, would have been undisguised by those extravagances and that nonsense with which they are frequently accompanied.[2]

The *extravagances* and *nonsense* to which Lord Chesterfield referred were instances of Shakespeare's supposed artistic irresponsibility, which militated against his being accepted as a classic and qualifying for comparison with the Ancients.

Even before Shakespeare began to write, his kind of play had been condemned, by anticipation, as artistically unacceptable. In *The Defence of Poesie* Sir Philip Sidney had little but contempt for the plays shown at that time. What he was condemning, in satirical terms, was the *form* of drama which we recognize as essentially Shakespeare's.

> Our Tragedies and Comedies [are] not without cause cried out against, observing rules neyther of honest civilitie nor of skilfull Poetrie . . . where you shal have *Asia* of the one side, and *Affrick* of the other, and so many other under-kingdoms, that the Player, when he commeth in, must ever begin with telling where he is, or els, the tale wil not be conceived. Now ye shal have three Ladies walke to gather flowers, and then we must beleeve the stage to be a Garden. By and by, we heare newes of shipwracke in the same place, and then wee are to blame if we accept it not for a Rock. . . . While in the meantime two Armies flye in, represented with foure swords and bucklers, and then what harde heart will not receive it for a pitched fielde? Now, of time they are much more liberall, for ordinary it is that two young Princes fall in love. After many traverces, she is got with childe, delivered of a faire boy; he is lost, groweth a man, falls in love, and is ready to get another child; and all this in two hours space: Which how absurd it is in sence even sence may imagine, and Arte hath taught, and all auncient examples justified.

But worse than the disregard of common sense in the representation of space and time was the artistic irresponsibility of Shakespeare shown by his lack of decorum, proved particularly by his marring tragic feeling with comic intrusions. This has been a most stubborn argument against Shakespeare's merits, far more stubborn than his neglect of the Unities.

> All theyr Playes be neither right Tragedies, nor right Comedies; mingling Kings and Clownes, not because the matter so carrieth it, but [they] thrust in Clownes by head and shoulders, to play a part in majesticall matters, with neither decencie nor discretion: So as neither the admiration and commiseration, nor the right sportfulnes, is by their mungrell Tragy-comedie obtained. . . . So falleth it out that, having indeed no right Comedy, in that comicall part of our Tragedy we have nothing but scurrility, unwoorthy of any chast eares, or some extreame shewe of doltishnes, indeed fit to lift up a loude laughter, and nothing els: where the whole tract of a Comedy shoulde be full of delight, as the Tragedy shoulde be still maintained in a well raised admiration.

In the same spirit and on precisely the same principles, Milton, in his preface to *Samson Agonistes* concerning the nature of Tragedy, drew attention to "the Poets error of intermixing Comic stuff with Tragic sadness and gravity; or introducing trivial and vulgar persons, which by all judicious hath bin counted absurd; and brought in without discretion, corruptly to gratifie the people."

What Shakespeare thought about all this, we cannot decide with certainty; we can only infer his opinions from his practice and from his incidental comments on literary art in his plays. From his practice, we conclude that he thought he possessed an art superior to the uniformity of tone desiderated by the classicizing critics. His dramatic form certainly became more free, more of a hybrid of tragedy and comedy, in his later years. *The Winter's Tale* not only has a gap of sixteen years between Acts III and IV. It is very near to tragedy in the first half of the play. There are some perilous clashings of tone and abrupt transitions. After the deaths of the young Mamillius and (as the audience must suppose) of the queen Hermione, and after the good Antigonus has been eaten by a bear, Autolycus enters, one of Shakespeare's glorious comic creations.

Shakespeare, then, apparently regarded the objections to the mongrel tragicomedy as pointless. The opinions he puts into the mouth of Polonius on several occasions seem to give an unfavorable view of conventional literary critics. It is difficult not to interpret Polonius' description of the dramatic entertainments which the players will provide as a joke against the Renaissance critical doctrine that the "forms" should be kept pure and that tragicomedy was illegitimate. The players who visit Elsinore are "the best . . . in the world, either for tragedy, comedy, history, pastoral, pastoral-comical, historical-pastoral, tragical-historical, tragical-comical-historical-pastoral, scene individable, or poem unlimited. Seneca cannot be too heavy, nor Plautus too light."

But, in spite of Polonius, for a long time Europe was to respect the genres and believe that the dramatists (especially the tragedians) who produced well-contrived plays surpassed the ignorant and artless Shakespeare. The "Art" that Shakespeare "wanted" was that of arranging dramatic material to obtain what Corneille called *les liaisons des scènes*—skillful connections between the different parts of the play, avoiding anything superfluous, and thereby achieving a concentration of effect. Shakespeare was a great and wonderful genius who (owing to his own ignorance and the barbarousness of his times) failed to manifest in his productions the technical control which a cultivated and enlightened reader demanded; and one of the great stumbling blocks in the acceptance of Shakespeare as a serious artist had, from his own time onward, been his introduction of comic scenes into his profoundest tragedies. It was not merely an offense against the "rules"; it was simply inhuman. When our feelings are excited, when our souls are sympathetically fulfilled with pity and terror and suspense, just at that moment the dramatist chooses to bring on to the stage a half-witted or scurrilous clown, who breaks jests, feeble, indecent, irrelevant, in order to raise a laugh from the lowest rabble in the audience. Extraneous comedy destroys illusion; it mars the unity of impression; it is absurd, offensive, gross, and contemptible.

On the stage, of course, such vile intrusions could be omitted; but the *reader* of Shakespeare's plays was confronted with the *niaiseries* of the grave-digger in *Hamlet*, the filthy porter in *Macbeth*, the intolerable fool in *King Lear*, the gross nurse in *Romeo and Juliet*; and the obtrusive imbecilities of the clowns in *Othello* (III. i and iv) and *Antony and Cleopatra* (V.ii). It was possible to exonerate Shakespeare partially (as did Pope and others) by declining to accept his responsibility and by supposing that some of this comic nonsense had been foisted into his writings by the players. But it was not possible to offer that excuse in, for example, *Hamlet*, *King Lear*, or *Romeo and Juliet*; and elsewhere comic incidents or turns of speech were incorporated too tightly into the context for them to be regarded as interpolatioňs. Excuses and parallels and condonements were inadequate. It carried no conviction to declare that Shakespeare did not know any better because his genius lacked cultivation. Even as a natural genius—indeed, especially as a natural genius—he ought to have known better; and many sensitive readers even in the later eighteenth century, who fully accepted Shakespeare's greatness in other respects, deplored the unsympathetic soul which he revealed by this inattention to his readers' feelings. "When I first, at a very early age," wrote Schiller in 1795, "became acquainted with Shakespeare, I felt indignant at his coldness, his hardness of heart, which permitted him in the most melting pathos to utter jests—to mar, by the introduction of a fool, the soul-searching scenes of *Hamlet, King Lear, Macbeth*, and other pieces; which now kept him still where my sensibilities hastened forward, now drove him carelessly onwards where I would so gladly have lingered. . . . He was the object of my reverence and zealous study for years before I could love himself."[3]

Something could be done, perhaps, in considering this problem by pointing out that there were hints of this kind of comic intrusion even in Greek tragedy: comic incidents, or even episodes. The vulgarity and lack of decorum attributed to Shakespeare had parallels even in Aeschylus, the most solemn of the Greeks. The nurse in *Romeo and Juliet*, whose coarseness was the subject of much disapproval, would have found a gossip in the nurse in the *Oresteia* who is so indiscreet in her confidences about the nursery life and bowel-actions of the infant Orestes.[4] Since Aeschylus could make a slip like that in cultivated Athens, Shakespeare might be more easily able to err in the uneducated London of his time, when (on the authority of Dr. Johnson) the English nation was yet struggling to emerge from barbarity.

Euripides, too, was obnoxious to censure in this matter. Recall the silly conduct of the chorus in the *Hippolytus* when poor Phaedra is hanging herself (ll. 776 ff.). A voice comes from within: "Anyone who is in the house, come and help; the Queen is hanging! . . ." And the Chorus comments, "Oh, oh! she has kept her word—the Queen hung high in a strangling rope!" And then the insistent voice within: "Come quickly. Bring a knife to cut this cord from her neck!" And the Chorus divides and debates:

> "Friends, what shall we do? Ought we to go inside and untie
> the noose and free her?"
> "Why, where are the young women who attend her? It is never
> safe to interfere."

The disgraceful behavior, too, of Heracles in the *Alcestis* (ll. 747 ff.)—getting drunk, and carrying on a conversation with a servant, including four lines in rhyme, to increase the tipsy effect—it was more like something in a Plautine comedy or in Shakespeare than in a Greek tragedy, and this, too, was derogatory to the reputation of Euripides.

But soon the tide of criticism began to turn. The "practice of blending comedy with tragedy," wrote Shelley in *A Defence of Poetry*, "though liable to great abuse in point of practice, is undoubtedly an extension of the dramatic circle" beyond what the Greeks had achieved; "but the comedy should be as in *King Lear*, universal, ideal, and sublime. It is perhaps the intervention of this principle which determines the balance in favour of *King Lear* against the *Oedipus Tyrannus* or the *Agamemnon*." Thus Shelley could express the opinion that it was the very appearance of a comic element in Shakespearean tragedy which gave it a superiority to Greek tragedy. The comic scenes (all the critics now begin to declare) do *not* interrupt the tragic feeling. On the contrary, they greatly enhance it. They deepen its degree, though they diminish its duration. The impression given of the agony of the tragic characters is far stronger than it would otherwise have been, and our sympathies are more forcibly awakened. Had the comic contrast been lacking in Shakespeare's tragedies, explained (for example) the young John Ruskin, only an impression of pain would have been transferred to us.[5] Mere selfish feeling, instead of our sympathy, would have been awakened. It is interesting to see this new view of Shakespeare's artistry not only becoming commonplace but also beginning to affect academic criticism of the Greek dramatists. John Keble was Professor of Poetry in Oxford from 1832 to 1841 and published his *Praelectiones* in 1844. He there accepts Shakespeare's introduction of comic characters into tragic situations and by analogy approves of similar episodes in Greek tragedies, giving as examples the Watchman at the beginning of the *Agamemnon* and the Nurse in the *Choephoroi*. He then surprisingly goes on to adjudge Sophocles inferior to Aeschylus because he was overfastidious in these matters.[6] Into the mouth of Aristophanes Browning puts an opinion of the limitations of Greek tragedy in general:

> *Euripides hangs fixed,*
> *Gets knowledge through the single aperture*
> *Of High and Right.*

But Aristophanes claims that he himself is the "best friend of man" because he reports the whole truth, and can "face Low and Wrong and Weak and all the rest." And he then gives his prophecy of the coming of a poet in future ages, perhaps in a remote corner of the known world, who will be

> stationed (by mechanics past my guess)
> So as to take in every side at once,
> And not successively,—may reconcile
> The High and Low in tragi-comic verse,—
> He shall be hailed superior to us both
> When born—in the Tin-islands![7]

There were other, equally serious, matters. Shakespeare's style, it had to be admitted, on many occasions compared unfavorably with the easy, unforced strain of simplicity and naturalness which ran through the compositions of the great Greek writers. Dryden said that his "whole style is so pestered with figurative expressions, that it is as affected as it is obscure";[8] and Dr. Johnson maintained that Shakespeare never had six lines together without a fault.[9] Shakespeare had, of course, immense powers of "invention" (as it was called in the early eighteenth century) or "imagination" (as it came to be called in the later eighteenth century). But his style was inadequate to his imaginative powers; and David Hume[10] coolly quoted, apropos of Shakespeare, the observation of the younger Pliny that even barbarians have powers of invention, but a person of taste and culture is required for adequate expression (*invenire etiam barbari solent, disponere et ornare non nisi eruditus*).[11]

But redundancy and some extravagance of diction are small faults of style compared with the crushing evidence of Shakespeare's literary irresponsibility: he was a punster. He put "quibbles" or "clenches" into the mouths of his characters, not merely clowns and fools, but serious and dignified characters as well; not merely in comedy, but also in tragedy. He cannot for long be pathetic (and Dr. Johnson in the famous passage in the preface to his edition was brilliantly expressing what oft was thought) without marring the effect by some "contemptible equivocation" of words; and often "terror and pity, as they are rising in the mind, are checked and blasted" by the intrusion of an inane pun. A verbal quibble, Johnson continued, had "some malignant power" over Shakespeare's mind, and he felt its fascination to be irresistible.

> Whatever be the dignity or profundity of his disquisition, whether he be enlarging knowledge or exalting affection, whether he be amusing attention with incidents, or enchaining it in suspense, let but a quibble spring up before him, and he leaves his work unfinished. A quibble is the golden apple for which he will always turn aside from his career, or stoop from his elevation. A quibble, poor and barren as it is, gave him such delight, that he was content to purchase it, by the sacrifice of reason, propriety, and truth. A

quibble was to him the fatal Cleopatra for which he lost the world, and was
content to lose it.

The pun had, in fact, for long been regarded with contempt; and as a literary
device it was intolerable. Pope in *The Dunciad* ironically quoted "a great critic"
(probably his old enemy John Dennis) as declaring that "he that would pun,
would pick a pocket."

Even among the Greeks, of course, the characteristic elegance of thought and
expression was, it soon came to be remembered, occasionally marred by a frivolous verbal quibble. For example, the name of Polyneices, one of Oedipus'
sons, means "much wrangling." In the altercations between the brothers, this
pun was employed by Aeschylus, Sophocles, and Euripides. "It is remarkable,"
observed Hume, "that so poor a conundrum could not be rejected by any of
these three poets, so justly celebrated for their taste and simplicity. What could
Shakespeare have done worse?"[12] Did not Sophocles, moreover, make Ajax in
his despair quibble upon his own name quite in the Shakespearean fashion?
The Greek exclamation of woe *aiai* corresponds closely to the name *Aias*, the
Greek form of Ajax. "Who would have thought," the hero cries, "how well my
name would fit my misery?"[13] This would bear comparison with Shakespeare's
exhibiting John of Gaunt as punning on his own name when King Richard addresses him as "Aged Gaunt":

> *O, how that name befits my composition!*
> *Old Gaunt indeed, and gaunt in being old ...*
> *Gaunt am I for the grave, gaunt as a grave.*

Whereupon the King, not unnaturally, exclaims:

> *Can sick men play so nicely with their names?*[14]

Furthermore, it was known that Aristotle, Cicero, and other rhetorical theo-
rists had treated puns seriously, dividing them into classes and recommending
their appropriate use by orators.[15] Still, for a long time, an occasional quibble
in Greek tragedy was not felt—any more than the examples of Christ, Moses,
Homer, Cato, Cicero, and Petrarch—to be an excuse for Shakespeare's odious
plenitude of puns. Coleridge thought that Shakespeare's use of puns would
stand up to philosophical analysis, and he defended some of them; the worst
he rejected or turned a blind ear to them. But throughout the nineteenth century the rejection of Shakespeare's puns (in tragic or serious contexts) was the
last stronghold of sanity, the last bulwark against bardolatry, the remaining

principle of classical grace and restraint. Only gradually has Shakespeare's wordplay been elevated to a serious artistic technique; and only slowly has the principle in the textual criticism been established that a reading which somehow incorporates a pun (however abhorrent) is likely to be a superior reading —trivial puns are (in James Joyce's phrase) all the better for being quadrivial.

One of the curious, and curiously persisting, ideas about Shakespeare in comparison with the Ancients, was his inferiority in the representation of women characters. This is difficult to understand nowadays, for it seems to contradict theatrical experience. The female characters in Shakespeare's plays had, ever since a woman appeared as Desdemona with Killigrew's company in 1660, provided scope in the theater for subtle and admired interpretations. Mrs. Betterton, Mrs. Barry, Mrs. Bracegirdle, Mrs. Clive, Mrs. Anna Maria Cibber, Mrs. Nancy Oldfield, Mrs. Pritchard, Mrs. Peg Woffington, culminating in the glorious Mrs. Siddons and Mrs. Jordan, had delighted the playhouses with a wide range of Shakespeare's women—although, to be sure, the parts were often fattened in the acting versions of the plays. It was well known, of course, in the eighteenth century that on Shakespeare's stage the women's parts were taken by boys, and this fact was sometimes brought forward to account for the comparative inferiority (as it was supposed) of Shakespeare's women-characters.

> What Grace or Master-strokes of Action [asked Colley Cibber in 1740] can we conceive such ungainly Hoydens to have been capable of? This Defect was so well considered by *Shakespeare,* that in few of his Plays he has any greater Dependance upon the Ladies, than in the Innocence and Simplicity of a *Desdemona,* an *Ophelia,* or in the short Specimen of a fond and virtuous *Portia.*[16]

The literary critics were sometimes much more censorious or imperceptive. In the later years of the seventeenth century Thomas Rymer published his tract, *The Tragedies of the Last Age Consider'd and Examin'd by the Practice of the Ancients, and by the Common Sense of All Ages,* a severe attack on the Elizabethan drama; and he followed it with his notorious *A Short View of Tragedy; its original, excellency, and corruption. With some reflections on Shakespear, and other practitioners for the stage* (1693). He gave a detailed discussion and analysis of Phaedra in Euripides' *Hippolytus*—quite a remarkable piece of character-study for that date. Shakespeare's females, by contrast, he treats with great severity. Of Brutus' Portia, for example, in *Julius Caesar:*

Portia, in good manners, might have challeng'd more respect: she that shines, a glory of the first magnitude in the Gallery of Heroick Dames, is with our Poet, scarce one remove from a Natural: She is the own Cousin German, of one piece, the very same impertinent silly flesh and blood with *Desdemona.*

And as for Desdemona herself, there is nothing in her "that is not below any Countrey Chamber-maid with us."

> *O good Iago,*
> *What shall I do to win my lord again?*

"No Woman bred out of a Pig-stye cou'd talk so meanly," was Rymer's comment. And he continues:

The Italian Painters are noted for drawing the *Madonna's* by their own Wives or Mistresses; one might wonder what sort of *Betty Mackerel Shakespear* found in his days, to sit for his *Portia,* and *Desdemona.*[17]

Although few critics went as far as Rymer, there were others who were sensitive to the indelicacies of some of the attractive heroines in the most popular plays. The vivacity of Ophelia's imagination was first nosed by Jeremy Collier in his notorious *A Short View of the Immorality, and Profaneness of the English Stage* in 1698. Phaedra's frenzy in the *Hippolytus* of Euripides, says Collier angrily,

is not lewd; She keeps her Modesty even after She has lost her Wits. Had *Shakespear* secur'd this point for his young Virgin *Ophelia,* the *Play* had been better contriv'd. Since he was resolv'd to drown the Lady like a Kitten, he should have set her a swimming a little sooner. To keep her alive only to sully her Reputation, and discover the Rankness of her Breath, was very Cruel.

Rymer, too, found that the Greek tragedians kept to a higher plane of seriousness in their representations of womanhood—though he finds a deterioration between Euripides and Seneca in their characterization of Phaedra.[18] Of course, the high seriousness of Greek tragedy was not necessarily to be discerned in Homer, who, it could be admitted, like Shakespeare had little sense of decorum, and made his Juno speak Billingsgate.[19] But the Greek tragic writers knew better.

It is odd that until the beginning of the nineteenth century Shakespeare was thought to be deficient and inferior in his representation of the female character. Only then were the tables turned; and it becomes customary to compliment the women characters in Greek tragedy by comparing them with Shake-speare's: Clytemnestra and Lady Macbeth, Antigone and Cordelia, and other pairs.

It would be natural to expect that Shakespeare's plays on Roman themes (*Julius Caesar, Antony and Cleopatra, Coriolanus*) might provide the closest parallel to ancient drama. At times Shakespeare is clearly trying very hard to *be* classical, to be authentic, to give a just impression of the most important civilization (humanly speaking) that the world had known. This is true espe-cially of *Coriolanus*, where Shakespeare is on his mettle, trying to produce a *mimesis* or representation of Rome at one of the most critical stages of its development. It was, certainly, the Roman plays in particular that in the nine-teenth century helped Shakespeare to become a classic in the educational sys-tem. English literature only gradually penetrated into the schools as a reputa-ble subject. In the boys' schools, the writings of the Greeks and the Romans remained the source of good taste and the groundwork of education. In his *Thoughts Suggested by a College Examination* Byron could deride the pedantic candidate who

> *Of Grecian dramas vaunts the deathless fame,*
> *Of Avon's bard remembering scarce the name.*

Even the Victorian educational reformers were in no doubt that a true and exact appreciation of the beauties of poetry was only to be gained by constru-ing it from a foreign language.

> My delight in going over Homer and Virgil with the boys [wrote Dr. Thomas Arnold of Rugby to a friend in 1836] makes me think what a treat it must be to teach Shakespeare to a good class of young Greeks in regenerate Athens; to dwell upon him line by line, and word by word, in the way that nothing but a translation lesson ever will enable one to do; and so to get all his pic-tures and thoughts leisurely into one's mind. . . . And how could this ever be done without having the process of construing, as the grosser medium through which alone all the beauty can be transmitted, because else we travel too fast, and more than half of it escapes us?

(By a curious coincidence, I can claim the interesting experience of thus teach-ing Shakespeare "to a good class of young Greeks in regenerate Athens.") Dr. Arnold, as late as 1836, could hardly envisage the replacement of the ancient classics by "English literature," which was, of course, too easy for educational purposes. "Shakespeare, with English boys, would be but a poor substitute for

Homer," he continued in the same letter; "but I confess that I should be glad to get Dante and Goethe now and then in the room of some of the Greek tragedians and of Horace; or rather not in their room, but mixed up along with them."[20]

But very soon the reformers, who foresaw the part that English literature was to play in education with the inevitable, if deplorable, decline of Latin and Greek, thought they saw in Shakespeare something that could be made as tough a discipline as Sophocles. The "school edition" of *Julius Caesar* soon made its appearance, with its abstruse philological notes and its elaborate explanation of allusions. The ominously named *School Shakespeare* by J. R. Pitman was published as early as 1822; it consists largely of *Julius Caesar*. The protean Shakespeare appeared in a new rôle, the examinable text. From the time of the foundation of the Oxford and Cambridge Local Examinations in 1858, a Shakespeare play appeared in the syllabuses.[21] Upon William Aldis Wright of Cambridge, a great scholar, who edited seventeen plays for the Clarendon Press between 1868 and 1897, fell the glory of having produced a school edition of Shakespeare which made him, for the first time, *look* like a classical text prepared (and expurgated) *in usum scolarum*. Such works as A. H. Gilkes's *School Lectures on the 'Electra' of Sophocles and 'Macbeth'* (1880) were indicative of what was going on everywhere.

An interesting example of the treatment of Shakespeare with the technique appropriate to an ancient classic was the *Shakespearian Grammar* which Edwin Abbott, head master of the City of London School and a leader in education, produced in 1869. His book was not primarily a work of disinterested scholarship, but an educational tool; or, rather, the two things were scarcely distinguishable. Like Homeric and Sophoclean grammars, it was directed to the more advanced pupils in schools and had value for students at all levels of work. It is astonishing that Abbott's *Shakespearian Grammar . . . For the use of Schools*, which, after nearly a century, is still often quoted by editors of Shakespeare as if it were the authoritative and standard work on the subject, should have had such a discreditable origin.

Abbott wanted to provide for the study of English in schools something as rigorous and systematic and definite as the Latin and Greek grammars which were approved and admired as disciplinary exercises for the young. To read Shakespeare critically, he asserts, we must be able to explain every idiom. If we fail to do that, "we are in danger of seriously lowering our standard of accurate study, and so far from training we are untraining our understanding." We must follow the course pursued in Latin and Greek: "Our native tongue should either not be studied critically at all, or be studied as thoroughly as the languages of antiquity." In brief, his book was, as he said in the preface to the first edition, an "attempt to apply rules of classical scholarship to the criticism of Elizabethan English."

Abbott's book was successful. Within a year a third edition had been demanded, and this the author thoroughly revised and expanded to three times its original size. In the preface to this third edition (1870) he gives some more candid indications of the motives behind his writing the book; it is prompted very largely by a desire to defend "English" against the champions of a purely classical education. English is easy and vague, the classical schoolmaster may say. Abbott quietly paraphrases this as "the want of some . . . distinct work, to give thoroughness and definiteness to an English lesson, has been felt by many teachers of experience." His *Shakespearian Grammar* is the answer. Surely, said the classical champions, there is no discipline like the study of Greek and Latin to encourage accuracy, exactness, and so on? "My own experience," Abbott interposed, "leads me to think that the Prosody of Shakespeare has peculiar interest for boys, and that some training in it is absolutely necessary if they are to read Shakespeare *critically*." Finally he tries to turn the tables upon his opponents and declares that the study of English would be a positive benefit to classical education: "Taking the very lowest ground, I believe that an intelligent study of English is the shortest and safest way to attain to an intelligent and successful study of Latin and Greek, and that it is idle to expect a boy to grapple with a sentence of Plato or Thucydides if he cannot master a passage of Shakespeare or a couplet of Pope."

It would be an exaggeration to say that Shakespeare killed classical education in England; he only gave the *coup de grâce*. Nevertheless the generous championship of English literature as an object of serious study received strong support from the annotated and grammaticized Shakespeare, which undermined the position of those who were now defending the unique educational value of Greek and Latin to the last ditch. A genuine, patriotic, and creditable enthusiasm developed for making the study of Shakespeare a part of every Englishman's education. After all, England was lucky enough to possess the poet generally acknowledged to be the greatest in the world. Surely all of us ought to know him as the Greeks knew their Homer. Were we not frequently told that for the glorious Athenians their Homer was the foundation of education, the inspiration of virtue, the school of taste? Could not our Shakespeare be the same to us? One of Furnivall's intentions in founding the New Shakspere Society in 1874 was, as he said in his opening speech as Director, to promote a really national study of Shakespeare; "which we have never had yet, which I am sure we ought to have, and which if we could but have,—all our young fellows being trained on Shakespeare's thoughts and words,—we should have a much finer nation of Englishmen than we have now!"[22]

Despite their defeats in the educational field, some of the champions of Greek and Roman literature in the later nineteenth century fought a rearguard action against the classic status of Shakespeare, principally on moral grounds. His "criticism of life" was thoroughly unsatisfactory. Lowes Dickinson, in his famous book *The Greek View of Life* (1896), characterizes Shakespeare:

> The tragedies of Shakespeare are devoid, one might say, or at least compara-
> tively devoid, of all preconceptions. He was free to choose what subject he
> liked and to treat it as he would; and no sense of obligation to religious or
> other points of view, no feeling for traditions descended from a sacred past
> and not lightly to be handled by those who were their trustees for the future,
> sobered or restrained for evil or for good his half-barbaric genius. He flung
> himself upon life with the irresponsible ardour of the discoverer of a new
> continent; shaped and re-shaped it as he chose; carved from it now the cyni-
> cism of Measure for Measure, now the despair of Hamlet and of Lear, now
> the radiant magnanimity of the Tempest, and departed leaving behind him
> not a map or chart, but a series of mutually incompatible landscapes.

There is some delicate malice here. Lowes Dickinson finds Shakespeare particularly vulnerable in the metaphysics of *King Lear*.

> To choose such a theme as Lear, to treat it as Shakespeare has treated it, to
> leave it, as it were, bleeding from a thousand wounds, in mute and helpless
> entreaty for the healing that is never to be vouchsafed—this would have
> been repulsive, if not impossible, to a Greek tragedian.[23]

A. E. Housman, too, following in Matthew Arnold's footsteps, came out against
Shakespeare in his Introductory Lecture in 1892.

> Virgil and the Greeks would have made Shakespeare not merely a great
> genius, which he was already, but, like Milton, a great artist, which he is not.
> He would have gained from the classics that virtue in which he and all his
> contemporaries are so wofully deficient, sobriety. He would have learnt to
> discriminate between what is permanently attractive and what is merely
> fashionable or popular. And perhaps it is not too much to hope that with
> the example of the classics before him he would have developed a literary

conscience and taken a pride in doing his best, instead of scamping his work because he knew his audience would never find out how ill he was writing.[24]

But it was too late. The ancient classics were beginning to come to terms with the English classic. The appropriate thing to do was to assert the similarity, to exert one's ingenuity to show that Shakespeare and the Greek tragedians were doing much the same sort of thing. Gilbert Murray in his British Academy lecture on *Hamlet and Orestes* in 1914 spoke of the unconscious traditions that lie behind great tragic creations. Hamlet and Orestes are, both of them, "traditional characters"; the "most famous heroes of the world's two great ages of tragedy" have both emerged from the "gradual shaping and reshaping of a primitive folk-tale."[25] And recently H. D. F. Kitto in his lecture "A Classical Scholar Looks at Shakespeare"[26] has spoken strikingly of the metaphysical similarities now apparent. The classical scholar who is familiar with Greek tragedy "very soon finds himself at home" with Shakespeare.

> For these are great tragic poets. They speak the same language, though in different dialects: those in Greek, this one in English. They speak about the same things; whether they tell us of an Agamemnon or a Creon, or of a King Richard or a Hamlet, they are speaking in the same grave and spacious way of nothing less than the terms on which the gods will let us live; and though each of them speaks in his own voice and with his own accent, about this one thing they do not speak differently.

The accommodation is thus complete. It would be interesting to speculate what Dryden or Dr. Johnson or even Matthew Arnold would have said concerning this easy-going enthronement of Shakespeare alongside the Greek tragedians, all "speaking in the same grave and spacious way of nothing less than the terms on which the gods will let us live."

Shakespeare Criticism 1900-1964

By Irving Ribner

The quantity of writings on Shakespeare produced in the sixty-four years of our century is so vast, and reflects so many different personalities and heterogeneous attitudes, that to attempt to draw from it some conclusions about the direction of Shakespeare criticism in our time is very difficult. Generally our twentieth-century Shakespeareans have seen themselves—and have been seen by others—as writing in reaction to the great Victorian critics, and such reaction, of course, was inevitable. I would suggest, however, a continuing influence which may be even more significant than any reaction—that in the work of five men who wrote about Shakespeare at the turn of the century we may find the sources of the more significant attitudes developed in the following sixty years. These men are Edward Dowden, A. C. Bradley, Richard Moulton, Walter Raleigh, and Robert Bridges. The first four wrote closely in the critical tradition of Samuel Taylor Coleridge, and Bridges brought to his criticism of Shakespeare the poet's own conception of his craft.

Of these, Bradley and Dowden had perhaps the widest influence among their immediate successors, Bradley with his attempt to define the moral world of Shakespeare through a naturalistic analysis of character, and Dowden with a focus upon Shakespeare the man which led him to emphasize the process of development and to see the plays as reflections of specific periods in their author's attitude toward life, to see in Shakespeare's conjectured joys and sorrows the difference between *As You Like It* and *Measure for Measure*. Dowden's approach[1] in more recent times has not fared so well as Bradley's. His biographical assumptions were attacked directly by C. J. Sisson in "The Mythical Sorrows of Shakespeare," his influential British Academy lecture for 1934. But Dowden's belief that we can see the man Shakespeare through his plays survives as recently as Edward G. McCurdy's *The Personality of Shakespeare* (New Haven, 1953), where the author attempts by means of a body of Freudian theory unknown to Dowden's generation to delineate the personality of whose fantasies the plays supposedly give evidence.

Such "psychological" criticism is of relatively slight importance—although a considerable bibliography could be compiled of the articles on Shakespeare's complexes and compulsions which appear in the psychoanalytic journals—but Dowden's assumptions have survived in our time in a much more important form than this. Caroline F. E. Spurgeon's analysis of imagery,[2] which may have had more influence than any other critical method of the last thirty years, began also with Dowden's assumption that Shakespeare the man could be discovered in his plays. She was no more successful in this discovery than Dowden had been, but her method was a new one with wide implications; a whole school of contemporary critics, with little interest in the personality of Shakespeare, has used imagery instead as an index to Shakespeare's themes and as the key to the poetic texture of his plays. The Dowden influence has led, through a strange metamorphosis, from a futile study of Shakespeare the man to a very fruitful study of Shakespeare the poet.

Although the character analysis of Bradley[3] is still the stock in trade of many teachers of Shakespeare, it is not this aspect of his work which has had the greatest influence upon more recent criticism. Indeed, Bradley carried character analysis probably as far as it could be carried, and L. C. Knights's important essay, "How Many Children Had Lady Macbeth?"[4] may have signalized its end as an important critical tool. Only one book has appeared since Bradley's time which makes a significant advance in character analysis. This is J. I. M. Stewart's *Character and Motive in Shakespeare* (London, 1949), which uses modern psychology (largely Freudian) and anthropology to argue a naturalistic fidelity to life in Shakespeare's characters more subtle than even Bradley had imagined. Stewart's book is cast as an answer to such historical critics as E. E. Stoll and Levin Schücking, who had stressed the artificial and conventional elements of Shakespeare's art, and it does much as an antidote to some of their excesses.

The great influence of Bradley has been rather in the view of Shakespeare he inherited from Coleridge: that is, the poet is treated as philosopher who, through the power of imagination, attempted in his plays to illuminate the mystery of life and did so in a way that was always profoundly moral. Bradley saw evil as an aberration in nature, and to relate it to human character he fell back upon the Aristotelian notion of *hamartia*, although the inadequacy of this concept is implicit in its very vagueness. Bradley failed to relate human disaster to human character in any way that was truly moral, as Lily B. Campbell pointed out in two important essays;[5] a world in which a Romeo or Hamlet must suffer through his own insufficiency as fully as a Macbeth or Othello is one in which it is difficult to find the kind of reconciliation and confidence in the naturalness of good that Bradley felt essential to tragedy. Many succeeding critics have accepted Bradley's view of tragedy's necessary philosophical dimension and inherent morality, and they have tried to find in Shakespeare a moral order more meaningful than Bradley could find.

The moral criticism of Shakespeare is, in fact, among the most important currents of our time. It is indebted to Bradley, but it often goes beyond Bradley to Coleridge and to Samuel Johnson, and it is often identified closely with Matthew Arnold's assumptions about literature. A lesser-known figure than either Dowden or Bradley is Richard G. Moulton, but Moulton's writings on Shakespeare were among the most original and important the Victorian era produced. In *Shakespeare as a Dramatic Artist* (London, 1885) and *Shakespeare as a Dramatic Thinker* (London, 1907) Moulton sought to apply what he called an inductive method to Shakespeare criticism; that is, he intended to approach each play without consideration of the other plays, but with a sympathetic appreciation which might enable the critic to comprehend the play fully and, independently of external fixed standards, judge it as a unique totality. Moulton in this was applying the Coleridgean principle of the self-sufficiency of the work of art, later to be so crucial to the *Scrutiny* group of critics in England and the "new critics" in America.

Moulton differed from Coleridge in a greater emphasis upon plot, and although he made full use of character analysis, it was primarily in the elements of story that he found Shakespeare's moral themes implicit. He thus approaches a modern mythographic view of Shakespeare, with the story, as the embodiment of idea, assuming a large symbolic function. Moulton, moreover, tried to systematize the moral philosophy of Shakespeare in a way Coleridge had never attempted. Through plot analysis he found certain root ideas to which Shakespeare returns again and again: the relation of heroism and morality, of sin and retribution, of wrong and restoration, the antithesis between man's relation to himself and to society. Moulton's readings of the plays in terms of these central ideas are often very rigid. Such rigidity, perhaps an inevitable aspect of his method, has frequently been the basis of complaint against more recent critics who have employed a similar technique.

We can see at once that Moulton's work rests upon assumptions which were unusual among his predecessors, but which have become fairly commonplace in Shakespeare criticism of the last quarter century. That the play must be studied as a unity to which all of its parts contribute has been emphasized very strongly by L. C. Knights among others, and in Knights's recent work[6] we have an examination of Shakespeare's recurrent moral themes which reminds one at once of Moulton. His influence can be seen also in such a book as John Lawlor's *The Tragic Sense in Shakespeare* (London, 1960), with its analysis of imagery and plot in terms of antithetical moral themes.[7]

Walter Raleigh and Robert Bridges wrote relatively little about Shakespeare, but what they did write is important, for these men represent the Victorian antecedents of the school of historical criticism which dominated Shakespeare study for the first forty or so years of this century, which is still very strong, and which may finally prove to be our century's most distinctive contribution to Shakespeare criticism. Raleigh was one of the titans whom E. E. Stoll singled out for attack in his "Anachronism in Shakespeare Criticism,"[8] the essay which may well be regarded as the manifesto of historical criticism; but in spite of this repudiation, there is much in Raleigh's slim volume, *Shakespeare*, published in London as part of the English Men of Letters series in 1907, which Stoll developed in his own work. Stoll found fault with Raleigh's carrying on Dowden's method, his seeking to portray Shakespeare's mind at work and holding that the plays may be an index to the character of their author. But Raleigh is also the only important critic of his time to see Shakespeare as the product of the theater, his plays governed by the requirements and physical conditions of the Elizabethan stage; and these concerns, after all, are the cornerstone of Stoll's own criticism.

Raleigh, moreover, parted company with Coleridge, Bradley, and Moulton in denying a philosophical dimension to Shakespeare's art. He saw the artistry of the plays only in their power to make an immediate emotional impression upon an audience in a theater. Raleigh also criticized the great concern with character analysis among contemporary critics, holding that such concentration obscured other elements in a play, which must be viewed as a total stage artifact. He censured those critics who would discuss character details outside of a play's context, and he argued for the influence upon Shakespeare of the tastes of his audience, holding that Shakespeare's greatness lay in his ability to cater to these tastes and at the same time triumph over the restraints and limitations they imposed upon him.

It was this theme which occupied Robert Bridges in his widely influential essay on "The Influence of the Audience on Shakespeare's Drama,"[9] but Bridges could not see Shakespeare as having triumphed over these supposed limitations. For the sensitive Victorian Bridges, Shakespeare was a great potential genius who had prostituted his talent by catering to the crude, low tastes of a degenerate audience interested only in sex, violence, and coarse buffoonery. That Bridges' conception of Shakespeare's audience was based upon lamentable misinformation has since been demonstrated by Alfred Harbage.[10] Bridges' greatest shortcoming, however, was that his was a historicism misapplied, for he had an inadequate conception of what any dramatist's relation to his audience must be in any age.

His views, nevertheless, attracted wide attention, and they may have been particularly influential upon E. E. Stoll. To Bridges, probably, Stoll owes the notion that the principal effect of Shakespeare's tragedies is in their power to shock by what Stoll calls "steep tragic contrast," revealing a hero performing an act of which the author has conditioned the audience to believe him incapable, such for instance as Macbeth's murder of Duncan or Othello's of Desdemona. The audience, for Bridges, demanded such shock, in defiance of logic, credibility, and morality, and Shakespeare sacrificed his art in order to give it to them. For Stoll, however, Shakespeare's true greatness as an artist lay in his very ability to hold an audience by such means.

Stoll began his lifelong assault upon the Victorian critics in two early essays,[11] and he continued to state his principles in a series of books, perhaps the most important of which are his *Shakespeare Studies* (New York, 1927) and *Art and Artifice in Shakespeare* (Cambridge, Eng., 1933). He went back to Longinus in his belief that the dramatist's mission is to "enthral" by means of the imagination, and to Aristotle in his belief in the primacy of plot. He broke with the nineteenth-century followers of Coleridge in denying a philosophical dimension and a concern with character in Shakespeare (Bradley), a moral content in the plays (Moulton), and our ability ever to know Shakespeare the man from his plays or our need to do so (Dowden). He stressed the conventional nature of drama, relating Shakespeare to his medieval heritage and to the physical conditions of the Elizabethan stage, the essential artificiality of drama and its need to distort physical reality in order to exist. Stoll is the father of twentieth-century historical criticism of Shakespeare, and his followers have extended his influence in many directions.

There has been, to begin with, an important critical movement which would reassert the essence of the plays as drama, and which would place Shakespeare specifically in the theatrical milieu of his own London. Probably the greatest theater-oriented critic of our time has been Harley Granville-Barker, who approached the plays in his *Prefaces to Shakespeare*,[12] not as a disciple of Stoll, but with his own rich theater experience to draw upon. More closely in the line of Stoll has been S. L. Bethell's *Shakespeare and the Popular Dramatic Tradition* (London, 1944), which has tried to see Shakespeare in terms of the requirements of popular drama, drawing often upon our modern cinema for analogies. Bethell has gone beyond Stoll in emphasizing the moral and religious elements of popular drama and the symbolism which Shakespeare's art carried on from the Middle Ages. Bethell has countered the naturalistic psychological critics in his contention that Shakespeare's chief interest lay in mankind rather than in the peculiarities of individual men.

In this general current we may place such books as Peter Alexander's *Hamlet, Father and Son* (London, 1955), which examines Shakespeare's play in terms of the modern thriller. More recently Bertrand Evans in his *Shakespeare's Comedies* (Oxford, 1960) has studied these plays in the light of a stage technique involving anticipation of action by the audience, explaining the comedies in terms of gaps between character and audience awareness. William Rosen in *Shakespeare and the Craft of Tragedy* (Cambridge, Mass., 1960) is interested also primarily in dramatic technique, the relation between actors and audience, by which Shakespeare presents character and moral issues.

Closely allied to Stoll's was the work of Levin Schücking.[13] He too was concerned with Shakespeare upon the stage, and to him we owe the concept of "episodic intensification," the notion that Shakespeare developed individual scenes for immediate effect, often sacrificing the structure, coherence, and logic of his total play for such impact. Schücking, who was interested also in primitive survivals in Shakespeare, explained *Hamlet* in terms of the brutal revenge story at its source. Schücking may be Stoll's most important follower, although he does not represent much development of Stoll's premises and he is even more narrow in their application.

The historical method had far-reaching results when it was extended beyond considerations of the stage to an examination of the entire social, political, and intellectual milieu in which Shakespeare worked. This movement was carried on in the middle years of our century by an important group of writers which included Hardin Craig, Lily B. Campbell, W. W. Lawrence, Theodore Spencer, Willard Farnham, and E. M. W. Tillyard. It is impossible to divide the work of these critics into clear-cut categories, for all overlap. All share Stoll's premise that Shakespeare must be seen as a product of his age, and in general they tend to see the English Renaissance as tied more closely to the Middle Ages than earlier writers had recognized. For them, Shakespeare's dramatic medium is the perfection of what had evolved out of earlier tradition and never entirely broken its medieval ties. Unlike Stoll, these critics have been concerned with Shakespeare's intellectual content, and they have studied his ideas in terms of what they found Elizabethans generally to have believed about the world.

Probably the most comprehensive argument for the continuity of Shakespeare's art form with its medieval forerunners has been Willard Farnham's *The Medieval Heritage of Elizabethan Tragedy* (Berkeley, 1936), which stressed the evolving morality play and *de casibus* story as they came to acquire the substance of real tragedy. In the same year appeared Theodore Spencer's *Death in Elizabethan Tragedy*, which though narrower in scope was similar in its assumptions, stressing the medieval gothic aspects of Shakespearean tragedy, while Howard Baker,[14] dealing only with *Titus Andronicus* among Shakespeare's tragedies, went even beyond Farnham in denying the Senecan influence in Elizabethan tragedy and relating it instead to the morality play. William Witherle Lawrence had already related Shakespeare's long-debated problem plays to the conventions of medieval romance and story.[15]

A somewhat similar—although less medievally cast—attempt to see Shakespeare in terms of conventional art form has been O. J. Campbell's effort to relate Shakespeare's work to contemporary, primarily Jacobean, notions of satire.[16] E. C. Pettet[17] has tried to do for Shakespeare's romantic comedies what Lawrence did for his more somber ones, relating them to the traditions of romance as they had developed among such predecessors as Lyly and Greene. Among the more important treatments of Shakespeare stressing the symbolic and allegorical traditions which shaped his art is W. B. C. Watkins' *Shakespeare and Spenser* (Princeton, 1950). A somewhat different and more original examination of the medieval antecedents of Shakespearean comedy has been C. L. Barber's *Shakespeare's Festive Comedy* (Princeton, 1959), which is concerned with the relation of Shakespeare to primitive fertility rites and May games. Russell A. Fraser, in *Shakespeare's Poetics* (London, 1962) has examined *King Lear* in terms of medieval and Renaissance iconography.

Scholars like Hardin Craig and E. M. W. Tillyard have further countered the assumption that there was any sharp break between the world views of sixteenth-century England and those of earlier centuries; they have suggested that Shakespeare's plays must be seen in terms of Elizabethan Christian humanism, with its religiously oriented conception of degree and order in the universe. Hardin Craig's *The Enchanted Glass* (New York, 1936), a pioneer work in its exploration of Elizabethan cosmology, was followed by Tillyard's widely influential *The Elizabethan World Picture* (London, 1943). Douglas Bush, although not primarily concerned with drama, has argued along similar lines in such works as *The Renaissance and English Humanism* (Toronto, 1939). Among the most brilliant and influential applications of this historical point of view to Shakespeare's plays were Theodore Spencer's Lowell Lectures,

Shakespeare and the Nature of Man (New York, 1942). Spencer described Shakespeare's age as one of conflict between the settled values which Christian humanism carried over from the Middle Ages and a new skepticism which was challenging them, and he saw Shakespeare's tragedies in particular as a product of this tension. Tillyard in *Shakespeare's History Plays* (London, 1946) examined the English histories in terms of the Tudor doctrines of order and the Tudor conception of how earlier history had reflected a divine plan for England's destiny. The importance of relating a Christian humanist view to the understanding of Shakespeare has been developed further in W. C. Curry's *Shakespeare's Philosophical Patterns* (Baton Rouge, La., 1937); and V. K. Whitaker in *Shakespeare's Use of Learning* (San Marino, Calif., 1953) has tried to examine Shakespeare's use of his sources in these terms, stressing primarily the work of Richard Hooker as representing the system in the light of which Shakespeare transformed his source materials.

In Craig's *Enchanted Glass* is also the first important attempt at understanding the "Elizabethan mind," at probing the ways of viewing things which belonged to a pre-Cartesian world. From this concern has sprung a large school of "history of ideas" criticism, which has applied to the understanding of Shakespeare's plays common Elizabethan notions of many things. Craig's student Ruth L. Anderson was probably the first to examine Shakespeare's plays in the light of popular treatises on psychology and moral philosophy,[18] and she was followed in this by Lily B. Campbell, whose *Shakespeare's Tragic Heroes: Slaves of Passion* (Cambridge, Eng., 1930) examined each of Shakespeare's major tragic heroes in terms of contemporary treatises on the passions.

Miss Campbell has had many followers. J. E. Phillips in *The State in Shakespeare's Greek and Roman Plays* (New York, 1940) examined these plays in terms of Elizabethan theories of statecraft and attitudes towards Roman history, as Miss Campbell herself was to treat the English histories in similar terms.[19] Paul A. Jorgensen used contemporary military treatises to throw light on some of the plays,[20] Franklin M. Dickey has studied some of the tragedies in the light of Elizabethan notions about love,[21] and Curtis B. Watson has examined the plays in the light of what he conceives to be Renaissance concepts of honor derived from classical sources.[22]

Shakespeare's morality has been approached with a historical perspective by Alfred B. Harbage. In *As They Liked It* (New York, 1947), he related the moral content of the plays to the tastes and expectations of the Elizabethan popular theater audience, and in *Shakespeare and the Rival Traditions* (New York,

1952) he differentiated between the folk morality of the public theaters and the more sophisticated tastes catered to by those who wrote for the private or coterie theaters. Paul N. Siegel has related Shakespeare's moral and religious point of view to the political and economic conflicts of his era.[23] There has been also a considerable interest in Shakespeare's language from a historical point of view, Sister Miriam Joseph's *Shakespeare's Use of the Arts of Language* (New York, 1947) being perhaps the most significant attempt to relate Shakespeare's usage to traditional rhetorical forms and concepts. Paul A. Jorgensen, in *Shakespeare's Redeeming Words* (Berkeley, Calif., 1962), has used Elizabethan connotations of Shakespeare's vocabulary to illuminate the plays.

The works of historical criticism continue to appear, but a reaction against this method of inquiry had already begun to be expressed in the early nineteen-thirties. It is perhaps ironic that much of this reaction was given impetus by the work of Caroline Spurgeon which, as we have seen, itself sprang from strong historical assumptions, the belief that through analysis of imagery the critic might attain a greater measure of true historical insight than ever before, determining the inner feelings and attitudes of Shakespeare himself as the methods of Dowden and Raleigh were incapable of doing. It cannot be said that Miss Spurgeon's work ever revealed much about Shakespeare the man, but in her analysis of imagery she was able to focus more closely upon the poetic texture of Shakespeare than any critic had done before,[24] and it was in terms of this poetic dimension of Shakespeare's art that the reaction against historical criticism began to develop, until we have among the *Scrutiny* critics in England and the "new critics" in America a focus upon Shakespeare not as a dramatist subject to the influences of his age and the requirements of a relatively unsophisticated theater, but rather as the author of "dramatic poems" which share the universality of all poetry and which must be studied by a technique of close textual analysis.

While Miss Spurgeon was developing her technique, G. Wilson Knight was evolving the critical method which he was to illustrate most notably in *The Wheel of Fire* (London, 1930). Knight examined poetic imagery, not as an index to the author's mind, but as his principal means of insight into the total conception of each play as a work of art. In the introduction to *The Wheel of Fire* Knight explained his method of "poetic interpretation" as opposed to criticism, with its distinction between the spatial and temporal aspects of drama; in that volume, in *The Imperial Theme* (London, 1931), and in others, he applied his method to specific plays. Knight's emphasis has always been upon the totality of the work of art, which may be obscured by concentration upon any one of its parts such as plot or character. He has proclaimed his interest in Shakespeare the philosophical poet rather than the man of the theater, linking his own work to the metaphysical tradition of Coleridge, Hazlitt, and Bradley, from which he has held that the stage-oriented criticism of Harley Granville-Barker must be excluded.

Knight has sought to arrive at a full response to Shakespeare, a total imaginative perception of each play, which only the critic of the most heightened sensibility may hope to achieve. Through imagery he has sought to approach the integrating themes in Shakespeare's plays and to define a pattern by which each play is unified. These themes Knight often has found to be conveyed by conventional Christian symbols, and it may be said that he has contributed more than any other critic of this century to an awareness of Shakespeare's symbolism and the relation of his plays to Christian tradition and belief. Sometimes Knight's work has been erratic and misguided—he has been overly fond of enthusiastic superlatives—but it has at times also been marked by a brilliance and clarity of insight which few critics have rivaled.

We find the influence of Knight most marked among those critics who contributed to *Scrutiny* magazine in England and have been associated with it as the *Scrutiny* group, and among the so-called "new critics" in the United States. They have shared Knight's assumptions about the totality of the work of art and the importance of poetic imagery as its key. They have worked by methods of close textual analysis, and they have ignored the assumptions of the historical critics that Shakespeare's art can be studied profitably in the light of his own theater and that its thematic content may be revealed by study of the Renaissance intellectual milieu.

Of the *Scrutiny* group, dominated by the views of F. R. Leavis, the two most important Shakespearean critics have been Derek Traversi and L. C. Knights. The controlling drive behind Leavis' own criticism has been a search for value, cultural and moral, since an age's culture and its morality are closely related aspects of a society's ordering and perception of its experience. He has regarded this search as imperative in our century, in which traditional aristocratic forms of culture are no longer operative and traditional values are no longer pertinent. Leavis has been a moralist essentially in the tradition of Matthew Arnold, who believed that literature must reflect the best of which man is capable, that the perception of literature is a moral activity, and that the moral value of literature must be made by the critic to pervade society. Leavis thus opposed the historical critics who would limit their understanding of Shakespeare to the meaning he may have had for his own age, holding that the process of ordering experience which is reflected in poetry is a universal process and not limited to one age: if the moral vision of a writer like Shakespeare had validity for his own age it must have that validity for our own age as well, and therefore the critic's focus must be on what poetry means today. Conjectures about what it may have meant in the past are irrelevant, and thus the great body of criticism stemming from E. E. Stoll and his followers was for Leavis and his followers beside the point.

Leavis himself has written little on Shakespeare, although his essays on *Measure for Measure* and *Othello* are classics.[25] His philosophy is manifest in the writings of L. C. Knights, who is concerned with describing the moral and cultural value of Shakespeare.[26] Since poetry best reflects an age's values, it is with Shakespeare the poet that Knights is most closely occupied, and with the ability of the poet to convey moral themes. To understand this poetry, Knights has used a method of close textual analysis, an exploration of language and the implications of image and symbol, which owes much to the methods of G. Wilson Knight. Knights is influenced also by I. A. Richards and Richards' pupil, William Empson, who has been concerned with the ambiguities and connotations of words, divorced usually from historical and biographical considerations. Knights has been also in the tradition of Coleridge and Bradley in that he has seen Shakespeare as the philosopher-poet whose plays embody an evolving view of life. Like Wilson Knight he has sought the integrating pattern which governs each play, and like T. S. Eliot he has held that no single play of Shakespeare's can be perceived fully without an awareness of the dramatist's entire artistic development. Knights has been particularly outspoken in his arguments against the historical critics,[27] denying the relevance of any specific historical setting to the universal truth of poetry, which is always a personal creation of the artist, and which can be perceived only by a direct experience of the poetry itself, exclusive of any external considerations.

Derek Traversi, although he has not written about his own critical premises so much as Knights or engaged so fully in countering the methods of other critics, has probably applied Leavis' principles to Shakespeare more consistently and comprehensively than any other of the *Scrutiny* critics. He has, like Knights, argued the importance of development in the total body of Shakespeare's work. In *An Approach to Shakespeare* (London, 1938) he explained his method and presented his view of the full development of Shakespeare's art; in subsequent volumes[28] he has elaborated his views of specific stages in Shakespeare's progression. He has sought an impersonal objectivity in his analysis of Shakespeare's language, holding that through language alone is the poet's vision of experience conveyed, and seeking finally to come to a perception of the total emotional experience which is the whole play. Traversi, more than Knights, has tended to emphasize plot as an instrument of poetry. He has been concerned with the symbolism of action and with a conception of the play, or "dramatic poem" as he calls it, as one large extended metaphor.

The "new critics" in America have not differed widely from the *Scrutiny* critics in their general assumptions and method, but thus far they have not concerned themselves with Shakespeare to a large extent. Cleanth Brooks's "The Naked Babe and the Cloak of Manliness"[29] is a classic essay on *Macbeth*, but of this group only Robert B. Heilman has devoted himself to Shakespeare in any extensive manner.[30] Heilman, like Bradley, has been concerned with the philosophical scope of Shakespeare, and he has tried to determine the central moral themes which give to the plays their unity; like the *Scrutiny* critics he has sought these themes by a close analysis of poetic imagery, using many of the techniques which critics like Ransom, Tate, and Brooks had developed in the criticism of lyric poetry. Heilman has dwelled upon image patterns— clothes and blindness in *King Lear*, for instance—through which Shakespeare poses paradoxes and creates tension between opposing systems of value. Heilman's criticism moves always toward the definition of a comprehensive vision by which all of the parts of the play are united, and the vision of the tragedies with which Heilman deals is found to be not unlike what Bradley discerned; Shakespeare for Heilman also embodies a faith that good is natural and evil the corruption of nature.[31]

Heilman, like the *Scrutiny* critics, has been concerned with the moral value of Shakespeare's art. The ability of Shakespearean drama—and tragedy in particular—to translate a moral vision into dramatic terms has been perhaps the dominant concern of the most recent Shakespeare criticism, and in the hands of various writers it has taken different directions. Some have approached Shakespeare's morality in secular terms, holding that Christianity and tragedy are essentially incompatible. Others, with perhaps a truer historical perspective, have argued that Shakespeare wrote with the assumptions of the Christian Renaissance about man's relation to God always in mind, and that thus we cannot ignore the religious dimensions of his art.

One of the wisest and most balanced studies of Shakespeare's moral ideas has been Donald Stauffer's *Shakespeare's World of Images* (New York, 1949), which uses all of the elements of drama—plot, character, and language—to arrive at Shakespeare's view of experience, believing that all great literature must reflect the ideas of its creator and that although these may be expressed in a form which transcends logical discourse, they may be discovered by analysis of the dramatist's "choice of subject, his shaping of sources, the judgments implicit or stated in the outcome of his plots, his ventriloquism when characters speak out of key, his undramatic set speeches, his repetitive ideas, his recurrent images, and his choric or touchstone figures." Stauffer, we can thus see, has been very eclectic in his methods, drawing upon the historical critics as well as upon those who have written in opposition to them. Also eclectic in its method, although objecting strongly to the historical bias of his contemporary critics, was H. C. Goddard's highly personal reading of the plays in his *The Meaning of Shakespeare* (Chicago, 1951).

More narrowly dogmatic in their approach were two important books which appeared in 1951, *The Dream of Learning,* by D. G. James, and *Character and Society in Shakespeare,* by Arthur Sewell. Both were concerned with Shakespeare's moral content and both at the same time committed to the thesis that tragedy and Christianity are incompatible. James and Sewell, each in his own way, argued that tragedy constitutes a unique way of knowing, distinct from both the religious and the scientific, that Shakespeare's plays must be viewed as unified structures—with character and plot properly subordinated to the whole—which by means of poetry translate a moral vision into drama. James and Sewell were followed in these contentions by Geoffrey Bush in *Shakespeare and the Natural Condition* (Cambridge, Mass., 1956). All three of these writers define Shakespeare's moral vision in terms of a terrible pessimism alien to Christian belief, with man the prey of terrible demonic forces against which his struggles must always be in vain. They are at the opposite pole from a critic like S. L. Bethell who in *Shakespeare and the Popular Dramatic Tradition* has argued that Shakespearean popular drama, as it emerged from the moral plays of the Middle Ages, was framed to present a moral argument and that in this Shakespeare was always Christian.

Bethell is one of many critics who have tried to study Shakespeare's moral vision within the intellectual context of his own age, holding that certain ethical and metaphysical assumptions are essential to tragedy, and that Shakespeare's plays were conceived against a common background of religious belief which the dramatist shared with his audience. John F. Danby in *Shakespeare's Doctrine of Nature* (London, 1949) has been historically oriented as well, for he has tried to examine *King Lear* in terms of the conflicting Renaissance ideas of nature revealed by historical critics like Craig and Tillyard; that is, on the one hand, the harmonious, divinely controlled nature of the Christian humanists, and, on the other, the chaotic, impersonal nature of skeptical philosophers, most fully expressed by Thomas Hobbes. Danby shares many of the assumptions of the *Scrutiny* critics—indeed, some of his early essays were published in *Scrutiny*—using their techniques of close textual analysis, and concentrating upon the play as a total unity. Danby concludes that Shakespeare is consistently Christian in his ethical and religious point of view.

One of the most original attempts to come to terms with Shakespeare's philosophical substance has been Harold S. Wilson's *On the Design of Shakespearian Tragedy* (Toronto, 1957). Wilson divided the major tragedies into three groups, those of the "order of faith" which explore the implications of a Christian providential world view, those of the "order of nature" which limit themselves to the finite observable experiences of man, without regard to supernatural considerations, and finally two plays, *Antony and Cleopatra* and *King Lear*, in which Shakespeare achieves a synthesis between the natural and providential orders, and in which his most profound tragic vision is therefore embodied. More consistently Christian in its point of view is M. D. H. Parker's *The Slave of Life* (London, 1955), which finds in Shakespeare's plays a Thomistic and Augustinian metaphysic by which Miss Parker supports her own argument that Shakespeare himself was a Roman Catholic recusant, a biographical supposition which though very questionable does not detract from the value of her book as criticism.

The books of G. R. Elliott on *Hamlet*, *Othello*, and *Macbeth*[32] have employed a technique of minute, scene-by-scene analysis to show how Shakespeare deliberately made use of Christian principles to create dramatic conflict and tension, affirming always an orthodox Anglican religious position. The religious orthodoxy of Shakespearean tragedy has been argued also by Roy Walker in his studies of *Hamlet* and *Macbeth*,[33] and by Robert Speaight in *Nature in Shakespearian Tragedy* (London, 1955). The influence of pagan ritual as well as Christian symbolism upon the plays has been studied by H. M. V. Matthews in *Character and Symbol in Shakespeare's Plays* (Cambridge, Eng., 1962).

This recognition of a religious dimension in Shakespeare has been a significant development in recent criticism. Its emphasis may have been carried to an extreme in the books of John Vyvyan,[34] where the plays tend to be regarded as little more than elaborate dramatic allegories in which Shakespeare proclaims a consistent and rigidly orthodox Christian moral philosophy. Perhaps the ultimate stage in the Christian reading of Shakespeare is reached in J. A. Bryant's *Hyppolita's View* (Lexington, Ky., 1961), where the plays are seen in terms of medieval typology as biblical analogies whose central theme is always the story of Christ. Beyond this it is difficult to go. A reaction has appeared in Roland M. Frye's *Shakespeare and Christian Doctrine* (Princeton, 1963), which argues that although Shakespeare often used contemporary theological writings and is generally Christian in his point of view, his plays were not written as Christian propaganda—something which none of those critics who have pointed to Shakespeare's Christian symbolism or to the Christian assumptions underlying many of his plays has ever suggested.

I have touched upon only a few of the many books of Shakespeare criticism which have appeared in the sixty-four years of this century, not aiming at a comprehensive bibliography, but seeking only to illustrate what seem to me to be the principal currents. The volumes continue to appear in ever increasing numbers, many of them frivolous and inconsequential, but some continuing to develop important new insights. If we are to draw any conclusions about our century's criticism of Shakespeare, one would have to be that the great tradition—extending from Coleridge down to our own times, and behind Coleridge back to Samuel Johnson and John Dryden—has been moral and philosophic, emphasizing always the value of Shakespeare's plays as the embodiment of important truth about human experience. The twentieth century has developed and amplified this great tradition in at least two important ways. It has contributed a historical point of view by which Shakespeare's meaning may be more fully perceived, and it has directed new attention to his poetry and developed methods by which this poetry may be more closely examined than ever before. Often the critics have tended to be partisan and acrimonious, but a new generation just ahead of us may recognize that even in seemingly contradictory approaches there has been room for reconciliation in terms of a common larger tradition. Even those most critical of Bradley have acknowledged their indebtedness to him, and the *Scrutiny* critics have accepted more of Stoll's assumptions about drama than they themselves are usually aware.

Notes on the Text

Ornstein   Character and Reality   pp. 3–18

1 A striking example is the sonnet which Romeo and Juliet speak together at Capulet's ball. On the page the antiphonal rhyme scheme seems impossibly literary. On the stage, however, it very effectively conveys the impression of a marriage of true minds; indeed, despite its formality, it captures with amazing naturalness and humor the self-conscious give and take of youthful courtship as Juliet's innocent guile matches Romeo's ingenuous ardor. We are often told that since conversation is ordinarily in prose, the use of verse in drama is necessarily conventional. It seems to me, however, that the issue is not how people ordinarily speak, but rather how dramatic verse sounds in a theater. Certainly one of Hamlet's soliloquies sounds eloquent and poetic to an audience; but its cadences are so natural, and it creates so immediate and spontaneous an impression of human thought and feeling, that the actor who plays Hamlet does not seem to be reciting poetry. In contrast, a reader of one of Donne's supposedly dramatic lyrics is obviously reciting a poem. For despite his nervous excitement, his colloquialisms, and his "dramatic" form of address, Donne's *persona* is not a dramatic character; he is a poet enunciating a poetic attitude. His lines do not mimic the spontaneous flow of thought and feeling; they are patterned by the necessities of Donne's chosen verse form. It seems to me that dramatic verse sounds artificially poetic, unrealistic, and therefore conventional only when it is not genuinely dramatic or genuinely poetic, or when as a choric speech it is not appropriate in style to its dramatic context.

2 See the chapter on "Characterization" in *Shakespeare Studies* (New York, 1927).

3 Many of Shakespeare's allusions to the theater express a satiric delight in the stage comparable to Pirandello's. The exaggerated style of acting which the Actors in *Six Characters* assume is paralleled by the fustian melodramatic style which Gloucester and Buckingham jokingly plan to assume in "counterfeiting the deep tragedian" in *Richard III*. It is somewhat extraordinary that this satiric description of the tragic style is cited as evidence of the stylization of Elizabethan acting. If anything, the passage from *Richard III* (III.v.1 ff.) suggests that the acting of Shakespeare's company at least was fairly naturalistic, because the fact that Gloucester and Buckingham intend to act out a tragicomic interlude within the play would be lost on an audience unless the style they are going to assume is different from their customary style of speaking and acting. So far as we can tell from Shakespeare, only a poor player struts and frets his hour upon the stage.

4 A striking exception is *The Widow's Tears*.

5 See *Shakespearean Tragedy* (London, 1952), p. 344.

6 See *Political Characters of Shakespeare* (London, 1952), pp. 103–4.

7 On the stage all is expressed if not spoken; even the silences of a Bolingbroke are explicit. I think it more accurate to say that Shakespeare's art grows more evocative and intrinsically dramatic than to say that it grows more implicit. The characterizations of *Antony and Cleopatra*, for example, are as rhetorically and poetically expressed as those of *Richard III*, but the poetry and rhetoric of the later play are, as needs be, far more subtle and imaginative. Where the characters in Shakespeare's early plays self-consciously declare their emotions in speeches that momentarily suspend the dramatic action, the characters in the later plays reveal themselves more naturally and unselfconsciously in dramatic situations. Cordelia's "No cause, no cause" does not move us because it hints of a great depth of unexpressed feeling; the line moves us because it expresses very immediately, though very simply, her deepest feelings. If Shakespeare's portrayal of character were genuinely implicit, his plays could not be acted.

8 Just as the minor characters in a play are not miniatures of the protagonists, so too the plotting of peripheral or minor incidents is not equivalent to the plotting of the central episodes of a play. An audience recognizes and accepts York's discovery of Aumerle's conspiracy in *Richard II* as a bit of dramatic shorthand. No doubt if the event were more significant and Shakespeare had had world enough and time he would have lent more credibility to the incident in the Chronicles. In the abstract, Iago's use of the handkerchief to "prove" Desdemona's guilt is far more improbable than Aumerle's carelessness. But because the handkerchief episode is part of the central drama of *Othello*, it is superbly realized as the final and masterful touch in Iago's corruption of Othello. To fasten on a minor detail of plot as evidence of Shakespeare's lack of realism is somewhat like insisting that the houses in the

background of a painting are unrealistic because they lack windows.

9   See Chapter IV of *Character and Society in Shakespeare* (Oxford, 1951).

Heilman   Manliness in the Tragedies   pp. 19–37

1   The limitation is arbitrary; a short essay could not deal with all of the plays.

2   All references are to the New Cambridge Edition of *The Complete Plays and Poems*, eds. William Allan Neilson and Charles Jarvis Hill (Boston, 1942).

3   *Hamlet* IV.vii.187, 190; *Lear* I.iv.319–26, II.iv. 280–81; *Antony and Cleopatra* IV.ii.36.

4   Cf. *Timon* I.ii.27, IV.iii.203; *Antony and Cleopatra*, I.iv.5–7.

5   Cf. Tybalt to Romeo, III.i.69, 135; Brutus and Cassius to Octavius, V.i.60–61; Aufidius to Coriolanus, and Coriolanus' consequent bitterness, V.vi.101, 104, 113, 117.

6   The idea of rational powers appropriate to man lies behind the Clown's gag when Desdemona asks him to carry a message: he agrees, since the job "is within the compass of man's wit" (III.iv.21–22).

7   Cf. Iago's adjustment of the concept to his own ends at III.iii.153–54 and IV.ii.134.

8   Without the association between the honorable and the manly in the minds of his hearers, Antony as funeral orator could hardly have played the tune of "honorable man" so effectively.

9   The various meanings are fully discussed in Curtis B. Watson, *Shakespeare and the Renaissance Concept of Honour* (Princeton, 1960).

10   Different editors read and punctuate the line differently, but in all the variations Goneril's attitude is unmistakable.

11   For other jokes that turn on the nature of man, see *Romeo and Juliet* IV.v.127; *Othello* III.iv. 21–22, IV.iii.101–2.

12   Granted, Kent is punning on the meaning of "man" as "servant." But the passage as a whole is an earnest definition; and the presence of the pun in the lines quoted does not exclude the serious thematic meaning.

13   For convenience I use "Coriolanus" throughout. Caius Marcius is given the name "Coriolanus" in Act II, scene i.

14   At this point, indeed, Volumnia carries her sense of values into a hyperbole that otherwise appears only in the first of these plays, *Titus Andronicus*: had she twelve sons, she would rather have "eleven die nobly for their country than one voluptuously surfeit out of action" (I.iii.26–27).

15   There is some anticipation of this early in the play when Timon declares that Apemantus' "humour . . . / Does not become a man" and stigmatizes Apemantus as "ever angry" (I.ii. 26–29). Cf. Alcibiades, "But who is man that is not angry?" (III.v.57). Apemantus shares Alcibiades' view of man, but with a different feeling: "I wonder men dare trust themselves with men. / Methinks they should invite them without knives" (I.ii.44–45).

16   John Bunyan, *The Pilgrim's Progress* (Rinehart ed.; New York, 1949), p. 74.

17   Thomas Hardy, *The Mayor of Casterbridge* (Riverside ed.; Boston, 1962), p. 235.

18   Joseph Conrad, *Victory* (Modern Library ed.; New York, n.d.), p. 200.

Hastings   Is Hamlet *a Hoax?*   pp. 38–49

1   E. E. Stoll says (*Art and Artifice in Shakespeare*, Cambridge, Eng., 1933, p. 121): "He is a dramatic figure, not a psychological study." He admits (p. 120): "By the present interpretation . . . some matters remain unexplained," among them the violence at the grave of Ophelia. That is to say, we are to take the character to be what others say of him, no more and no less; we are to take his action and non-action as purely dramatic. We are not to seek to find any central unity of mind and heart to which all his acts and non-acts can be referred and in which they find explanation.

Bowers   Moment of Final Suspense in Hamlet
pp. 50–55

1   That Osric is innocent is demonstrated by his surviving the catastrophe. Elizabethan tragic justice would have disposed of him if he had been one of Claudius' accomplices.

2   Kittredge would seem to overrefine the meaning by reading into the two lines "It must be shortly known to him from England / What is the issue of the business there" a tacit comment that Hamlet's action will be in self-defense. On the contrary, since self-defense can scarcely be defined in any legal (or in any ethical) manner as anticipatory, or preventative of the actual fact, Horatio is only suggesting, quietly, that time is of the essence: Hamlet must act for himself during the short interval that he will be a free agent before the counteraction is mounted against him.

3   Bowers, "Hamlet as Minister and Scourge," *PMLA*, LXX (1955), 747, n. 7.

4   It may follow logically what is apparent to any student of dramatic structure, that the famed temperamental hesitation and inability to act have, actually, nothing to do with the essential plot of the play insofar as this comprises the tragic action. For an elaboration of this point, see Bowers, "Dramatic Structure and Criticism: Plot in *Hamlet*," *SQ*, XV (1964), 207–18.

5   The intention seems to be present to suggest to the audience that the delay in Creon's acceptance, accompanied by his accusations against Teiresias, uses up valuable time. If he had humbled himself immediately, instead of too late, Antigone might have been saved.

6   Augury and the consequences of a too late recognition appear less causally in Sophocles' *Ajax*, where they are seemingly divorced from characterization.

7   Bowers, "The Death of Hamlet," *Studies in the English Renaissance Drama in Memory of Karl Julius Holzknecht* (New York, 1959), pp. 41–42.

8   Something of this ennoblement may be faintly seen in classical tragedy, as perhaps in Creon's final religious fear, or in Ajax' last soliloquy, but it is elementary compared to the Shakespearean apotheosis.

9   "Hamlet as Minister and Scourge," pp. 746–49.

10   *Ibid.*, p. 748. It is tempting to connect the practical advice that Horatio gives here with Hamlet's "There are more things in heaven and earth, Horatio, / Than are dreamt of in your philosophy" (I.v.166–67). Kittredge glosses *your philosophy* as "this philosophy that people make so much of." The unemphatic and generalized use of "your" is well known, as in *Hamlet* IV.iii.21 ff., cited by Kittredge. Nevertheless, the early emphasis in I.i on Horatio as a skeptic, and the hint at I.v.166–67 that he is at least acquainted with the skepticism of natural science, may join with his prudent superstition here to suggest a contrast between him and Hamlet in some ultimate matters of belief. Certainly Horatio's materialism (if that is a proper word) mistakes the point of the augury and it is clear that—though acquainted with all the facts —he fails to interpret them as does Hamlet. The final worldly contrast occurs in his mistaken attempt at suicide from which Hamlet saves him. Horatio is a sympathetic character, but all the contrasts favor Hamlet.

11   If, as I have suggested, the tragic error creating the play's climax was Hamlet's killing of Polonius, an act performed in his own instead of in God's time and therefore an alienation, the defiance of augury restores him to a trust in Providence that he had rejected in the closet scene. In this manner Hamlet refuses to repeat his initial tragic error and therefore merits his victory in the catastrophe, even at the price of death. To illustrate: if the classical protagonist had taken the right advice or had correctly understood the omen, he could have altered his course of action and escaped the threatened consequences. In Shakespeare's Christianization of the device, Hamlet understands the omen and—by choice—accepts the consequences. If he had moved to avoid them (as Horatio urges) he would have been repeating his initial tragic error. Hence the classical protagonist repeats his initial fault and dooms himself by blindly failing to heed the omen, whereas Hamlet saves himself by ignoring the omen with open eyes. (In the contrast drawn in this paper between Shakespeare's and the classical use of this device, no intention holds to suggest any influence from the Greeks. We have no means of knowing whether Shakespeare had ever read a Greek tragedy.)

Myrick   Christian Pessimism in King Lear
pp. 56–70

1   See "On the Tragedies of Shakespeare," *Works of Charles and Mary Lamb*, ed. E. V. Lucas (London, 1903), I, 107; Hiram Haydn, *The Counter Renaissance* (New York, 1950), pp. 636–51; A. C. Swinburne, *A Study of Shakespeare* (London, 1880), p. 172; Hazelton Spencer, *The Art and Life of William Shakespeare* (New York, 1940), p. 330; Prosser Hall Frye, *Romance and Tragedy* (Boston, 1922), pp. 155, 297; A. C. Bradley, *Shakespearean Tragedy* (2nd ed.; London, 1922), p. 252. For Hermann Ulrici on Cordelia, see his *Shakespeare's Dramatic Art*, [trans. A. J. W. Morrison] (London, 1846), pp. 187–88. More useful are his remarks on "the suicidal nature of sin" and the providential pattern as revealed in the fall of the wicked (p. 197). (The translator's name, which does not appear on the title page, is taken from a note signed by W. J. Rolfe, in a copy in the Harvard Library.)

2   Hardin Craig, "The Ethics of *King Lear*," *PQ*, IV (1925), 97–109. See also *Shakespeare* (21 plays), ed. Craig (rev. ed.; Chicago, 1958), p. 720; and notes on III.iv.114 (p. 873); IV.i.38–39 (p. 879); O. J. Campbell, "The Salvation of Lear," *ELH*, XV (1948), 93–109; R. B. Heilman, *This Great Stage* (Baton Rouge, La., 1948), pp. 150, 271, 255–75; G. I. Bickersteth, *The Golden*

World of "King Lear," Annual Shakespeare Lecture of the British Academy, 1946 (London, 1947), pp. 9, 26, 27.

3 *The Tempest* V.i.201–4. All quotations from Shakespeare are from *The Complete Works*, 1 vol., ed. G. L. Kittredge (Boston, 1936).

4 "The Theme of Damnation in Shakespearean Tragedy," *SP*, XXXVIII (1941), 221–45.

5 Clifford Leech, *Shakespeare's Tragedies and Other Studies in Seventeenth Century Drama* (New York, 1950), p. 18; *A [Booke] of Christian Exercise, by R. P., perused by Edm. Bunny* (London, 1596), pp. 385, 337, 342, 355; *Henry V* IV.iii.28–29; *Hamlet* III.iv.61–62; Parsons, pp. 379–80.

6 S. L. Bethell, *The Winter's Tale—A Study* (London and New York, 1947), p. 14.

7 *Christian Exercise*, pp. 379–80.

8 *King Lear* IV.vi.155–63. Cf. Craig's note on l. 109.

9 Henry Smith, *Sermons* (London, 1618), pp. 238–39.

10 Richard Hooker, "A Learned Sermon on the Nature of Pride," *Works*, ed. John Keble (3rd ed.; Oxford, 1845), III, 620, 629.

11 Boethius, *The Consolation of Philosophy*, eds. H. F. Stewart and E. K. Rand, Loeb Classical Library (Cambridge, Mass., 1953). See esp. Bk. iii.xii ff.; and Bk. iv *passim*. Thomas Aquinas, *Summa theologica*, trans. Fathers of the English Dominican Province (London, 1912–22), Pt. I, No. 1, Qu. xix, Art. 5; Vol. I, pp. 266–67.

12 Howard R. Patch, *The Goddess Fortuna in Mediaeval Literature* (Cambridge, Mass., 1927), pp. 24–26; Douglas Bush, *English Literature in the Earlier Seventeenth Century* (Oxford, 1952), p. 11; Justus Lipsius, *Discourse of Constancy*, trans. Nathaniel Wanley (London, 1670). Lipsius calls Fate "a decree of Providence" (p. 113), repudiates the Stoic doctrine that God is subject to Fate (pp. 118–20), and says of the murderous tyrant, "God by a secret indiscernible thread (while he thinks and wills nothing less) shall guide him to his end" (pp. 171–72); Georg Brandes, *William Shakespeare: A Critical Study* (London, 1898), I, 141.

13 Hooker, "Fragments of an Answer to the Letter of Certain English Puritans," *Works*, II, 560–61; Raleigh, Preface to *The History of the World*, in *Works* (Oxford, 1829), II, xlvii.

14 John Calvin, *Institutes*, trans. John Allen (Philadelphia, 1921), I, 185, 188–89 (Bk. I, Chap. XVI, Secs. 2, 5–6); Hooker, *Ecclesiastical Polity*, *Works*, I, 203, 208.

15 "A Sermon found among the papers of Bishop Andrews," *Works*, III, 707.

16 *Romeo and Juliet* V.ii.17; V.iii.146, 153–54, 292–93. *Hamlet* V.ii.10, 48–50.

17 Joseph Hall, *Works*, ed. Philip Wynter (Oxford, 1863), "The First Century of Meditations and Vows," VII, 448, and "Satan's Fiery Darts Quenched, or Temptations Repelled," VII, 238; Parsons, *Christian Exercise*, p. 294. Cf. William Perkins, "A Golden Chaine," *Works* (London, 1612–13), I (1612), 23; and William Negus, *Man's Active Obedience* (1619), p. 167.

18 Richard Greenham, "Godly Instructions for . . . Al Men," *Workes*, ed. H. H. (London, 1605), p. 446; John Norden, *A Progress of Piety* (Cambridge, Eng., 1847), p. 139; Hooker, *Ecclesiastical Polity*, V, xlvi, in *Works*, II, 195 ff.

19 "The Fall of Nebuchadnezzar," *Sermons*, p. 184.

20 Smith, p. 184; G. L. Kittredge, *Shakspere: An Address* (Cambridge, Mass., 1921), p. 19.

21 *King Lear* IV.iii.78–80; V.iii.170–71, 231–32.

22 V.iii.172–73; Hooker, "A Sermon found among the papers of Bishop Andrews," *loc. cit.*

23 *Gods Revenge Against Murther* (London, 1670), pp. 11, 30–31, 43, 21.

24 Aristotle *Poetics* ix. 11; Bradley, p. 256.

25 Spencer, p. 330.

Brooke   The Ending of King Lear   pp. 71–87

1 Johnson's comments are quoted from *Johnson on Shakespeare*, ed. Walter Raleigh (Oxford, 1925), pp. 161–62.

2 *Spectator*, No. 40.

3 "Characters of Shakespeare's Plays," in Hazlitt's *Complete Works*, ed. P. P. Howe (London and Toronto, 1930), IV, 270.

4 "On the Tragedies of Shakespeare, Considered with Reference to Their Fitness for Stage Representation," in *Lamb's Criticism*, ed. E. M. W. Tillyard (Cambridge, Eng., 1923), p. 46.

5 Quotations from *King Lear* are made from the Arden edition, ed. Kenneth Muir (Cambridge, Mass., 1952).

6 Cambridge, Eng., 1960, p. l.

7 J. F. Danby, *Shakespeare's Doctrine of Nature: A Study of* King Lear (London, 1949).

8 *Some Shakespearean Themes* (London, 1959); see especially pp. 118–19.

9 "*King Lear* and the Great Tragedies," in the *Pelican Guide to English Literature*, ed. Boris Ford, Vol. II, *The Age of Shakespeare* (London, 1955).

10 London, 1930, pp. 223–26.

11 *The Dream of Learning* (Oxford, 1951), pp. 92–93.
12 A. C. Bradley, *Shakespearean Tragedy* (London, 1904), Lecture VIII, p. 325.
13 *The Story of the Night* (London, 1961). Also skeptical of Christian allegory are: Barbara Everett, "The New King Lear," in *Critical Quarterly*, II, 1960; and J. Stampfer, "The Catharsis of King Lear," in *Shakespeare Survey*, XIII, 1960.
14 Baton Rouge, La., 1948, pp. 286–87.

Bonjour   Shakespeare and the Toil of Grace
pp. 88–94
1 S. L. Bethell, *Shakespeare and the Popular Dramatic Tradition* (London, 1944).
2 E. E. Stoll, " 'Multi-Consciousness' in the Theatre," *PQ*, XXIX (1950), 12, 14.
3 See *Essays in Criticism*, III (1953), 115.
4 J. I. M. Stewart, *Character and Motive in Shakespeare* (London, 1949), p. 72.
5 Kenneth Muir, "Some Freudian Interpretations of Shakespeare," *Proceedings of the Leeds Philosophical Society*, VII (1952), 50.
6 Stewart, p. 77. Though in his recent study Professor Irving Ribner still asserts that "in terms of rational psychology it is difficult to make sense of Cleopatra," he nevertheless acknowledges that "within the total structure of the play, her role is perfectly consistent" (*Patterns in Shakespearian Tragedy*, London, 1960, p. 169). This brings us closer to an artistic unity which, as soon as we consider the play from an esthetic viewpoint, in fact extends to the psychology of the heroine. As Mr. Stewart's essay indeed implies, the limitations of a so-called rational psychology are due to a set of preconceived notions that sorely fall short of the total reality of human nature.
7 I.ii.107 and V.ii.218–19. All references to *Antony and Cleopatra* are from the text of J. Dover Wilson's edition (Cambridge, Eng., 1950).
8 IV.viii.17–18.
9 V.ii.345–47.
10 Bethell, p. 131.
11 V.ii.333–34.
12 L. C. Knights, *Some Shakespearean Themes* (London, 1959), p. 145. It is only fair to acknowledge that Mr. Bethell clearly perceived how strongly Shakespeare tipped the balance in favor of Egyptian values. But his suggesting that this had something to do with the fact that it is easier for your strong sinner to enter the kingdom of Heaven than for the pru-

dent legislator, is hardly convincing. For one thing there is no possible way of ascertaining, on the strict basis of our text, whether the lovers' vision of their meeting after death is a pathetic illusion, a moving piece of wishful thinking (as it may well be), or the poet's way of stating the reality of a heavenly kingdom (whether in conformity with the Christian doctrine or not).
13 On this point, of course, the imagery of the play provides an excellent test: in *Antony and Cleopatra*, "The Roman world is set forth in an austere imagery of hard, cold, material objects and the practical business of state; it is only the imagery of Egypt that is luxuriant" (Maurice M. Charney, *Shakespeare's Roman Plays*, Cambridge, Mass., 1961, p. 16).
14 Ernest Schanzer, *The Problem Plays of Shakespeare: A Study of* Julius Caesar, Measure for Measure, Antony and Cleopatra (London and New York, 1963). I here express my gratitude to Mr. Schanzer, who generously sent me the manuscript of his chapter on *Antony and Cleopatra*.
15 This has been pointed out again lately by Professor Ribner, who, writing about the final Roman plays, declares that "in neither of these plays does Shakespeare stress the after-life or the soul's ultimate fate" (p. 168).
16 As J. F. Danby (quoted by Ribner, *loc. cit.*) pleasantly puts it, "Both *Antony and Cleopatra* and *Coriolanus* follow North's Plutarch without benefit of clergy" (*Poets on Fortune's Hill*, London, 1952, p. 149).

Foakes   Shakespeare's Later Tragedies
pp. 95–109
1 For a full discussion, see my essay, "John Marston's Fantastical Plays: *Antonio and Mellida* and *Antonio's Revenge*," *PQ*, XLI (1962), 229–39.
2 O. J. Campbell, *Shakespeare's Satire* (London and New York, 1943), p. 216. The phrase is from the essay on *Coriolanus*, reprinted in *Shakespeare: Modern Essays in Criticism*, ed. Leonard Dean (New York, 1961); see also H. S. Wilson, *On the Design of Shakespearian Tragedy* (Toronto, 1957), p. 113.
3 Willard Farnham, *Shakespeare's Tragic Frontier* (Berkeley, Calif., 1950), pp. 7–8. In a long review-article on this book, "Another World of Shakespeare," *MP*, XLIX (1951–52), 42–61, Robert Roth criticized Farnham's attempt in it to show Shakespeare writing "under the in-

spiration of a sophisticated development in Jacobean moral thinking" (p. 45).

4 Farnham, p. 37.

5 *The Moral Vision of Jacobean Tragedy* by Robert Ornstein (Madison, Wis., 1960) closes with a long section on Shakespeare's tragedies; *Jacobean Tragedy: The Quest for Moral Order* by Irving Ribner (London, 1962) is designed, the author says, as a companion volume to his *Patterns in Shakespearian Tragedy* (London, 1960).

6 P. 224.

7 Pp. 226–27.

8 L. C. Knights, *Shakespeare's Politics*, British Academy Lecture, 1957 (London, 1957), p. 2.

9 P. 11.

10 Ornstein, p. 155; Ribner, *Jacobean Tragedy*, p. 12.

11 Irving Ribner insists that De Flores and Beatrice are damned, and that the play shows a "vindication of divine justice" at the end, in which Beatrice's "commitment to evil" is punished (*Jacobean Tragedy*, pp. 125–29). This is to ignore the lack of moral direction in the casual world in which she is shown to exist. The only virtue lies in the insipid Alsemero, and most of the characters are indifferent, so that De Flores stands out, not as evil, but as possessing a tenacity of purpose and power of mind that make him the central figure in the play. The action is not concerned with damnation or divine justice.

12 In his later, and weaker, plays, Chapman proclaims himself a moralist, and consciously examines the relation between "A mighty merit and a monstrous crime" (*The Tragedy of Biron*, V.ii.277). But Bussy is, morally, a confused and equivocal figure. Even in the later plays, Chapman is concerned not with the good man driven to the sin of murder or revenge (like Macbeth or Hamlet), but with the man of natural power and ability learning to distinguish between the moral and the politic course, and to command himself—so that he may at last, as Clermont does, commit suicide in triumph. Chapman and Ben Jonson both announced their concern with morality, and may have unduly influenced critics writing on Jacobean tragedy; their work would be more important for a general estimate if they were in the mainstream, or if either of them had written a really good tragic play.

13 *An Approach to Hamlet* (Stanford, Calif., 1961), p. 68.

14 Shakespeare may also have felt that he needed to provide some hint of a frame of reference for a play which does not follow the moral pattern of his previous tragedies, and so made the Poet moralize and foreshadow the action of the play. The play's opening, like its unfinished state, suggests that he was not altogether sure of what he was doing at this stage.

15 Alcibiades and Coriolanus were the subject of a comparison in Plutarch, which Shakespeare doubtless knew; it follows the life of Coriolanus in Sir Thomas North's translation.

16 Una Ellis-Fermor, seeing Coriolanus as initially a noble character, who like Othello or Macbeth forfeits his integrity and honor, finds in the greeting to Virgilia a hint of a longing in Coriolanus for a poetry of living, a wisdom and grace beyond military glory (*Shakespeare the Dramatist*, London, 1961, pp. 60–77). I find this as odd a reading as that of Irving Ribner, who writes, "For Coriolanus there can be no meaningful renunciation of evil, nor any regeneration, for the sin which destroys him is the inevitable concomitant of all that makes him great" (*Patterns in Shakespearian Tragedy*, p. 201). The play does not show Coriolanus in these terms, as a noble figure longing for wisdom, or as a man who sins, but as a man who is psychologically incapable of fulfilling his proper role in society. See Millar MacLure, "Shakespeare and the Lonely Dragon," *University of Toronto Quarterly*, XXIV (1955), 109–20.

17 J. Leeds Barroll, "Shakespeare and Roman History," *MLR*, LIII (1958), 327–43, has shown to what extent Augustus, i.e., Shakespeare's Octavius, was generally applauded by medieval and Renaissance historians, while the aspirations of Antony and Cleopatra were just as generally condemned.

18 The phrase is from Ian Watt, *The Rise of the Novel* (Berkeley and Los Angeles, 1957), p. 11. The development of Jacobean tragedy seems to me to have some connection with the development of realism in literature as sketched in the first chapter of this book; and Shakespeare's later tragedies bear this out in their new sense of a "realistic particularity" (Watt, p. 17). This does not mean simply a Baconian disenchantment, as in his essay "Of Suspicion": "What would Men have? Doe they thinke, those they employ and deale with, are Saints? Doe they not thinke, they will have their owne Ends, and be truer to Themselves, than to them?" It is true that these plays have no room for saints

like Duncan, or demidevils like Iago, but they have room for magnanimity, loyalty, and love, for figures like Antony, Enobarbus, and Virgilia.

Tillyard   *The Fairy-Tale Element in* The Taming of the Shrew   pp. 110–14

1   *Narrative and Dramatic Sources of Shakespeare* (London and New York, 1957), I, 61–62.
2   In "Zu Shakespeare's *The Taming of the Shrew*," *Jahrbuch der Deutschen Shakespeare-Gesellschaft* (1868), pp. 397–401.
3   An exception is in a story in the Spanish *Conde Lucanor* of Don Juan Manuel, where all the men keep off the shrew, except one who is poor and wishes to better himself. See Karl Simrock, *Die Quellen des Shakespeare in Novellen, Märchen und Sagen* (2nd ed.; Bonn, 1870), I, 343.
4   *Shakespeare's Life and Art* (London, 1939), p. 71.
5   For an English translation, see *Grimm's Household Tales*, by Margaret Hunt (London, 1884), I, 203–7.
6   See J. Bolte and G. Polívka, *Anmerkungen zu den Kinder- und Hausmärchen der Brüder Grimm* (Leipzig, 1913), I, 443–49.
7   Published in *La Revue des Traditions Populaires* (1907), pp. 321–23.

West   *Ariel and the Outer Mystery*   pp. 115–23

1   For my argument that we cannot tell where the "ghost" is "from," see my "King Hamlet's Ambiguous Ghost," *PMLA*, LXX (1955), 1107–17, and on the "witches," my "Night's Black Agents in *Macbeth*," *Renaissance Papers* (Columbia, S.C., 1956), pp. 17–24.
2   Curry, *Shakespeare's Philosophical Patterns* (Baton Rouge, La., 1937), chap. vi. See also C. J. Sisson, "The Magic of Prospero," *Shakespeare Survey* 11 (Cambridge, Eng., 1958), 70–77; Virgil Whitaker, *Shakespeare's Use of Learning*, (San Marino, Calif., 1953), pp. 321, 322; Bonamy Dobrée, "The Tempest," in English Association, *Essays and Studies*, New Ser. V (Toronto, 1952), 13–25; and Robert R. Reed, Jr. "The Probable Origin of Ariel," *SQ*, XI (Winter, 1960), 61–65. Everyone is indebted in some degree to Thomas A. Spalding, *Elizabethan Demonology* (London, 1880). For an opposed opinion see Brander Matthews, *Shakespeare as a Playwright*, (New York, 1913), p. 341.

3   See such widely-read daemonologists as Pierre Le Loyer, *A Treatise of Specters* (London, 1605), ii, especially p. 19; James I, *Daemonologie* (London, 1597), III, ii, 65; Jean Bodin, *De la Demonomanie des Sorciers* (Paris, 1598), II, i, 112, and vii, 229. See also Minor White Latham, *The Elizabethan Fairies* (New York, 1930), p. 46; Edward Langton, *Supernatural* (London, 1934), p. 241; Spalding, *op. cit.*, p. 125.

4   See Dover Wilson's well-known discussion in *What Happens in Hamlet* (3rd ed.; Cambridge, Eng., 1951), pp. 55 ff., with his references to his predecessors; and my "King Hamlet's Ambiguous Ghost," note 1 above.

5   Cornelius Agrippa, *De occulta philosophia* (Cologne, 1533?), III, xxiv, 256, and xxviii, 271. See also Robert Fludd, *Utriusque cosmi historia* (Oppenheim, 1617), II, I, II, IV, III, vii, 93; and Caesar Longinus, *Secretorum magicorum opus* (Frankfort, 1630), II, vi, 423. This edition is much expanded over that of 1616, which does not contain the name. Strozzio Cicogna, in *Magiae omnifariae* (Cologne, 1607), II, xii, 240, 241, and R. P. P. Valderama, in *Histoire Générale du Monde* (Paris, 1618), ii; xii, 261, are among Catholics who expound Cabalistic pneumatology with more or less orthodox motives. All these men have nearly identical information on Ariel as angel of earth, not air. Quite different but no more enlightening for Shakespeare's use is the listing of the name by Trithemius in his odd pseudocryptographic work *Steganographia*. For more detail on the name in daemonology, see my *Milton and the Angels* (Athens, Ga., 1955), pp. 152–54.

6   Platonistic daemonologists usually seem to think spirits dichotomous, and describe them as existing always each in his own elementary "vehicle," which may require nourishment and may know pain induced by worldly objects such as swords and, presumably, cloven pines. The Calvinist theologians, resisting the well-known Scholastic idea that spirits are wholly immaterial and present themselves to us only in "assumed" bodies which are entirely without vital functions, incline to say that spirits have real body of ether or the empyrean but do not need food or rest or know temporal pain. For three varieties of the Platonistic view see Agrippa, *De occulta philosophia* III, xix, 257; Robert Fludd, *Philosophia sacra* (Frankfurt, 1626), I, IV, II, I, I, i, 207 ff.; and Michael Psellus, *De operatione daemonum* (Paris, 1615), pp. 28 ff. For the anomalous Calvinistic view

see Jerome Zanchy, *De operibus Dei* I, II, iv, 70 ff. in Vol. III of *Operum theologicorum* (Geneva, 1613); and John Deacon and John Walker, *A Dialogicall Discourse of Devils and Spirits* (London, 1601), iii, 89–93. For a summary of the whole question of spirits' substance and bodily powers, see my "The Substance of Milton's Angels," *SAMLA Studies in Milton* (Gainesville, Fla., 1953), pp. 20–53.

7   See K. M. Briggs, *The Anatomy of Puck* (London, 1959), p. 53; Frank Kermode's Appendix B to his Arden edition of *The Tempest*; Curry, pp. 175, 190; G. L. Kittredge's Introduction to his edition of *The Tempest*; Sisson, p. 75; and many others.

8   See Paracelsus, *Of the Supreme Mysteries of Nature*, trans. R. Turner (London, 1655), pp. 51–53; and Paracelsus, *A Book on Nymphs, Sylphs, Pigmies, Salamanders, and on the Other Spirits*, trans. Henry Sigerist, in *Four Treatises of Theophrastus von Hohenheim*, ed. Henry Sigerist (Baltimore, 1941), pp. 228–41.

9   Michael Psellus, *De daemonibus*, trans. Marsilio Ficino (Lyons, 1577), vi, 334 ff. and especially 360–61. In the sixteenth and seventeenth centuries Psellus was probably the most widely noticed non-Scholastic authority on daemons. Trithemius, Agrippa, Cardan, Zanchy, and innumerable others quote, paraphrase, and refer to him, attack him, defend him, adjust him, and steal from him.

10 Scholars have noticed before me that the conception of Ariel seems derived from widely various sources. See, for instance, W. Stacy Johnson, "The Genesis of Ariel," *SQ*, II (1951), 205–11; Reed, note 2 above; and Briggs and Kermode, note 7. They are all, perhaps, less concerned with the picture we finally have of Ariel than with the materials for it. I have touched on p. 117, above, their further point of the fairy strain in Ariel.

11 Briggs, p. 54, says that "following the usual practice of magicians and animal tamers of his period [Prospero] was extremely rude, peremptory, and unconciliatory to the spirits he raised, so as to preserve his dominion over them," and cites a MS conjuration *To a disobedient spirit*. Prospero speaks more often lovingly to Ariel and complimentarily than angrily and rudely; besides that, we never hear him conjure, and if we did he certainly *might* have picked some conciliatory charm such as abound in The Key of Solomon, The Lemegeton, The Magical Elements ascribed to Peter of Abano, and other

rituals. Still, the point is good that the position of a magus resembled that of a lion tamer.

12 For a detailed account of Renaissance views on ceremonial magic, see my *The Invisible World: A Study of Pneumatology in Elizabethan Drama* (Athens, Ga., 1939), pp. iii and vii, and especially 124–34.

13 The fact of Ariel's moral impassivity, a well-known trait of daemons, has been noticed by many scholars. See Hardin Craig, *An Interpretation of Shakespeare* (New York, 1948), p. 354; L. Gillet, "Ariel et Caliban," *La Revue Hebdomodaire* (1930), p. 338; Curry, p. 176; and Kittredge, Introduction, p. xx, and Kermode, Appendix B, to their respective editions of *The Tempest*. In this impassivity lies the strongest as well as the most subtle suggestion of Ariel's existence in the unhuman "outer mystery."

Butler and Fowler   Time-Beguiling Sport

pp. 124–33

1   *Short Time's Endless Monument* (New York, 1960).

2   E.g. Gunnar Qvarnström, "Dikten och den nya vetenskapen. Det astronautiska motivet," *Acta Reg. Soc. Humaniorum Litterarum Lundensis*, LX (Lund, 1961); reviewed by Maren-Sofie Röstvig in *Seventeenth-Century News*, XIX (1961). Qvarnström discusses the numerology of Benlowes' *Theophila* and of Milton's *Paradise Lost*. See also Miss Röstvig's "The Hidden Sense," *Norwegian Studies in English*, IX (1963), 1–112, and a study of *The Faerie Queene* by one of the present authors (Alastair Fowler, *Spenser and the Numbers of Time*, London, 1964).

3   The epigraph occurs in a context which might even be interpreted as presenting the idea of poetry as "short time's endless monument"; for, in the course of a discussion of the enduring quality of art, Ovid mentions the astronomical poet Aratus: "With the sun and moon Aratus will ever exist."

4   *Ovid's Metamorphosis. Englished Mythologiz'd And Represented in figures by G[eorge]. S[andys].* (Oxford, 1632), pp. 366–67. Cf. Valeriano, *Hieroglyphica*, IX, xx–xxiii (Frankfort, 1613), p. 106; and Macrobius, *Saturnalia*, I, xxi, 1–4, ed. Eyssenhardt (Leipzig, 1868), pp. 117–18.

5   For convenience, the text here followed is that of F. T. Prince's Arden edition (London, 1960). The 1593 text differs in no particular material to our purpose.

6   This operation of basing calculations upon the time from noon to sunset can be paralleled in contemporary astronomical writing. See, for example, Giov.-Battista Riccioli, *Almagestum novum*, I, xxvii (Bologna, 1651, Vol. I, pp. 33–34): "De Invenienda quantitate Semidiurna, et Seminocturna; cognitis Altitudine Poli, et gradu Eclipticæ, in quo Sol versatur."

7   Significantly, the modulus is an integer; a fact which much facilitates the reader's calculations. Other figures would have produced complicated fractions. The probability of such an integer's occurring is one in twenty-four.

8   That is, somewhat north of the seventh of the zones or climes of earth for which Sacrobosco gives the solstitial durations of day and night. See *The "Sphere" of Sacrobosco and Its Commentators*, ed. Lynn Thorndike (Chicago, 1949), p. 140.

9   Riccioli gives a convenient account of measurement by temporal hour in *Almagestum novum*, I, xxviii, "De diversis Dierum Naturalium Initiis, unde Horarum quasi species quatuor; et de mutua illarum Conversione" (Vol. I, pp. 34–35).

10 According to the modulus given, a temporal nocturnal hour would be little more than half a natural hour.

11 Adonis is discovered dead in st. 172.

12 I.e., ll. 178–530, and ll. 531–856, inclusive.

13 The lunar sidereal year is twelve times the sidereal period, that is, the time taken by the moon to return to the same apparent position with respect to the zodiac; while the lunar synodic year is twelve times the synodic period or lunation, that is, the time from new moon to new moon.

14 Also, the total stanza count for the summer's day of the poem, which is also incomplete, is eighty-nine, one short of the ninety degrees of the (summer) quarter of the sun's revolution through the zodiac.

15 Cf., for example, Christ's mounting his chariot at the exact center of *Paradise Lost*, by line-count: a matter discussed at some length by Qvarnström.

16 One might note also that at sts. 50 and 150, the midpoints of the two halves of the poem, its symmetrical balance about st. 100 is most emphatically struck. In st. 50 comes the only direct description of Adonis' courser; it concludes with the lines "Look what a horse should have he did not lack, / Save a proud rider on so proud a back," which find an echo in "He will not manage her, although he mount her," in

the central stanza. In st. 150 comes the first appearance of the horse's antitype: "And with that word she spied the hunted boar." These two stanzas epitomize the contrast between summer and winter, on which the poem is based; the generative power of the horse emblemizes summer; the destructiveness of the boar, winter. Verbal links between sts. 100 and 150 should also be observed: with "All is imaginary she doth prove" cf. "cheering up her senses all dismay'd, / She tells them 'tis a causeless fantasy."

17 " 'Ten kisses short as one, one long as twenty' " (l. 22); " 'Is twenty hundred kisses such a trouble?' " (l. 522); "Were beauty under twenty locks kept fast, / Yet love breaks through, and picks them all at last" (ll. 575–76); " 'If love have lent you twenty thousand tongues' " (l. 775); " 'Ay me,' she cries, and twenty times, 'Woe, woe,' / And twenty echoes twenty times cry so" (ll. 833–34).

18 *Petri Bungi Bergomatis numerorum mysteria* (Paris, 1618), p. 424, where many instances are given from Homer, and a few from Genesis (e.g., that "Jacob servit annis viginti"). A briefer but similar account of the number appeared earlier in the same author's *Mysticae numerorum significationis liber* (Bergamo, 1585), pt. II, p. 46.

19 This stanza appears to mingle the Petrarchan rhetoric of love with allusion to an astronomical state of affairs. Mythologically, Phoebus was accustomed "to steepe / His fierie face in billowes of the west" (*Faerie Queene* I.xi.31) at close of day; so that Venus, in close proximity to the setting or rising sun, would be simultaneously in Sol's "fire" and in the drenching ocean.

Adonis' presence after sunset is probably to be accounted for in terms of the *crepusculum*: that is, the interval between the setting of the sun ("His day's hot task hath ended in the west," l. 530) and the departure of its light ("Confounded in the dark she lay, / Having lost the fair discovery of her way," ll. 827–28).

20 Twenty times "Woe, woe" would come to forty utterances of the word "woe." But each of these is echoed twenty times; so that a total of 800 sounds is arrived at.

Stirling   Sonnets 127–154   pp. 134–53

1   I have used double quotation marks for excerpts from the sonnet text, and single marks for other quotations.

2 Sonnets 131–32 are not unrelated to the poet's swearing, in later sonnets, that black is fair; see Group III, p. 145, especially sonnet 147. But the tone is indulgent in 131–32 and extremely bitter in the Group III series. Besides, 131–32 is plainly linked with 133–34 and the latter pair is on a theme (the poet, friend, mistress triangle) not specifically present in the later sonnets on forswearing. The relationship between 131–32 and 133–34 is cogent, or 'clear' (p. 135); that between 131–32 and sonnets like 147 is general.

3 The possible connection 134–35 is broken to produce the restored sequence 143, 135–36. But compare 134–35 with either of the closely knit clear pairs 133–34 and 135–36. The potential connection 130–31 is also broken, but I cannot regard it as a clear sequence. Compare its 'plausible' links with the close, specific ones ("swear," "black," plus couplet echo) in the clear pair 131–32. On p. 145, however, I relate the restored pair 130, 127 (I–C) collaterally to the group including 131–32, and if a more direct link is desired, the restored pair can be placed actually within Group II, between 135–36 and 131–32. This would maintain any 130, 131–32 connection and would also produce something like a syntactical 'run-on' from 127 to 131. The change would not materially affect the manuscript hypothesis (see n. 14).

4 To avoid confusion, I use the symbol > instead of an en dash in linking sonnets of a restored pair or sequence. It means 'followed directly by.' If the en dash were used, as in '137–41,' a sequence of two sonnets would be misconstrued as a series of five.

5 In 140.14, "Bear thine eyes straight" echoes 139.14, "Kill me outright with looks." In its context of 139.5–12, "looks" means a "straight" gaze. When the sonnets are reversed, as I suggest (p. 145), the couplet echo remains. Of the six clear pairs (p. 135), only 149–50 appears to lack couplet echo, although an effect quite like the echo appears.

6 Among clear pairs of the larger group (1–126), note 27–28, 46–47, 57–58, 59–60, 69–70, 123–24. Couplet echo does not appear in all Shakespearean pairs, but it is characteristic, especially in 127–54. In the Q sonnet order 1–126 some widely separated sonnets have echoing couplets: 93 and 69–70 with highly similar phrasing; 36 and 96 with identical phrasing. In both instances the couplet echo combines with strong additional evidence in favor of linkage.

See my essay, "More Shakespeare Sonnet Groups," *Essays on Shakespeare and Elizabethan Drama in Honor of Hardin Craig* (Columbia, Mo., 1962), pp. 129–31, 123–26. Apparent couplet echo without other parallel elements does not establish pairing. See the discussion of 148–49, p. 144.

7 Throughout the essay Q numbers have this restricted function; obviously they are unrelated to any text of the Sonnets prior to the Q assemblage of 1–154.

8 There is no instance in which a Q variation from the modern text would affect issues discussed here. Thus an archaic text would serve no purpose.

9 Omitted from 146.2 is an obviously repeated phrase from l. 1. The repetition is a 1609 printing error.

10 Without question the two sonnets are paired, but their combined meaning is a puzzle. The Q, or unreversed, order seems to say, "Kill me by telling me the brutal truth, so I may be rid of pain" (139), "but don't tell me the truth, lest I go mad and slander you" (140). On the other hand, when taken in the order 140, 139 the pair is held together by syntax, and is climactic.

11 It is hard to see any rapport between 138 and 137. The two opening lines of 139 may appear to continue 138. "O call not me to justify the wrong" (139.1) seems at first a reference to the condoning of deceit in 138.9–14. But at 139.3 it becomes clear that a different reference is intended: "Wound me not with thine eye, but with thy tongue." Thus, in context, 139 declares, "O call not me to justify the wrong" your wounding eye inflicts. And this refers to nothing in 138. If there is a reference to another sonnet, it must be to 140.14 (see n. 3). Brooke places 138 and 151 together, and the bawdy *double entendre* found in both makes for an interesting pair. But tonal similarity of this kind is a standard that invites a good many combinations. Besides, 151 clearly leads into 152 which is hard to link with the indulgent 138. Sonnet 138 in a variant form appeared in *The Passionate Pilgrim* with 144, and there is a vague relationship between the two similar to that Brooke found between 138 and 151. Nevertheless, 144 is strongly tied to the Group II sequence (see the table and p. 136).

12 They need not be responsible for all surviving clear sequences. We can say that 132–33 (in even-odd order) survives not because it was on

a single leaf but because two leaves containing clear pairs (131–32, 133–34) remained together. I retain this sequence in the restoration. I must also clarify another matter. Clear surviving units have been identified, and they show the odd-even number pattern. Is the identification arbitrary? It would be foolish to deny the presence in Q of seeming links running from even-numbered sonnets to odd-numbered ones. But compare the general, and at times questionable, unity they achieve with the pointed cohesion found in units of two having an odd-even numerical order. See the examples in n. 3; also compare 142–43 with 143–44. On 148–49 see p. 144. I am convinced that if we wish to begin with Q links that are undeniable survivals, we are limited to the ten listed on p. 135. The merely acceptable Q links are of a kind that can often be achieved by 'shuffling' sonnets at random.

13 It is difficult to express this without appearing to muddle or compromise the odd-even number theory of leaf identification. With reference to 143–44, the statement means simply that the manuscript leaf containing sonnets 144 (recto) and 143 (verso)—without Q numbers, of course—was turned over, so that when Q numbers were imposed later the leaf became identifiable by the number order 143, 144.

14 The variant restoration of Group II (n. 3) would not materially affect the process. Instead of an independent pair, I–C (130>127) would be a separable unit or 'leaf' of the original Group II. As such it could just as readily have been displaced and then mingled with Group III.

15 Witness Benson's 1640 edition of the Sonnets.

16 See Joan Grundy, ed., *The Poems of Henry Constable* (Liverpool, 1960), pp. 101–2. A photographic reproduction of the first leaf recto appears opposite p. 183.

17 See Grundy, pp. 87–89 and the table, pp. 255–56.

18 A rather constricted allowance of four inches per sonnet (including space between sonnets) would require a sheet nearly four feet long.

19 Apparently by discarding 5ʳ before copying, and proceeding to 6ʳ (the eleventh sonnet). As Muir points out, the first of these begins "Thyne eye . . ." and the second "Myne eye. . . ."

20 See Muir and Grundy for evidence of editorial rearrangement in 1594.

21 Miss Grundy concedes that the Harington sonnet order is clearly superior to that of 1592

only "in one small point" (p. 89). Further, it is plain that none of the three Constable texts—Harington, 1592, or 1594—approximates the order of these sonnets in the authoritative Todd manuscript. Thus my explanation would imply not that the 1592 scribe or compositor produced the right sonnet order, but that he copied accurately from the text placed before him.

Muir "A Lover's Complaint"   pp. 154–66

1 J. M. Robertson, *Shakespeare and Chapman* (London, 1917).

2 John M. Murry, *Countries of the Mind*, 2nd ser. (London, 1931), p. 115.

3 In *Essays and Studies of the English Association*, III, 51 ff.

4 H. Granville-Barker and G. B. Harrison, *Companion to Shakespeare Studies* (Cambridge, Eng., 1934), pp. 102–3. The views of Malone, Swinburne, Butler and J. D. Wilson are cited in the New Variorum edition.

5 Mackail lists thirty, together with sixteen words used in a different sense by Shakespeare; but he does not mention the compound epithets, and his list is not complete. Since Mackail wrote his essay, Robert Gittings has suggested (*Shakespeare's Rival*, London, 1960) that the Rival Poet was Gervase Markham. He uses many unusual words. In *Devorax*, for example, his vocabulary includes *gadge, globy, invoke(n), intold, insearchable, ornefy, spelder, unrecurable, unconjoined, unavoid, valeyd,* and such compounds as *honor-loosing, helpe-attayning, thin-leau'd, poyson-painted, clowd-fashond, golden-spurd, demy-god-like, marish-shaken.* But, apart from a few stanzas formerly ascribed to Marlowe, the general level of the poem is low, and it contains some absurd lines, e.g., "Stoning to death these shadowes with my teares." This Rival Poet, at least, could not have written "A Lover's Complaint."

6 See below, p. 158.

7 Alfred Hart, *Shakespeare and the Homilies* (Melbourne, 1934), *passim*.

8 Cf. K. Muir, *Shakespeare as Collaborator* (London, 1960), pp. 13, 101–2.

9 Mackail comments on the last of these lines:
    . . . it is not un-Shakespearian; it is a real case of what I called the shorthand notation of Shakespeare's later manner. But of course the point is that (1) Shakespeare does not use this highly compressed shorthand in his poems; and (2) where he does use it, his use of it is masterly.

To which one could retort that if five or ten years separated *Lucrece* and "A Lover's Complaint," one would expect some difference of style; that Shakespeare's use of such shorthand notation in the plays is not always masterly; and that, in any case, the line may well be textually corrupt.

10 *William Shakespeare* (Oxford, 1930), I, 550.

11 *out-storm* Steevens; *out-scorne* Q; *om.* F.

12 W. L. Rushton, *Shakespeare's Testamentary Language* (London, 1869). Cf. K. Muir, *NQ*, CCII (1957), 285–86.

13 *M.M.* IV.iv.29; *W.T.* I.ii.142.

14 Some editors emend unnecessarily to *bawds*.

15 Pandarus, for instance, is called a broker.

16 The following parallels may be added: they are not given in the New Variorum. The idea of a battery of sighs (277) occurs also in *3 Henry VI* III.i.37; the idea of the eyes being glazed by tears (286) appears also in *Richard II* II.ii.16; the inundation of tears (290) appears twice (*K.J.* V.ii.48; *R.J.* IV.i.12); and the contrast between a false jewel and its rich setting (153) occurs in *Richard III* V.iii.250. *Henry VI* and *King John* had not yet been published.

17 The printing of the line (Sonnet 129) "Made In pursut and in possession so" may be explained by the theory that Shakespeare originally wrote "In pursut and in possession so," and that he inserted "Made" without altering the capital letter of the next word.

18 E.g. *tottered* (26), *chrusht* (63), *could* (94), *mynuits* (14), *hower* (126), *inhearce* (86), *pibled* (60).

19 Thorpe also acquired the MS of Marlowe's translation of Lucan, and he published three plays by Chapman and four works by Ben Jonson.

20 W. J. Craig and C. K. Pooler. There are, in fact, no indisputable verbal echoes of Holland's translation; the author of the poem could have read the original; and the information about precious stones was in any case available elsewhere. The relevant lines are:

The diamond—why 'twas beautiful and hard,
Whereto his invis'd properties did tend;
The deep-green em'rald, in whose fresh regard
Weak sights their sickly radiance do amend;
The heaven-hu'd sapphire and the opal blend
With objects manifold.

The parallel passages in Holland's translation are:

Wonderful and inenarrable is the hardnesse of a Diamant.   (II.610)

True it is, that we take great delight to behold greene hearbes and leaves of trees, but this is nothing to the pleasure wee have in looking upon the Emeraud, for compare it with other things, be they never so greene, it surpasseth them all in pleasant verdure   (611)

Nay, if the sight hath beene wearied and dimmed by intentive poring upon any thing else, the beholding of this stone doth refresh and restore it againe.   (611)

The stones called Opales.   (614)

Borea, like unto the morning skie in the time of Autumne. . . . Saphires are likewise sometime blew.   (620)

21 Cf. F. C. Kolbe, *Shakespeare's Way* (London, 1930), p. 87, and *Much Ado* I.i.76, II.i.340, II.iii.18, III.ii.31–37, III.iii.124–52, etc.

Craig   Shakespeare and the Trivium   pp. 167–76

1 *Timber*, in *Works* (London, 1641), II, 87–88; Fuller's *Worthies* (Warwickshire, 1662), p. 126.

2 *Works*, ed. Nicholas Rowe (London, 1709), I, xiv.

3 *The Shakespeare Allusion Book*, ed. John Munro (London, 1932), I, 455, 483, *et passim*. There were also a few defenses, such as that of John Aubrey (II, 260–62).

4 2 vols. (Urbana, 1944).

5 Material is to be found in *Protagoras* and other dialogues, and in *Republic* and *Laws*.

6 An excellent account of the genesis of the Roman grammar school will be found in J. W. Duff, *A Literary History of Rome* (London and Leipzig, 1910), *passim*, materials being gathered from Quintilian, Suetonius, and various other Latin writers.

7 See the author's "Shakespeare and Formal Logic," *Studies in English Philology . . . in Honor of Frederick Klaeber* (Minneapolis, 1929), pp. 380–96.

8 *An Essay concerning Human Understanding*, mainly Book II.

9 *Adventures of Ideas* (Mentor ed.; New York, 1959), pt. 3, sec. xvi, pp. 237–38.

10 *Shakespeare the Dramatist* (London, 1961), pp. 34–39, 126–57, *et passim*.

Spencer   The Great Rival   pp. 177–93

1   Ed. D. C. Allen (Urbana, 1933), p. 76.
2   *Letters*, ed. Bonamy Dobrée (London and New York, 1932), III, 1131.
3   *Über naive und sentimentalische Dichtung*, selection in Roy Pascal, *Shakespeare in Germany* (Cambridge, Eng., 1937), p. 122.
4   *Choephoroi*, ll. 749 ff.
5   "The Poetry of Architecture" (1838), *Works*, eds. E. T. Cook and A. Wedderburn (London and New York, 1903–12), I, 173–74.
6   *De poeticae vi medica. Praelectiones Academicae Oxonii habitae* (Oxford, 1844), pp. 337–38, 566.
7   *Aristophanes' Apology* (London, 1875), pp. 329, 331.
8   Preface to *Troilus and Cressida*, in *Essays*, ed. W. P. Ker (Oxford, 1900), I, 203.
9   Boswell's *Life of Johnson* (19 Oct. 1769), eds. G. B. Hill and L. F. Powell (Oxford, 1934; 1950), II, 96.
10 *The History of England* (London, 1778), VI, 192 (Appendix to chap. xlix).
11 *Epist.* III.xiii (roughly quoted).
12 *The History of England*, VI, 190.
13 *Ajax*, l. 430.
14 *Richard II* II.i.72 ff.
15 Aristotle *Rhetorica* III.xi; Cicero *De oratore* ii.63.
16 *Apology*, chap. iv.
17 *Critical Works*, ed. C. A. Zimansky (New Haven, 1956), pp. 50–58, 134, 158, 169, 170; *Othello* IV.ii.150–51.
18 *Critical Works*, pp. 55 ff.
19 Charles Gildon, "Some Reflections on Mr. Rymer's Short View of Tragedy and an Attempt at a Vindication of Shakespear," *Miscellaneous Letters and Essays* (London, 1694), p. 84.
20 Letter to Justice Coleridge, 23 September 1836, A. P. Stanley, *The Life and Correspondence of Thomas Arnold, D. D.* (London, 1845), II, 51.
21 John D. Jones, "Shakespeare in English Schools," *Shakespeare Jahrbuch*, XLII (1906), 114.
22 *Transactions of the New Shakspere Society*, Pt. I (1874), p. ix.
23 Sixth ed. (1907), pp. 210, 214.
24 Repr. Cambridge, Eng., 1937, p. 23.
25 *The Classical Tradition in Poetry* (Cambridge, Mass., 1927), pp. 224, 235.
26 In *More Talking of Shakespeare*, ed. John Garret (New York, 1959), p. 54.

Ribner   Shakespeare Criticism 1900–1964
                                                  pp. 194–208

1   His *Shakespeare: A Critical Study of His Mind and Art*, first published in London in 1875, has gone through many editions.
2   *Shakespeare's Iterative Imagery* (London, 1931); *Shakespeare's Imagery and What It Tells Us* (Cambridge, Eng., 1935).
3   *Shakespearean Tragedy* (London, 1904).
4   In *Explorations* (London, 1946). The essay was first published in Cambridge, Eng., in 1933.
5   "Bradley Revisited: Forty Years After," *SP*, XLIV (1947), 174–94, and "Concerning Bradley's Shakespearean Tragedy," *HLQ*, VII (1949), 1–18. Both are reprinted in the New York, 1951, edition of her *Shakespeare's Tragic Heroes*.
6   *Some Shakespearean Themes* (London, 1959).
7   In the analysis of plot as the vehicle f moral statement, the present writer has flected Moulton's influence in *Patterns in Sha spearian Tragedy* (London, 1960).
8   *MP*, VII (1910), 557–75.
9   First published in the "Shakespeare Head" edition of Shakespeare's plays in 1907 and reprinted in *Collected Essays* (London, 1927).
10 *Shakespeare's Audience* (New York, 1941).
11 "The Objectivity of the Ghosts in Shakespeare," *PMLA*, XXII (1907), 201–33, and "Anachronism in Shakespeare Criticism," *loc. cit.*
12 These were written originally for *The Players' Shakespeare*, then printed separately in London at various times and finally issued in two volumes by the Princeton University Press in 1946 and 1947.
13 His most important books, translated from the German, are *Character Problems in Shakespeare's Plays* (New York, 1922) and *The Meaning of Hamlet* (New York, 1937).
14 *Induction to Tragedy* (Baton Rouge, La., 1939).
15 *Shakespeare's Problem Comedies* (New York, 1931).
16 *Comicall Satyre and Shakespeare's Troilus and Cressida* (San Marino, Calif., 1938) and *Shakespeare's Satire* (New York, 1943).
17 *Shakespeare and the Romance Tradition* (London, 1949).
18 *Elizabethan Psychology and Shakespeare's Plays* (Iowa City, 1927).
19 *Shakespeare's Histories: Mirrors of Elizabethan Policy* (San Marino, Calif., 1947).
20 *Shakespeare's Military World* (Berkeley, 1956).

21 *Not Wisely But Too Well: Shakespeare's Love Tragedies* (San Marino, 1957).

22 *Shakespeare and the Renaissance Concept of Honor* (Princeton, 1960). Among the more important historical studies should be included also Madeleine Doran, *Endeavors of Art* (Madison, Wis., 1954), which attempts to see Elizabethan drama in terms of contemporary critical theory and has much valuable light to throw upon Shakespeare. Little need be said of the voluminous writings of J. W. Draper, including *The Hamlet of Shakespeare's Audience* (Durham, N.C., 1938), *The Humours and Shakespeare's Characters* (Durham, N.C., 1945), and *The Twelfth Night of Shakespeare's Audience* (Palo Alto, Calif., 1950). All attempt to see Shakespeare in the light of his own age. Perhaps the most comprehensive attempt ever to see a single play from a strictly historical point of view has been H. N. Paul, *The Royal Play of Macbeth* (New York, 1950).

23 *Shakespearean Tragedy and the Elizabethan Compromise* (New York, 1957).

24 For one assessment, see Stanley E. Hyman, "The Critical Achievement of Caroline Spurgeon," *Kenyon Review*, X (1948), 92–108, and "Caroline Spurgeon and Scholarship in Criticism" in *The Armed Vision* (New York, 1955).

25 In *The Common Pursuit* (New York, 1952).

26 His most important writings are contained in *Explorations* (London, 1946); *Some Shakespearean Themes* (London, 1959); *An Approach to Hamlet* (London, 1960). The inevitable reaction against Knights's method has appeared in John Halloway's *The Story of the Night* (London, 1961).

27 See, for instance, "On Historical Scholarship and the Interpretation of Shakespeare," *Sewanee Review*, LXIII (1955), 223–40.

28 *Shakespeare: The Last Phase* (London, 1955); *Shakespeare: from Richard II to Henry V* (London, 1957); *Shakespeare: the Roman Plays* (London, 1963).

29 In *The Well Wrought Urn* (New York, 1947).

30 *This Great Stage* (Baton Rouge, La., 1948) and *Magic in the Web* (Lexington, Ky., 1956), studies of *King Lear* and *Othello* respectively.

31 Other noteworthy attempts to discover Shakespeare's themes through his imagery include Brents Stirling, *Unity in Shakespearian Tragedy* (New York, 1956) and John Russell Brown, *Shakespeare and His Comedies* (London, 1957). Wolfgang H. Clemen, *The Development of Shakespeare's Imagery* (London, 1951) more closely than the others relates Shakespeare's imagery to the immediate dramatic context in which it occurs and attempts to show Shakespeare's growth in ability to make dramatic use of poetic imagery. A historically oriented study is John E. Hankins, *Shakespeare's Derived Imagery* (Lawrence, Kansas, 1953), which is concerned with the traditional nature of Shakespeare's imagery, Shakespeare's use of imagery to evoke concepts with which the specific images long had been associated.

32 *Scourge and Minister* (Durham, N.C., 1951); *Flaming Minister* (Durham, N.C., 1953); and *Dramatic Providence in Macbeth* (Princeton, 1958, rev. 1960).

33 *The Time Is Out of Joint* (London, 1948) and *The Time Is Free* (London, 1949).

34 *The Shakespearean Ethic* (London, 1959); *Shakespeare and the Rose of Love* (London, 1960); *Shakespeare and Platonic Beauty* (London, 1961).

Notes on the Contributors

ADRIEN BONJOUR: Professor of English, University of Neuchâtel (Switzerland). Major publications: *The Structure of "Julius Caesar"* (1958) and essays on Shakespeare; *Coleridge's "Hymn before Sunrise"* (1942); *The Digressions in "Beowulf"* (1950); *Twelve "Beowulf" Papers, with Additional Comments* (1962).

FREDSON BOWERS: Alumni Professor of English, University of Virginia. Major publications: *Elizabethan Revenge Tragedy* (1940, reprinted 1959); *The Fairy Knight: A MS Play Attributed to Thomas Randolph* (1942); *Principles of Bibliographical Description* (1949, reprinted 1963); *George Sandys: A Bibliographical Catalogue* (1950); ed., *The Dramatic Works of Thomas Dekker*, 4 vols. (1953–61); *On Editing Shakespeare and the Elizabethan Dramatists* (1955); *Textual and Literary Criticism* (1959); *Bibliography and Textual Criticism* (1964).
Work in progress: "The Works of Christopher Marlowe"; "The Beaumont and Fletcher Canon" (general editor); "A Descriptive Bibliography of the Restoration Printed Drama."

NICHOLAS BROOKE: Senior Lecturer in English Literature, University of East Anglia. Major publications: Edition of Chapman's *Bussy D'Ambois* in The Revels Plays series (1963); essays on "The Moral Tragedy of *Dr. Faustus*" (1952), "Marlowe as Provocative Agent in Shakespeare's Early Plays" (1961); *Shakespeare: King Lear*, Studies in English Literature, No. 15 (1963).
Work in progress: a book on "Shakespeare's Early Tragedies."

CHRISTOPHER BUTLER: Graduate student, Brasenose College, Oxford University. Co-author with Alastair Fowler of the essay on *Venus and Adonis*.

HARDIN CRAIG: Research Associate, Henry E. Huntington Library and Art Gallery; formerly Scholar in Residence, Stephens College; Professor of English Emeritus, Stanford University, University of North Carolina, University of Missouri. Major publications: *Shakespeare —Twenty-One Plays* (1931); *An Interpretation of Shakespeare* (1948); *Complete Works of Shakespeare* (ed., 1950); *English Religious Drama of the Middle Ages* (1955); editions of individual plays by Shakespeare and other English classics; numerous contributions to learned journals.

Work in progress: third of a series of books on the Renaissance in sequence to *The Enchanted Glass* (1936, 1950) and *New Lamps for Old* (1961).

R. A. FOAKES: Senior Lecturer in English, University of Durham. Major publications: editions of *King Henry VIII* and *The Comedy of Errors* for the Arden Shakespeare (1957, 1962); edition (with R. T. Rickert) of *Henslowe's Diary* (1961); *The Romantic Assertion, a Study of the Language of Nineteenth-Century Poetry* (1958).
Work in progress: edition of *The Revenger's Tragedy*, for the Revels Plays series.

ALASTAIR FOWLER: Fellow of Brasenose College, Oxford University. Major publications: edition and translation of Richard Wills, *De re Poetica*, Luttrell Reprints (1958); *Spenser and the Numbers of Time* (1964); "The Image of Mortality: *The Faerie Queene*, II.i–ii" (1961), and other essays on Spenser.
Work in progress: an edition of *Paradise Lost*, for Longmans' Annotated English Classics series.

WILLIAM T. HASTINGS: Professor of English Emeritus, Brown University; Chairman, Advisory Board, *Shakespeare Quarterly*. Major publications: numerous essays on Shakespeare; *Conrade Webb of Hampstead* (1958); edited *Man Thinking*, Phi Beta Kappa Orations (1962).
Work in progress: a study of *Timon of Athens*, "Shakespeare's Sleight of Hand" (tentative title).

ROBERT B. HEILMAN: Professor of English, University of Washington, and Chairman of the Department of English since 1948. Major publications: *This Great Stage: Image and Structure in King Lear* (1948); *Magic in the Web: Action and Language in Othello* (1956). This book won the *Explicator Award* as the outstanding volume of critical explication in 1956. Chapters of both books frequently reprinted in anthologies.
Work in progress: a study of structure in tragedy and melodrama.

KENNETH MUIR: King Alfred Professor of English Literature, University of Liverpool. Major publications: *John Milton* (1955); *Shake-*

speare's Sources I (1957); *Shakespeare as Collaborator* (1960); *Life and Letters of Sir Thomas Wyatt* (1963); edited *Collected Poems of Sir Thomas Wyatt* (1949), *Unpublished Poems* of Sir Thomas Wyatt (1961), *Macbeth* (1951), *King Lear* (1952), *Richard II* (1963); *Shakespeare: Hamlet* (1963).
Work in progress: "Shakespeare's Tragedies."

KENNETH MYRICK: Professor of English Literature, Tufts University, and Chairman of the Department of English, 1957–62. Major publications: *Sir Philip Sidney as a Literary Craftsman* (1935); "The Theme of Damnation in Shakespearean Tragedy" (1941).
Work in progress: "Shakespeare and Christian Humanism," a series of essays.

ROBERT ORNSTEIN: Professor of English, University of Illinois. Major publications: *The Moral Vision of Jacobean Tragedy* (1960); edited *Discussions of Shakespeare's Problem Comedies* (1961); "The Comic Synthesis in Doctor Faustus" (1955); "Donne, Montaigne, and Natural Law" (1956); "Historical Criticism and the Interpretation of Shakespeare" (1959).
Work in progress: a book on Shakespeare's history plays.

IRVING RIBNER: Professor of English, University of Delaware. Major publications: *The English History Play in the Age of Shakespeare* (1957); *Patterns in Shakespearian Tragedy* (1960); *Jacobean Tragedy: The Quest for Moral Order* (1962); edited *The Complete Plays of Christopher Marlowe* (1963) and *The Atheists' Tragedy* by Cyril Tourneur (1964).

T. J. B. SPENCER: Professor of English Language and Literature, and Director of the Shakespeare Institute, University of Birmingham; General Editor, *Modern Language Review.*

Major publications: *Fair Greece, Sad Relic: Literary Philhellenism from Shakespeare to Byron* (1954); *The Tyranny of Shakespeare* (British Academy Lecture, 1959); edition of *Shakespeare's Plutarch* (1964).
Work in progress: a collection (with other contributors) of masques of the Jacobean and Caroline period; an edition of John Ford's *The Broken Heart*, for the Revels Plays series.

BRENTS STIRLING: Professor of English, University of Washington. Major publications: *The Populace in Shakespeare* (1949); *Unity in Shakespearian Tragedy* (1956); one of three special editors of the Variorum Spenser, Books VI and VII; numerous articles on Shakespeare and Spenser.
Work in progress: studies of Shakespeare's sonnets and tragedies.

E. M. W. TILLYARD: Late Master of Jesus College, Cambridge University; Fellow of the British Academy; President of the International Association of University Professors of English, 1953–56. Died May 24, 1962. Major publications: *Milton* (1930), and other works on Milton; *Shakespeare's Last Plays* (1938); *The Elizabethan World Picture* (1943); *Shakespeare's History Plays* (1944); *Shakespeare's Problem Plays* (1950); *The English Renaissance: Fact or Fiction?* (1952); *The English Epic and Its Background* (1954); *Essays Literary and Educational* (1962). Book on some Shakespearean comedies (probably to be published in 1964).

ROBERT H. WEST: Professor of English, University of Georgia. Major publications: *The Invisible World: A Study of Pneumatology in Elizabethan Drama* (1939); *Milton and the Angels* (1955).
Work in progress: a book on Shakespeare and the supernatural.